Possessed by the Spirits
Mediumship in Contemporary Vietnamese Communities

T0339155

 Cornell University

Karen Fjelstad and Nguyen Thi Hien, editors

Possessed by the Spirits
Mediumship in Contemporary Vietnamese Communities

SOUTHEAST ASIA PROGRAM PUBLICATIONS
Southeast Asia Program
Cornell University
Ithaca, New York
2006

Editorial Board
    Benedict R. O'G. Anderson
    Tamara Loos
    Stanley J. O'Connor
    Keith Taylor
    Andrew C. Willford

Cornell Southeast Asia Program Publications
640 Stewart Avenue, Ithaca, NY 14850-3857

Southeast Asia Program Series No. 23

Printed in the United States of America

ISBN-13: 978-0-877271-71-0 hc / ISBN-10: 0-877271-71-2 hc
ISBN-13: 978-0-877271-41-3 pb / ISBN-10: 0-877271-41-0 pb

Cover Design: Marie Tischler. **Art:** This woodblock print portrays the well-defined hierarchy of the Mother Goddess religion. A contemporary artisan made this print after a black and white illustration. American Museum of Natural History, reprinted with permission.

CONTENTS

CONTENTS

INTRODUCTION

Karen Fjelstad and Nguyen Thi Hien[1]

Contemporary Vietnam is witnessing a revitalization of popular ritual. In 1986 the Vietnamese government instituted a series of economic and social reforms known as Renovation (*doi moi*), which loosened state controls on religious practice and reinserted Vietnam into the global market system. Since then, Vietnamese have more confidently engaged in open displays of ritual and are now constructing temples and renovating places of worship, buying and selling religious objects, and participating in public and private rituals. Popular ritual practices, including many that had previously been viewed by the state as "social evils," are now flourishing in Vietnam. The intensification of ritual has reshaped religious practice so that rituals have been modernized and the number of ritual specialists is increasing. This book is a compilation of articles that focuses on the revitalization of one of the most popular rituals in Vietnam—*len dong* (spirit possession rituals).

Len dong spirit possession rituals are associated with the Mother Goddess religion (*Dao Mau*), one of the oldest religious traditions of Vietnam. Temples dedicated to mother goddesses, including temples for spirit possession rituals, are found in every region of Vietnam and among communities of overseas Vietnamese. Practitioners of the *len dong* ritual worship the goddesses of the four palaces of the universe (*Tu Phu*)—sky, earth, water, and mountains and forests. Each goddess has a number of spirit helpers, many of whom are cultural heroes, that are incarnated during spirit possession ceremonies. *Len dong* spirit mediums possess the spirit root or calling (*can*) of at least one spirit that is identified through horoscopy or divination by religious masters. During the *len dong* ritual, approximately thirty-six spirits possess or descend into mediums over the course of several hours. During the time that the spirits possess mediums, they dance, enjoy listening to songs, distribute blessed gifts (*loc*), interact with the audience, and bestow spirit blessings.

Although *len dong* is currently growing in popularity, it "has often been looked down upon by men and the so-called established society."[2] Spirit possession has been illegal in Vietnam and, until recently, was condemned as a superstitious

---

[1] The editors wish to thank Laurel Kendall, Deborah Homsher, Michael Wakoff, and all the contributors for their comments and feedback on this collection of essays. We especially thank all the mediums who have shared their thoughts, their time, and their experiences with us.

[2] Nguyen Khac Kham, "Vietnamese Mediums and Their Performances," *Asian Folklore Studies Group Newsletter* 11-12 (1983): 26-33.

practice by the current government.[3] Perhaps because Vietnam is a poor country, some state authorities felt that people should not be wasting their hard-earned money on so-called charlatans who specialize in the sale of false hopes. However, in spite of campaigns to eradicate superstition, the Vietnamese government did not prevent people from practicing many kinds of rituals, including spirit possession, during the pre-Renovation period.[4] In the past, when sanctions were strictly enforced, some spirit possession ceremonies were held without songs for the spirits (*chau van*) that might alert the police, and other ceremonies were held at night. Possession ceremonies continued in this relative secrecy until the Vietnamese government instituted *doi moi*.

As noted above, one consequence of Renovation has been the strengthening of rituals and an increase in the business of buying and selling religious objects. Instead of hiding ritual paraphernalia from the authorities, people now sell it openly on the streets. Instead of having small possession ceremonies in secret or out of the view of authorities, ceremonies are now held in larger temples, both in the country as well as in cities such as Hanoi, Hue, and Ho Chi Minh. Within a short period of time following Renovation, new temples were built and old temples refurbished, the production and sale of votive offerings began to flourish, and clothes and accessories for spirit mediums were sold in the markets. Today *len dong* spirit possession is in the process of revitalization.

Doi moi has also led to a resurgence of scholarly interest in Vietnam, resulting in a proliferation of social science research in Vietnam as well as a rise in Vietnamese studies among Western scholars. However, much of the information about the Mother Goddess religion and spirit possession rituals is still not readily available. A few Vietnamese scholars, most notably Ngo Duc Thinh, have written about *Dao Mau* and the *len dong* ritual, but much of this work has not been translated from the original Vietnamese.[5] Maurice Durand's book *Technique et panthéon des médiums viêtnamiens (Dông)* and Pierre Simon and Ida Simon-Barouh's *Hau Bong: Un culte viêtnamien de possession transplanté en France* were, until recently, the only in-depth Western-language accounts of Vietnamese spirit possession ceremonies.[6] A special issue of *Vietnamese Studies* focused on the Mother Goddess religion and spirit possession rituals, but the works were preliminary general descriptions and the publications are not readily accessible.[7] However, beginning in the 1990s, several contributors to this volume began dissertation research that focused on *len dong* spirit

---

[3] See Barley Norton, "'The Moon Remembers Uncle Ho': The Politics of Music and Mediumship in Northern Vietnam," *British Journal of Ethnomusicology* 11,1 (2002): 71-100.

[4] Shaun Malarney, *Culture, Ritual, and Revolution in Vietnam* (London: RoutledgeCurzon, 2002); Nguyen Thi Hien, "The Religion of the Four Palaces: Mediumship and Therapy in Viet Culture" (PhD dissertation, Indiana University, 2002); Norton, "'The Moon Remembers Uncle Ho.'"

[5] See Ngo Duc Thinh, *Dao Mau o Viet Nam* [The Mother Goddess Religion in Vietnam] (Hanoi: Nha Xuat Ban Van Hoa-Thong Tin, 1996) and "*Len dong*: Spirits' Journeys," in *Vietnam: Journeys of Body, Mind, and Spirit*, ed. Nguyen Van Huy and Laurel Kendall (Berkeley, CA: University of California Press, 2002), pp. 253-72; Nguyen Khac Kham, "Vietnamese Mediums and Their Performances"; Nguyen Huu Thong, *Tin nguong Thanh Mau Mien Trung Viet Nam* [The Mother Goddess Religion in Central Vietnam] (Hue: NXB Thuan Ho, 2001).

[6] Maurice Durand, *Technique et panthéon des médiums viêtnamiens (Dông)* (Paris: École Française d'Extrême-Orient, 1959); Pierre Simon and Ida Simon-Barouh, *Hau Bong: Un culte viêtnamien de possession transplanté en France* (Paris: Mouton & Co. 1973).

[7] "The Cult of the Holy Mothers in Vietnam," *Vietnamese Studies* 131 (1999).

possession. Karen Fjelstad explored the relationship between spirit possession and gender among Vietnamese living in Silicon Valley, California, Barley Norton examined *chau van* music and possession in Vietnam, and Nguyen Thi Hien studied Vietnamese mediumship as a form of therapy.[8] At the same time, Kirsten Endres began to write about her field research in Hanoi.[9] Even so, the works of Shaun Malarney and Thien Do were, until recently, the only published book-length treatments of religion and ritual in contemporary Vietnam, and they only devoted a few pages to *len dong* spirit possession.[10] *Goddess on the Rise: Pilgrimage and Popular Religion in Vietnam* provides a fascinating description and analysis of pilgrimages to *Ba Chua Xu*, a goddess worshipped in Chau Doc province, but the book does not discuss the *len dong* ritual, although spirit possession is one way of serving *Ba Chua Xu*.[11]

The idea for this book was born in the fall of 2002. Nguyen Thi Hien had just finished writing her doctoral dissertation titled "The Religion of the Four Palaces: Mediumship and Therapy in Viet Culture," a topic similar to one that Karen Fjelstad had studied among Vietnamese living in California.[12] After much correspondence, Nguyen and Fjelstad decided to bring together most of the international scholars who have studied the ritual. We wanted to compile multidisciplinary information about *len dong* into a single volume, provide firsthand ethnographic accounts of ritual practice in multiple settings, including Vietnam and the United States, and document changes in religious practice that have resulted from recent socioeconomic, political, and historical events. This book is a result of that decision. It assembles articles by nine international scholars, most of whom are pioneers in the study of *len dong* spirit possession, compiling most of the contemporary work on *Dao Mau* and the *len dong* ritual into a single reference.

These articles stem, in part, from a panel presented at the American Anthropological Association annual meetings and a symposium on the Mother Goddess religion held at the Center for Southeast Asian Studies, University of California, Los Angeles. These panels were organized to facilitate interaction between the contributors who are European, Vietnamese, and American anthropologists, ethnomusicologists, and folklorists. At all three venues, questions from the audience, which included laypersons and professionals, stimulated discussion and further deepened our commitment to the creation of this book. Questions ranged over a variety of topics: How common is spirit possession? What are the differences between spirit possession of the Mother Goddess religion and

---

[8] Karen Fjelstad, "Tu Phu Cong Dong: Vietnamese Women and Spirit Possession in the San Francisco Bay Area" (PhD dissertation, University of Hawaii, 1995); Nguyen Thi Hien, "The Religion of the Four Palaces"; Barley Norton, "Music and Possession in Vietnam" (PhD dissertation, SOAS, University of London, 2000).

[9] Kirsten Endres, "Local Dynamics of Renegotiating Ritual Space in Northern Vietnam: The Case of the Dinh," *Sojourn: Journal of Social Issues in Southeast Asia* 16,1 (2001): 70-101 and "Beautiful Customs, Worthy Traditions: Changing State Discourse on the Role of Vietnamese Culture," *Internationales Asienforum* 33,3-4 (2002): 303-22.

[10] Shaun K. Malarney, *Culture, Ritual, and Revolution in Vietnam*; Thien Do, *Vietnamese Supernaturalism: Views from the Southern Region* (London and New York, NY: RoutledgeCurzon, 2003).

[11] Philip Taylor, *Goddess on the Rise: Pilgrimage and Popular Religion in Vietnam* (Honolulu, HI: University of Hawaii Press, 2004).

[12] Nguyen Thi Hien, "The Religion of the Four Palaces"; K. Fjelstad, "Tu Phu Cong Dong."

calling the souls of the dead? Who gets possessed more often, men or women, and why are these practices gendered? Why is spirit possession increasing in Vietnam? This book seeks to answer these questions and more, meeting the interests of scholars and students, educators and travelers. The majority of articles are based on recent field research, and they present the voices of their subjects to convey the sense of firsthand field experience.

The distribution of blessed gifts (*loc*) is an important part of the ceremony.
Photo by Viveca Larsson.

Contributors to the volume discussed terminology at the UCLA symposium. One topic we considered was whether we should refer to members of the pantheon as gods or spirits. We agreed to use the term *spirits* in reference to members of the pantheon in general, and *goddess* for the mother goddesses in particular. We wanted to acknowledge the high status of the mother goddesses but use gender-neutral terms for other members of the pantheon, and we wanted our terminology to fit with the existing body of research on *len dong*. Another discussion focused on the difference between the terms *incarnation* and *performance*. What, for example, do we mean when we say that "the spirit of *Cau Be* was incarnated into the medium" or that "individuals worship the spirits by performing them?" Is one term more correct than another? Whereas *incarnation* implies that a medium gives bodily form to a spiritual being, *performance* refers to a presentation before an audience. The contributors to this volume agree that *len dong* involves performance as well as incarnation, a view that is close to the emic perspective of mediums. Whenever mediums are possessed, they are giving the spirit a bodily form and, at the same time, they are pleasing the spirits by wearing attractive clothing or dancing in a beautiful way. In fact, spirit mediums often talk about the importance of having nice clothing and jewelry for the ceremony. A third area of concern had to do with the translation of the term "*loc*" (blessed gifts). "*Loc*" commonly refers to material goods offered to the spirits before or during a *len dong* ceremony. Spirits infuse the goods with spiritual power, and these goods are then distributed to individuals in the temple. Members of the symposium wrestled with various translations of "*loc*." Is *loc* a gift or a blessing? Do we mean to imply that only spirits give *loc*, or can other supernatural beings distribute *loc* as well? Finally, we asked, does "*loc*" refer only to material goods, or can it also refer to nonmaterial blessings such as talent or good fortune? We decided to use the translation "blessed gifts" because this expression can include anything, material or not, that is auspicious and distributed by supernatural beings.

The articles in this book can be divided according to the ways the authors treat their respective subjects. There are two broad approaches. One deals with *len dong* and the individual, exploring how and why individuals become spirit mediums and the stories and personal histories of the women and men who participate in spirit possession ceremonies. The second approach studies *len dong* as a sociocultural phenomenon, covering such topics as the history of *Dao Mau* and the *len dong* ritual, the relationship between *len dong* and the political economy, regional variation in ritual practice, and *len dong* as a reflection and a re-creation of Vietnamese culture and society. Several common themes run through all of the articles. These include the contemporary revitalization of popular ritual, the syncretic nature of the religion and its many variations, individual and group responses to formal and informal stigmatization of the ritual, conflict and competition within the religion, *len dong* as therapy and a vehicle for personal transformation, and the effects of global processes on ritual practice. The final chapter by Laurel Kendall contextualizes the several chapters within a larger frame of East Asian popular religion, enabling a fresh look at some common themes of religious practice.

Ngo Duc Thinh, author of the first chapter, is a pioneer in the study of the Mother Goddess religion and the *len dong* ritual. One of the first Vietnamese scholars to focus on this form of popular religion, he is the author of the two-volume work *Dao Mau o Viet Nam*.[13] He also organized the 2001 International Conference on *Dao Mau* held in Hanoi, which marked the first collaborative work on the topic in Vietnam and the West. Ngo Duc Thinh has tirelessly sought to elevate the status of the Mother Goddess religion, and his work has helped to educate and influence state authorities, perhaps contributing to the lessening of formal strictures against the religion.

Ngo Duc Thinh's essay places the *len dong* ritual within the larger context of goddess worship. Although Vietnamese history, society, and religious practices are rich with goddesses, only some goddesses have attained the higher rank of mother goddess. This book focuses on the mother goddesses of *Tu Phu* (the Four Palaces) or *Tam Phu* (Three Palaces) and their spirit possession rituals. As Ngo Duc Thinh explains, the mother goddesses of *Tu Phu* are part of a large pantheon of spiritual

---

[13] Ngo Duc Thinh, *Dao Mau o Viet Nam.*

beings that is arranged in a hierarchical order and is reminiscent of a royal court replete with princes, mandarins, princesses, and ladies.

The Mother Goddess religion is syncretic, and, as Ngo Duc Thinh asserts, the cosmology reflects nature worship that is combined with elements from Chinese Taoism and Buddhism. In addition, the pantheon is full of historical and legendary figures representing individuals of several ethnicities, many of whom are cultural heroes. Regional variations, the tendency of the religion to adopt new members into the pantheon, and the incorporation of new religions complicate the picture so that *Dao Mau* and the *len dong* ritual have perhaps hundreds of local variations.

The Mother Goddess religion and the *len dong* ritual are in a constant state of flux, always changing and adapting to new circumstances, as shown by the relationship between the Mother Goddess religion of Four Palaces and the cult of Saint Tran. Tran Hung Dao was a Vietnamese general who fought and vanquished Mongol invaders in the thirteenth century. In the following centuries, he became a highly revered cultural hero who is sometimes worshipped through spirit possession rituals. According to the French and Vietnamese literature written in the first half of the twentieth century, there was a strong separation between the Mother Goddess religion and that of Saint Tran. However, Pham Quynh Phuong's essay, based on recent ethnographic fieldwork in Hanoi, shows that the two religions are merging. The spirits of Saint Tran and his two daughters sometimes possess spirit mediums of the Mother Goddess religion, and sections of altars for the mother goddesses are often devoted to Tran Hung Dao. The pantheon of the Mother Goddess religion easily incorporates new deities.

The syncretic nature of the religion sometimes leads to obfuscation of spirit identities, something Kendall describes as "the very stuff of an adaptable, dynamic, and vital popular religion." Ngo Duc Thinh and Pham Quynh Phuong respectively discuss the merging identities of the Great King of Eight Oceans (*Bat Hai Dai Vuong*) and General Tran Hung Dao. Long before the existence of Tran Hung Dao, the Great King fought foreign invaders with his army of dragons, crocodiles, and snakes. Then, many years later, Tran Hung Dao fought Mongol invaders in the same region. Nowadays, Tran Hung Dao and the Great King are often superimposed upon each other—they are each called "Holy Father" and are celebrated in the eighth month of the lunar calendar.

Spirit identities also merge in response to sociopolitical concerns. Rituals of the Mother Goddess and Saint Tran religions are blended, according to Pham Quynh Phuong, in the attempt to gain legitimacy at macro and micro levels. Whereas Saint Tran and the Mother Goddess religions each had rituals involving interactions with spirits, several twentieth-century authors cited vast differences between them. Followers of Saint Tran, a high-status group, were male practitioners of exorcism. The predominantly female followers of *Tu Phu* practiced spirit mediumship, and their status was much lower. These status differences continue today and are exemplified in official views that bestow a higher value on temples dedicated to worshipping national heroes. Spirit mediums of *Tu Phu* thus gain greater status and legitimacy when they are associated with Tran Hung Dao.

Empowerment, at all levels, is a recurring theme of many of the essays in this book. *Len dong* rituals enact transactions with spiritual beings who occupy varying degrees of power and authority in the pantheon, and, at the same time, these rituals are mechanisms for the empowerment of individuals, including those who might otherwise lack access to formal power structures. One dimension of empowerment concerns the representation and strengthening of national identity. Ngo Duc Thinh's essay refers to the *len dong* ritual as a theatrical performance representing Vietnamese national culture. In the eyes of the Viet, the pantheon of *Dao Mau* provides an inclusive view of the nation for it does not just include ethnic Viet peoples but also members of several minority groups, such as the Muong, Nung, Tay, and Dao. It should be noted, however, that ethnic minorities are often portrayed stereotypically, and they themselves are not empowered by representation in the *Tu Phu* pantheon. Also, as Norton says, "The development of a national Vietnamese culture imbued with the character of the Vietnamese people, including 'ethnic minority' groups, has long been a part of the Party's project of nation building."[14] In fact, the idea of *len dong* as a national theater fits so well with Party ideology that it may have contributed to the state's greater acceptance of the *len dong* ritual.

The pantheon of the Mother Goddess religion emphasizes protection of the nation by including deified historical figures that helped to save Vietnam from foreign aggressors. Tran Hung Dao fought Mongol invaders, the First Prince (*Ong Hoang De Nhat*) is the deified figure of Le Loi who fought for Vietnam's independence from Ming Dynasty China, and the Tenth Prince helped to expand the nation. Other members of the pantheon have made equally important contributions to the welfare of the nation. The essays by Ngo Duc Thinh and Pham Quynh Phuong discuss the significance of *Dao Mau* and *len dong* to Vietnamese national identity, and Kendall looks at this "historical imaginary" through an East Asian perspective. Cultural heroes and heroines are significant, not only because they help people to imagine who they have been and who they are, but also because they help people to imagine who they might become. Fjelstad, in her essay, and Fjelstad and Lisa Maiffret, in their jointly authored contribution, look at how spirits have become role models for Vietnamese living in the United States.

A second dimension of empowerment is concerned with gender. The Mother Goddess pantheon is, in many ways, a female complement to other religious practices (such as Confucian-based rituals) or social domains (such as kinship) that tend to be more male oriented. As several contributors to this volume indicate, the Mother Goddess religion worships spirits that are both male and female, and ritual roles are open to members of both sexes. Ngo Duc Thinh suggests that the Mother Goddess religion represents a primeval respect for, and acknowledgment of, female contributions to human welfare. Additionally, the importance of a balance of male and female and yin and yang is formally represented in ceremonies that venerate Lieu Hanh or Goddess of the Sky (*Thanh Mau Thuong Thien*) and Tran Hung Dao as spiritual parents of the Viet.

Although men and women both have ritual roles in *len dong* ceremonies, one cannot help but notice that the majority of mediums are female. Norton's essay examines the gendered implications of Vietnamese mediumship, providing several emic explanations for this discrepancy. An ethnomusicologist, Norton explores how *chau van* (mediumship music) helps to construct gendered identities and facilitate gender traversing, a common feature of *len dong* rituals. The music of female and male spirits is quite distinct and is differentiated by melody, rhythm, and syncopation, as well as text. Although gender traversing enables individuals to move between gender categories, Norton asserts that the categories themselves are comprised of conservative gender constructions. *Len dong* spirit possession thus

---

[14] Norton, "'The Moon Remembers Uncle Ho,'" p. 85.

provides a space to performatively negotiate established stereotypical gender categories.

The process of becoming a spirit medium is, in itself, a form of empowerment. Two essays describe the emic perspective of individuals who have become spirit mediums. Endres's essay is based on ethnographic fieldwork in Hanoi, and the essay by Fjelstad and Maiffret is based on field research among Vietnamese living in Silicon Valley, California. Both essays report similar explanations for the call to mediumship. Individuals are selected by spirits to become mediums, and they cannot refuse without facing severe retribution from those spirits. Thus, from the perspective of the medium, very little choice is involved in the decision to become a medium. A precipitating event often causes the individual to seek counsel from other mediums and to learn that they themselves have been selected to become a medium. Endres and Fjelstad and Maiffret reveal that diverse experiences can be perceived as precipitating events. These include physical and mental illness, bad luck, financial stress or job loss, grief, exposure to the religion, or even philosophical ponderings about the meaning and purpose of life. Although there are many similarities between mediums in Vietnam and the United States, there are also some differences in how individuals become mediums. Many mediums in the United States received their "calling" during the boat trip from Vietnam to America.

Ethnographic studies of emic perspectives often reveal diverse interpretations of religious experience. That is certainly the case here as spirit mediums describe the experience of possession very differently. Whereas some mediums say they are completely possessed, others say they are not. Also, some mediums say they feel as if they are looking out the window of a car, while others describe themselves as a "loudspeaker for the spirits." Mediums also differ in their interpretations and descriptions of spirits. Whereas one of Endres's consultants describes the Third Princess (*Co Bo*) as someone who will never forgive, Fjelstad and Maiffret's consultants claimed that she was always kind and empathetic!

Whether individuals who become mediums are engaging in a process of "personal transformation that entails restructuring of the self" or constituting "personal identities and their relationship to the world through the ritual embodiment of divine entities," one thing is certain—spirit mediums inevitably claim that their lives have changed for the better.[15] Endres's consultants in Hanoi and Fjelstad and Maiffret's consultants in Silicon Valley each emphasize the strongly held belief that one's life will improve with mediumship. Whether mediums say they are healthier, more at ease with life, happier, or more peaceful, they all share in common a feeling that life has gotten better. When individuals become spirit mediums, they join a social group that is led by a master medium (*dong thay*). Viveca Larsson and Endres explore how communities of mediums are formed and the roles of the various community members. Although membership in a social group can be supportive and even therapeutic, there is also a great deal of conflict within and between communities of mediums.

Some of the essays in this volume allude to the darker side of mediumship. Although becoming a spirit medium may be a source of empowerment, it can also make one vulnerable to attack. Spirit mediums have often been accused of fakery,

---

[15] See K. Fjelstad and L. Maiffret, "Gifts from the Spirits: Spirit Possession and Personal Transformation among Silicon Valley Spirit Mediums," and K. Endres, "Spirit Performance and the Ritual Construction of Personal Identity in Modern Vietnam," in this volume.

and they risk losing ritual goods and, in Vietnam, identification cards. Fjelstad's essay describes some of the criticism faced by mediums in Silicon Valley, and Norton describes domestic conflicts that arise when husbands learn that their wives have become spirit mediums. Pham Quynh Phuong says that some women are able to lessen the severity of their husbands' criticisms if they emphasize a connection between the mother goddesses and Saint Tran. Spirit mediums sometimes feel that they are tied to the temple and have very little free time, partly because of their responsibilities to the temple and the spirits. Isn't it true, Norton asks, that women have just attained a new master? Instead of being subservient to their husbands, they are now subservient to spirits. Several essays describe the financial and interpersonal stresses that are associated with mediumship.

Reaction to formal and informal stigmatization of the *len dong* ritual is another theme of the essays in this book. Since 1986, Renovation has brought tremendous changes to Vietnamese society, and ritual specialists are not bothered or arrested by local authorities as often as they were in the past.[16] However, practice of the ritual is still not officially allowed. State instructions on cultural and religious activities consider *len dong* spirit possession as a "social evil," and a list of condemned superstitious practices released by the Ministry of Culture and Information in 1998 states that astrology, horoscopy, ghost calling, spirit petitioning, making amulets, performing exorcism, and magical healing are superstitious practices. This ban was supported by a 2003 resolution that "strictly forbids using religion and belief to carry out superstition." How, then, has the *len dong* ritual managed to survive?

Several essays describe the survival strategies of spirit mediums and other ritual specialists. Larsson and Endres describe the time before Renovation as "the hard times" when spirit mediums risked custody terms, fines, and the confiscation of ritual goods. However, these sanctions did not prevent individuals from having ceremonies, and several of the articles in this volume present cases of army officials or communist party cadres who put their occupations at risk by attending ceremonies or becoming mediums. One way that individuals managed to continue having ceremonies was to hide their rituals from authorities by having *len dong* in temples that were both small and private. Vietnamese living in Silicon Valley in the 1980s employed a similar strategy. Fjelstad describes Silicon Valley temples that were well hidden from the public eye, perhaps because of the mediums' experiences of persecution in Vietnam and their fear of similar treatment in the United States.

Nguyen Thi Hien's essay describes another strategy, which is to ignore official pronouncements and continue whatever one is doing. The producers of votive offerings, many of whom are spirit mediums themselves, are subject to continual supervision by the local police and officials because they have been officially banned from making these items. Although manufacturers face detainment and harassment by the police and risk having their tools confiscated, they manage to continue their work by "not worrying" about government prohibitions.

A third strategy for dealing with stigmatization is to develop connections with people in power. This tactic is found in the blending of the Saint Tran and the Mother Goddess religions. It is also exemplified in Nguyen Thi Hien's advice to a maker of votive offerings that she develop good relations with local authorities. Fjelstad's study of Silicon Valley mediums describes a similar phenomenon, but in

---

[16] The official status of the religion is changing in Vietnam. A decree was passed on June 18, 2004, that gives the right to practice folk religions. It went into effect on November 15, 2004.

this case, spirit mediums are benefiting from their relationships with scholars. Fjelstad describes how the first international conference on *Dao Mau* helped to legitimize the religion in Silicon Valley.

Len dong and *Dao Mau* are not just rituals and religions of Vietnam; they are also practiced by Vietnamese living in several other countries. Since the Vietnamese diaspora of 1975, *len dong* has traveled to Australia, France, Great Britain, and the United States.[17] Fjelstad's essay explores transnational aspects of *len dong*, focusing on ritual practices in Vietnam and the United States. The global spread of *len dong* has influenced religious practice in both countries, and one result is that people sometimes refer to the expansion of the ritual as proof of its worthiness. The transnational movement of ritual specialists and goods also contributes to the revitalization of *Dao Mau* and *len dong* in Vietnam and the United States.

The past decade has witnessed an increase in the availability and consumption of ritual goods. *Dao Mau* and *len dong*, like many other religions and rituals, involve the use of a tremendous number of ritual objects. *Dao Mau* altars require representations of the spirits, and incense, flowers, and foods, and *len dong* ceremonies require music, clothing, spirit gifts, and votive offerings. Nguyen Thi Hien, Larsson and Endres, and Fjelstad interviewed spirit mediums who reminisced about the old days when there were fewer material goods available. They contrasted this with the present, when there is an abundance of material goods. Fjelstad reports an increase in ritual goods used in the United States, explaining that this increase was caused by Renovation as well as by the lifting of the US trade embargo.

Nguyen Thi Hien's study of the production of votive offerings documents the significance of ritual goods. Votive offerings have always been an important part of the *len dong* ritual, and they were missed when people did not have access to them. However, the use and production of votive offerings have been increasing since Renovation. Fjelstad interviewed Silicon Valley mediums who tried to explain the importance of ritual goods by drawing analogies with shopping for birthday presents at high-quality stores. Would anyone really want to give his or her mother a low-quality birthday gift?

Nguyen Thi Hien's essay raises the topic of religion as business. Many individuals, including ritual specialists (*thay cung*), cooks, musicians, seamstresses, and the manufacturers of ritual objects such as votive offerings, are earning a livelihood from religion. Nguyen Thi Hien explores the relationship between business and religious practice and devotion. Each consultant she interviewed is a spirit medium. However, one individual became a medium to help with his business, and another turned to business to help her practice as a medium!

Several essays discuss the *len dong* ritual as a mechanism for generating income in the new market economy. Endres says that *len dong* are common among female traders and market vendors in Hanoi, and these people are "particularly vulnerable to sudden economic booms and slumps." Nguyen Thi Hien, who has conducted research in several different regions of Vietnam, has found that *len dong* is popular among rich and poor, urbanites and peasants alike. Many essays report that individuals become mediums or attend possession ceremonies to enhance personal well-being, including their financial well-being, regardless of the social class of mediums. Pham Quynh Phuong asserts that there is a growing division of labor between Saint Tran and *Dao Mau*. Whereas Saint Tran is considered to be good for

---

[17] Fjelstad, "Tu Phu Cong Dong"; P. Simon and I. Simon-Barouh, *Hau Bong*.

healing, the mother goddesses are considered good for economic well-being. However, mediums do not necessarily agree on the appropriateness of asking the spirits for help with personal finances. Fjelstad claims that some Silicon Valley mediums say so many people are trying to make money from *len dong* that it is "more like a business than a religion."

The increased use of material goods has led to divisions between temples and mediums. Endres reports that groups of mediums in Hanoi are differentiated by socioeconomic background, so that there are master mediums with a predominantly rich clientele and those whose clientele includes less affluent members. Fjelstad and Maiffret found a similar ranking for mediums in the United States. Although wealthy mediums and temples may have a higher socioeconomic status, they risk being accused of excessive materialism or "buying and selling spirits" (*buon than ban thanh*). Wealthy mediums are also more likely to be called "show-off mediums" (*dong dua*), and Fjelstad says that wealthy mediums in the United States are more likely to be accused of sorcery. She also states, however, that mediums in the United States have developed strategies to mitigate conflicts created by these differences in wealth.

The essays in this volume indicate that many ritual specialists are concerned with the direction of ritual change in post-Renovation Vietnam. Several of the essays report an increased concern with materialism, and Larsson and Endres's essay describes mediums who look back to the "good old days" when groups of mediums had to be close because they were poor and in danger of being imprisoned. However, although many mediums reminisce about the past, spirit mediums also look to the future. Larsson and Endres tell of a medium who wants to develop an organization that teaches about the religion, Nguyen Thi Hien describes manufacturers who seek to develop spirituality along with their business, and Fjelstad describes spirit mediums who want to make sure that the *len dong* rituals reflect contemporary values. If this is indicative of the future, *len dong* and *Dao Mau* will continue to flourish and grow.

THE MOTHER GODDESS RELIGION: ITS HISTORY, PANTHEON, AND PRACTICES

Ngo Duc Thinh

The veneration of mother goddesses plays a prominent part in the folk beliefs of the Kinh (Viet) and other ethnic groups of Vietnam. Meeting the spiritual demands and everyday desires of ordinary people, the worship of female spirits has spread widely from the north to the south and from the lowlands to the highlands of Vietnam. More than a system of beliefs, the religion has embellished its rituals with music, fashion, and dance. One might even say that the Mother Goddess religion constitutes a distinct subculture with cultural nuances varying locally with its practitioners. This essay provides an ethnographic description of the main features of the religion, its pantheon, and practices. Taking an evolutionary perspective, it also describes how the Mother Goddess religion (*Dao Mau*), a syncretic belief system, emerged from general goddess worship to incorporate elements from indigenous religious traditions as well as Buddhism and Taoism.

THE WORSHIP OF GODDESSES

Vietnamese myths and legends often refer to goddesses, but it is difficult to list all the goddesses who have been worshipped throughout Vietnam. The book *Goddesses in Vietnam* lists seventy-five goddesses that are worshipped throughout the country.[1] According to *Vietnamese Historico-cultural Vestiges*, 250 of the 1,000 known places of worship are dedicated to goddesses.[2]

According to Vietnamese myth, some Vietnamese goddesses were active in the creation of the universe and its features. These include the sun goddess, moon goddess, and lady Nu Oa (and her esquire Tu Tuong) who created mountains and rivers and patched up heaven with stones. Local Vietnamese peoples have also

---

[1] Do Thi Hao and Mai Thi Ngoc, *Chuc Nu Than Viet Nam* [Goddesses in Vietnam] (Hanoi: Nha Xuat Ban Phu Nu, 1984).

[2] The Institute of Han-Nom, *Vietnamese Historico-cultural Vestiges* (Hanoi: Social Sciences Publishers, 1991).

deified and feminized clouds, rain, thunder, and lightning. Even the five elements are called Lady Metal, Lady Wood, Lady Water, Lady Fire, and Lady Earth.

Goddesses also symbolize the country or the nation. For example, Mother Au Co is said to have given birth to the one hundred children who lived in the mountainous and coastal regions, creating the multiple ethnic groups of Vietnam. Powerful female historical figures who drove away foreign invaders and those who have reigned over the country also became cultural heroines and goddesses: the Trung sisters, Trieu Au, Duong Van Nga, Y Lan, Bui Thi Xuan, and De Tham's wife.[3] Kings have bestowed the status of "deities of the first standing" upon these women.

The creative powers of goddesses have, according to popular myth, given birth to culturally important foodstuffs—Rice Mother and Mother Sugar Cane are both examples. Indigenous peoples have conceptualized the ancestresses of various professions, including weaving, sericulture, carpentry, and confectionery as goddesses. Whether the narratives of these women are based on historical fact or remain as unverifiable myths and legends, the role of Vietnamese women in building and safeguarding the country cannot be neglected. The contributions of women are well established by a comprehensive survey of the natural environment, productive activities, struggles waged by the people, and the traditional society of the Kinh and other ethnic groups living in Vietnam.

Goddesses have either heavenly or human origins; that is, they either emerge from Kinh myth or represent historical persons. A number of goddesses have been elevated to the rank of *mau* (mothers). Although the mothers are goddesses, not all goddesses are mothers. Mother goddesses are distinct from other goddesses in their higher ranking and their association with creation and regeneration. Mother Au Co, Rice Mother, and Mother Sugar Cane are examples of mother goddesses.

ORIGINS OF THE MOTHER GODDESS RELIGION

The Mother Goddess religion is a distinct religion that evolved from the generalized worship of goddesses. A mother goddess presides over each one of the four realms or "palaces" (*tu phu*): Heaven (*thien phu*), Earth (*dia phu*), Water (*thoai phu*), and Forests and Mountains (*nhac phu*). Practitioners of the Mother Goddess religion maintain public temples (*den*) and private temples or shrines (*dien tho*) and engage in practices of devotional worship and spirit possession.

Some scholars think goddess worship evolved from popular beliefs that have prevailed from primeval times.[4] Vietnamese peoples initially venerated the forces of nature, which later were linked to processes of wet-rice agriculture and then to other activities. The Granary Queen (*Ba Chua Kho*) is one such example.[5] The Granary Queen probably originated as an anthropomorphized force of nature, which then became the Rice Goddess, a deity common to many rice-cultivating peoples of Southeast Asia. In the 1980s and 1990s, the Granary Queen became popular among urbanites who seek to "borrow" her money, represented by gold and red papers, at

---

[3] Ngo Duc Thinh, *Dao Mau o Viet Nam* [Mother Goddess Religion in Vietnam] (Hanoi: Nha Xuat Ban Van Hoa Thong Tin, 1996).

[4] See, for example, ibid., p. 12; Nguyen Phuong Thao, *Van Hoa Dan Gian Nam Bo* [The Folk Culture of the Southern Vietnamese] (Hanoi: Nha Xuat Ban Giao Duc, 1994), p. 181.

[5] Ngo Duc Thinh, "The Belief in Granary Queen and the Transformation of Vietnamese Society" (paper, American Anthropological Association annual meetings, Chicago, 2004).

the beginning of the year. They believe the goddess constantly replenishes the money, helping their incomes to grow.

As the above example indicates, views of goddesses and their relative popularity change over time. Whereas the Rice Mother may have been an important figure to agricultural peoples, the Granary Queen is popular in contemporary Vietnam because she provides people with money and wealth. In *Goddess on the Rise*, Philip Taylor discusses the growing popularity of another goddess, the Lady of the Realm (*Ba Chua Xu*), who has also "come to be seen as a spirit of financial increase."[6]

The Mother Goddess religion contains some elements of Taoism. The supreme divinity is the Mother Goddess (*Thanh Mau*), but she is sometimes supervised by the Taoist Jade Emperor (*Ngoc Hoang*). According to many scholars,[7] Taoism was introduced into Vietnam very early, perhaps during the Chinese domination. In the times of the Dinh (968-80), early Le (980-1009), Ly (1010-1225), and Tran (1225-1400) dynasties, Taoism was one of the three major religions (*tam giao*) in Vietnam. The kings appointed Taoist priests, and Taoism was mentioned in some examination papers. Numerous members of the royal court practiced Taoism, among them Tran Hung Dao, and other members of the royal family became Taoist priests. The Taoist doctrine was ingrained in many intellectuals, and Taoist magical practices were widely practiced among common people.[8] During the Le dynasty, Confucianism prevailed over Taoism, but Taoist philosophy and magic were still held in high esteem. Taoist elements of the Mother Goddess worship include the identification of humankind with nature, the implantation of Taoist divinities (such as the Jade Emperor and the north and south stars) in its pantheon, the practice of exorcism, and the concept of the four palaces.

The concept of the four palaces (*phu*) has many connotations, as each palace corresponds to a domain of the universe: heaven, earth, water, or mountains and forests. Perhaps the division of the universe into four palaces originated with the worldview of the Kinh people regarding the Yin (*am*) and Yang (*duong*) principles that bring harmony and balance to the universe. According to Taoist views of the evolution and structure of the cosmos, the primordial essence of the universe (the Tao) evolved into Yin and Yang, which were respectively associated with earth and heaven. The four seasons evolved from heaven and earth, and the five elements emerged from the four seasons.[9] As applied to central aspects of the Vietnamese landscape and experience, the Yin (female) principle gradually split into the realms of the earth, water, and the mountains and forests, whereas the Yang (male) principle remained associated with the realm of heaven. As the cosmology of the Mother Goddess religion evolved, the oppositional relationship of the heavenly and earthly realms receded, and heaven became one of the four realms ruled by mother goddesses.[10] Each of the four palaces corresponds to one of the four directions of the

---

[6] Philip Taylor, *Goddess on the Rise: Pilgrimage and Popular Ritual in Vietnam* (Honolulu, HI: University of Hawai'i Press, 2004), p. 88.

[7] Van Tan et al., *Thoi Dai Hung Vuong* [Hung Vuong Dynasty] (Hanoi: Nha Xuat Ban Khoa Hoc Xa Hoi, 1973).

[8] Phan Huy Le, Tran Quoc Vuong, et al., *Lich Su Viet Nam* [Vietnamese History], vol. 1 (Hanoi: Nha Xuat Ban Dai Hoc va Trung Hoc Chuyen Nghiep, 1976).

[9] Michael Saso, *Taoism and the Rite of Cosmic Renewal* (Seattle, WA: Washington State University Press, 1972).

[10] Ngo Duc Thinh, "The Pantheon for the Cult of Holy Mothers," *Vietnamese Studies* 12 (1999): 21-22.

universe and is represented by one of the four primary colors: red for the palace of heaven, white for water, yellow for the earth, and green for the mountains and forests. Mediums wear costumes in one of these four colors when they perform *len dong*, or spirit possession rituals, the main practice of the religion.

The Mother Goddess religion also incorporates some aspects of Buddhism as well as indigenous religions. Most noticeably, the Mother Goddess sometimes shares her altar with the Lady Buddha Kwan-yin (*Phat Ba Quan Am*), and altars to the mother goddesses are often found in Buddhist temples. The religion also incorporates aspects of indigenous Vietnamese religions, such as the use of possession trance during rituals and the representation of ethnic minorities in the pantheon.

THE PANTHEON OF THE MOTHER GODDESS RELIGION

Mother Goddesses (Thanh Mau)

Distinct from other religious folk beliefs, the Mother Goddess religion has its own complete and well-articulated hierarchy. Among the mother goddesses, the Mother of Heaven (*Mau Thuong Thien*) reigns over the sky and takes control of clouds, rain, thunder, and lightning. The incarnation of this mother is identified with Lieu Hanh, the major and the most venerated figure in the pantheon. Lieu Hanh, daughter of the Jade Emperor and transfigured as a girl in the earthly world, lived during the sixteenth century.[11] Worshipping the Mother Goddess fulfills the needs of people for supernatural assistance, particularly for women who pray for prosperity and good health in their daily lives. According to their beliefs, the Mother Goddess is feared and loved at the same time. She can bring good luck and bestow blessings on her followers if she is properly worshipped. However, if neglected, she can bring misfortune and illness.

In the highlands of Vietnam, the goddess Au Co became identified as the Mother Goddess of Mountains and Forests. In the most enduring Kinh myth of the origin of the ethnic groups of Vietnam, Au Co—kidnapped and married by the Lac Dragon Lord, *Lac Long Quan*—took fifty of her children to the mountains (in some versions of the myth, Mount Tan Vien) where they became the founding ancestors of the different ethnic minorities.[12] Over the centuries, Au Co has attained the status of a holy mother who protects the mountainous regions of the country. Peoples of the Tay Nguyen region venerate her at temples throughout the highlands. The two principal temples dedicated to this mother are found at Suoi Mo (Bac Giang province) and Bac Le (Lang Son province).

According to another version of this legend, the Mother Goddess of Mountains and Forests (*Mau Thuong Ngan*) has been associated with the historical figure of Princess La Binh, who, according to legend, is a daughter of the genie Son Tinh and Princess My Nuong and a granddaughter of a Hung king. As befits her manner, she

---

[11] Ibid., p. 23.

[12] Keith Taylor discusses the sources and narratives of the legend of *Lac Long Quan* and *Au Co*. See Keith Taylor, *The Birth of Vietnam* (Berkeley and Los Angeles, CA, and London: University of California Press, 1983), pp. 303-5.

enjoyed nature, its vegetation and wild animals. She brought well-being to the population and became a guardian spirit of mountainous regions, villages, and hamlets.

The legend concerning the Mother Goddess of Water (*Mau Thoai*) shifts according to locality, but the variants all share common ground. As the goddess who takes care of rivers, lakes, and seas, she was a descendant of the lineage of the Dragon or Great King, which thus connects her to the founding ancestor of the Kinh people.

Thus, in the Mother Goddess religion, cosmological views about heaven, earth, and water, mythical concepts about the gods of these elements, and the oral history of the Kinh people about the Hung kings blend and intermingle to create this distinctive, localized religion of the Vietnamese.

Five Great Mandarins (Ngu Vi Quan Lon)

In the folk beliefs of the Mother Goddess religion, ten mandarins rank below the mother goddesses. Among them, five great mandarins, being either heavenly or human divinities, have close connections with the mundane world, but little is known of the origins of the other five.

The First Mandarin and the Second Mandarin originate in the celestial realm. The Jade Emperor, ruler of Heaven, ordered the First Mandarin to come down to the earth to protect people from evil spirits and the Second Mandarin to guard over forests and mountains.

The Third Mandarin and the Fifth Mandarin are specially revered and have special temples devoted to them. Folk legend claims that the Third Mandarin was the son of the Eighth Ocean King. Legends surrounding the Fifth Mandarin, called *Quan De Ngu*, vary in different locations. Some narratives depict him as originating as a snake living on the Do Tranh River in Hai Hung province. Other stories identify him as Cao Lo, a lieutenant of a Hung king, or as Tran Quoc Tang, one of Tran Hung Dao's sons. Believers now worship the Fifth Mandarin incarnated as Tran Quoc Tang at Cua Ong (Quang Ninh province) or at a temple in the province of Lang Son.

Ladies (Chau Ba)

There are twelve ladies of the pantheon, who are said to be reincarnations of the mothers. The first, second, third, fourth, fifth, sixth, and the youngest are often incarnated by spirit mediums. The first four ladies represent incarnations of the four mother goddesses.

Princes (Ong Hoang)

The ten princes are often identified with mortals, frequently famous generals who have fought against invaders and thus contributed to the independence of the country and its peoples. Spirit mediums often incarnate six of the ten princes, especially the Third Prince (*Ong Hoang Ba*), Seventh Prince (*Ong Hoang Bay*), and the Tenth Prince (*Ong Hoang Muoi*).

Many female spirits are associated with ethnic minorities. Photo by Viveca Larsson.

Princesses (Co)

The twelve princesses serve as handmaidens of the mother goddesses. When incarnated, these cheerful figures dress colorfully and perform graceful, fluttering dances. The proper names of some princesses derive from the places where they are worshipped, such as the Youngest Princess (Bac Le) (Lang Son province), or the Second Princess (Cam Duong) (Lao Cai province). As a group, the princesses are native to upland areas and thus belong to the realm of mountains and forests. When they are incarnated in spirit mediums, they dress as women of the Tay, Nung, Dao, and Muong ethnic groups.

Young Princes (Cau Be)

Among the ten or twelve young princes, ranging from one to nine years old, mediums often incarnate the third and the youngest princes. Being mischievous children, when incarnated, the princes usually wear bizarre costumes and speak a childish language.

Animal Spirits

Animal spirits, those of tigers (*Quan Lon Ngu Ho*) and the snake (*Ong Lot*) also belong to the Mother Goddess pantheon. The five great tiger mandarins rule the jungle, while the holy snake rules over the waters. Mediums rarely incarnate these two animals. Practitioners of the religion believe that tigers are always hostile to the evil spirits who do harm to both the living and the dead. People sometimes pray to the tigers to exorcise evil spirits that might cause epidemics or for protection against theft. When communicating with the five tigers, the medium pretends to spit fire by chewing burning incense sticks. He (or she) mimics the tiger sitting or imitates the tiger rushing at its prey.

We have seen that some spirits have been associated with historical figures, and the Mother Goddess religion reflects endurance of the nation's traditions. In the pantheon of the Mother Goddess religion, folk belief also recognizes a realm of the Tran dynasty (*Phu Tran Trieu*) associated with the worship of General Tran Hung Dao, who vanquished the Mongols in the thirteenth century. Some Mother Goddess temples include the worship of Tran Hung Dao along with other deities, and some even honor him as the highest spirit, equating him with the Jade Emperor.[13] When mediums incarnate Tran Hung Dao and his attendants, they punish evil ghosts and demons and cure diseases.

In addition to the Goddess of Heaven and the Mother Goddess of Mountains and Forests who are associated with Princess Lieu Hanh and Princess La Binh, both historical persons, the First Prince (*Ong Hoang De Nhat*) embodies the brilliant general Le Loi, who won national independence from the Chinese Ming dynasty in the fifteenth century. The Tenth Prince (*Ong Hoang Muoi*) was a mandarin of the early Le dynasty (fifteenth century) who helped expand the territory of the nation. This historicization of the spirits of the Mother Goddess religion links the concerns of daily life with national history, expressed through the needs and desires of worshippers and during the rituals of spirit possession. Mother Goddess worship thus simultaneously evokes the nation's history and deifies aspects of patriotism.

A Worldview of Complementary Opposites

The number of divinities of each type in the four palaces has symbolic significance. The female goddesses of the religion are in even-numbered groups—four mothers, twelve ladies, and twelve princesses. Conversely, the male gods appear in odd-numbered groups—five princes and ten (a multiple of five) young princes. Vietnamese folk belief conceives of odd numbers as "fixed" (*so co*) or stable and closely connected with the Yang, or male principle, whereas the even numbers are "nonfixed" (*so ngau*), unstable, and associated with the Yin, or female principle. Sacred as well as symbolic, the odd/even aspects of numbers represent the binary opposition of the King Father (*Vua Cha*) and male spirits to the Mother Goddess (*Thanh Mau*) and female spirits.

The pantheon, the appellation of divinities, and the worship of gods and goddesses in temples reveal a specific conception of life and the world at both the macro- and microcosmic levels. First, the pantheon represents a miniature cosmology

---

[13] See Pham Quynh Phuong's essay, "Tran Hung Dao and the Mother Goddess Religion," this volume.

with binary oppositions: heaven-earth and forest-water, of which the heaven-earth opposition forms the pillar of the four palaces system. The sacred odd/even numbers repeat the conception of the four directions of north, south, east, and west (*tu phuong*) and the five elements (*ngu hanh*) of metal, wood, water, fire, and earth. In such a model of the universe, many believe that, among their many abilities, the mother goddesses exercise power over creation and fertility.

On the microcosmic level, the pantheon resembles a family but one modeled upon the royal court. Spirit mother Lieu Hanh and spirit father Tran Hung Dao represent supreme rulers; beneath them in the hierarchy, we find the mandarins, ladies, princes, young princesses, and young princes. Adherents commemorate the deaths of Lieu Hanh and Tran Hung Dao, just as each family celebrates the anniversaries of the deaths of the husband's own father and mother. In the Viet folk belief, young princesses and princes are the incarnations of boys and girls who die young (*ba co, ong manh*). Parents often worship their deceased children and dedicate altars to them.

The appellation of divinities and the costumes worn by mediums when they incarnate the spirits of the pantheon also reinforce the conceptualization of the religion's deities as members of a royal court. A number of the deities—mothers, king fathers, princes, princesses, and mandarins—originated from historical members of Vietnamese royalty, specifically the Nguyen dynasty. The decoration of the palaces, with alcoholic offerings placed on the altars, and the use of certain ritual paraphernalia, like the swords that the spirits dance with while incarnated in the mediums, suggest practices similar to those of the royal court. These aspects of the Mother Goddess religion reinforce the idea that human society is mirrored in the "divine society."

MAIN PRACTICES OF THE MOTHER GODDESS RELIGION

Wherever the Kinh people have settled—from the north to the south and from the plains to the mountains of Vietnam—they worship the deities of the Mother Goddess religion in temples or at shrines. In general, each spirit is worshipped at a principal temple and several subordinate ones. Although the principal temple of the Mother Goddess Lieu Hanh is situated in Phu Giay (Nam Dinh province) and that of the Mother Goddess of Mountains and Forests at Bac Le in Lang Son province, people worship these goddesses in many other localities.

The practices of the religion are varied. At temples or shrines associated with a particular deity, lay people who follow the religion pray to the gods or have a ritual performed for very pragmatic reasons to fulfill this or that wish. At the temples and shrines, spirit mediums also perform the *len dong* possession rituals, in which they incarnate the members of the pantheon of gods and goddesses. The following two subsections highlight two main practices: the *len dong* spirit medium rituals and the festivals that honor the Mother Goddess and Father God.

Len Dong Spirit Possession Rituals

Len dong (going into trance) rituals, also called *hau bong* (service to the spirits) or *hau dong* (medium's service), are performed throughout Vietnam as the main practice of the Mother Goddess religion. In this ritual, the mediums represent only the "skeletons" (*cot*) or the empty bodies, or "seats" (*ghe*), into which the souls or shades of the goddesses and gods are incarnated.[14] There are about seventy spirits of the Mother Goddess religion, but only a certain number of these spirits descend (*giang*) or incarnate (*nhap*) into mediums.

Spirit mediums are obliged to perform one or two *len dong* rituals a year. In addition, they may perform *len dong* rituals on days celebrating specific spirits of the Mother Goddess religion, such as the twelfth day of the sixth lunar month, honoring the Third Princess, the seventeenth of the seventh month, dedicated to the Seventh Prince, the twentieth of the eighth lunar month for Tran Hung Dao, or the eleventh day of the eleventh month for the Second Mandarin.

The journey of a spirit into the body of the medium is called an incarnation (*gia*). The process includes the spirit's coming down and either hovering briefly or moving into the medium and the medium's changing costumes to indicate which goddess or type of attendant has arrived and then burning incense sticks, dancing, granting favors, and listening to songs about the spirits (*chau van*). The spirit then leaves.

Before a *len dong* ritual, the spirit mediums make careful preparations. They must choose an auspicious day for the ritual and invite a ceremony master (*thay cung*) for a petition ceremony, singers for performing *chau van*, and friends and relatives to attend. Before performing the *len dong*, the mediums must purify themselves and eat vegetarian food.

During the performances, ritual assistants (*hau dang*) and musicians specializing in *chau van* music (*cung van*) assist the medium. *Hau dang* help them to burn incense sticks, pass around cigarettes and alcohol to those in attendance, and change the medium's costume before the medium proceeds to the next incarnation. *Cung van* play musical instruments and sing religious songs throughout the ritual.

The ritual involves a minimum of two musicians—one who plays a two-stringed, moon-shaped lute (*dan nguyet*) and a percussionist. The percussionists might also use bamboo clappers (*phach*), a small two-headed drum (*trong*), or a small cymbal (*canh*). The musicians place the percussion instruments on the floor and strike them with wooden beaters. Additional percussion instruments include a small gong (*thanh la*), a large barrel drum, and a small wooden slit drum (*mo*). If the band is larger, the ensemble might add a sixteen-string zither (*dan tranh*), a two-stringed fiddle (*dan nhi*), and bamboo flutes (*sao*).[15]

The opening and closing of a red veil (*khan phu dien*) signals the arrival and departure of a spirit. Spirits manifest themselves in two ways: they descend and briefly hover over the medium or they take possession of, and are incarnated into, mediums. Because the mother goddesses descend and hover but do not incarnate, the mediums do not open the red veil. Only Tran Hung Dao and the spirits of the ranks below the goddesses actually take possession of mediums. From the entire pantheon of spirits, between ten and forty of the deities either descend and hover or incarnate into mediums, in hierarchical order from the mother goddesses to

---

[14] See Ngo Duc Thinh, "*Len Dong*: Spirits' Journeys," in *Vietnam: Journeys of Body, Mind, and Spirit*, ed. Nguyen Van Huy and Laurel Kendall (Berkeley and Los Angeles, CA, and London: University of California Press, 2003), pp. 253-72.

[15] Barley Norton, "Music and Possession in Vietnam" (PhD dissertation, SOAS, University of London, 2000). See also his essay, "'Hot-Tempered' Women and 'Effeminate' Men: The Performance of Music and Gender in Vietnamese Mediumship," in this volume.

mandarins, ladies, princes, young princesses and princes, and then sometimes to the spirits of the five tigers or snakes.

When the spirits enter (*nhap*) or leave (*thang*), the mediums signal with their fingers—right fingers for female spirits and left fingers for males—and then open the red veil. Then the *hau dang* help the medium to change costumes to suit the appropriate spirit. Changing costumes takes time because each divinity has his or her own costume appropriate to his or her status and character. On the whole, spirits of the same rank dress in the same style, but the costumes differ in color and details, which indicate their origins in different ethnic groups.

Female mediums offer incense sticks by going down on their knees and kowtowing three times, whereas male mediums merely kneel when raising the incense sticks. The sound of a bell accompanies each kowtow. This offering of incense sticks works as a silent prayer. Burning incense sticks, wearing perfume, and offering fragrant fruit not only delight the divinities but also show the medium's veneration.

The spirit incarnations also are enacted through dances that the mediums perform to music, creating an exciting and lively atmosphere. As well as changing costumes to indicate specific spirits, the mediums dance in the style appropriate to each spirit. Some of the spirits dance with oars as if rowing a boat or engage in actions suggesting the gathering of herbs or fishing with nets. Others dance with fans. After dancing, the medium sits while the singers perform songs telling the history of the spirit who has descended and praising his or her beauty and merits.[16] For princes, for example, the singers declaim old verses, and the princes manifest their satisfaction by giving the singers some money as a reward. The medium's assistants offer the spirit alcohol, cigarettes, betel nuts and areca leaves, or tea. At this point in the ritual, members of the audience move closer to the spirit medium to listen to the messages she utters pertaining to the future or to pray for protection, wealth, or recovery from illness.

The visiting spirit grants favors while listening to the religious music. The attendees often request that the divinity give favors or special attention to their families. They might offer a tray of fruit, candy, or money to the spirits. With the help of the attendants, the medium redistributes these and other items as "blessed gifts" (*loc*) in the form of a burning incense stick, a lighted cigarette, a betel nut, an areca leaf, a cake, a piece of fruit, a mirror, a comb, a hairpin, or some money. These previously mundane objects are now imbued with the power of the spirit, having gained meaning and potency by passing through the hands of the spirits.

When the medium sits motionless, starting slightly, with her hands joined before her forehead or with a fan covering her head, the audience recognizes the moment of the spirit's departure. Assistants then cover the medium's head with the red veil, and the singers play their instruments and sing the song, "The spirit comes back to his palace." Afterwards, the medium prepares to become the agent for another spirit coming down.

After the last spirit has left, the medium takes off her spirit costume and thanks both the divinities and the audience. Following the *len dong* ritual, the medium invites the audience to join in eating the meal consisting of the dishes already offered to the spirits. Returning home, the participants take a bag of *loc* for good luck.

---

[16] For an ethnographic description of one specific *len dong* ritual, performed for the Thuong Nguyen Festival in Hanoi, see Ngo Duc Thinh, "*Len Dong*: Spirits' Journeys," pp. 253-72.

Festivals of the Mother Goddess Religion: Death Anniversaries of Father and Mother

The celebration of the anniversaries of the deaths of the fathers lasts from the twentieth to the twenty-eighth day of the eighth lunar month when "Yin prospers at the expense of Yang." Legends say that Tran Hung Dao passed away on the twentieth day of the eighth month and *Bat Hai Dai Vuong* (the Great King of Eight Seas) died on the twenty-eighth of the same month. Exuberant festivals last from the fifteenth to the twentieth day of the eighth month at Kiep Bac, where Tran Hung Dao is worshipped, and another from the twentieth to the twenty-eighth day of the same month at Dong Bang, where both the Great King of Eight Seas and Tran Hung Dao are worshipped.

Stories of the Great King recount that when foreign aggressors threatened the country, King Hung called upon everyone to drive away the enemy.[17] The biggest snake turned into a human being and marched to the front to lead his army of dragons, crocodiles, and snakes. After the army of creatures vanquished the enemy, the king granted the snake the title of the Great King of Eight Seas. Dao Dong villagers have worshipped the Great King ever since.

In the thirteenth century, Dao Dong village was located in the military region where Tran Hung Dao fought against the Mongolians. Legends tell that Tran Hung Dao and his assistants, among whom was Pham Ngu Lao, came to the Great King temple to call on the spirit of the king to help them. After Tran Hung Dao's death, this temple was consecrated to him.

People sometimes identify the Great King directly with Tran Hung Dao. This explains the concurrent celebration of the anniversary of the spiritual father's death with that of Tran Hung Dao. Some villagers consider Tran Hung Dao to be the spiritual father, the male counterpart of Lieu Hanh, the spiritual mother. The identification of the two male gods as the spiritual father is not a "misconstruction" but partly reflects the people's differing frames of reference. Tran Hung Dao maintains a status not only as a great national hero but also, in the beliefs of many, long ago became a god. Tran Hung Dao came from a family line that was originally composed of a goodly number of fishermen. He then gained his triumph in naval battles against the Mongols. Being deified, Tran Hung Dao was seen by the people as a water god or dragon king.

As one of the main activities of the festival, villagers reenact the battle, led by Tran Hung Dao, that drove off the Mongolian aggressors. On one festival day, hundreds of boats from the local villages travel in procession on the Dong Bang River, with one boat carrying a palanquin with a chair and a table representing the Great King and Tran Hung Dao. After the procession, the villagers hold a boat race. The village that wins the race is granted spiritual good luck, good health, and prosperity for the whole year.

The anniversary of the death of the Mother Goddess is celebrated at every temple devoted to the Mother Goddess religion, but the main place of worship remains Phu Giay in Tien Huong village (Nam Dinh province), where Lieu Hanh

---

[17] Hung Vuong, the first Hung king, established the country of the Kinh or Viet, Van Lang, about 2,000 to 2,500 years ago. During this period, there were eighteen reigns of the Hung kings. The Kinh consider Hung Vuong as their founding ancestor. His death anniversary (*gio to*) has become a national commemoration. See Van Tan et al., *Thoi Dai Hung Vuong*.

was born. Instead of the procession of boats that commemorates the anniversary of the Father's death, on the anniversary of the Mother Goddess's death, people march from her temple to the Buddhist pagoda nearby where she took her vows. As one story goes, in a battle between Lieu Hanh (who became the Mother Goddess) and priests from a Taoist sect, Lieu Hanh fell into a trap. Suddenly the Lady Buddha Kwan-yin appeared to aid her in this critical situation. To pay homage to Kwan-yin, Lieu Hanh converted to Buddhism. This legend suggests the interpenetration of the Mother Goddess beliefs and a popular Buddhist sect, paving the way for the appearance of representations of members of the Mother Goddess pantheon in Buddhist pagodas.

Thus, celebrating the Fathers' death anniversary in the eighth month and the Mother Goddess's death anniversary in the third month brings together the most distinguished features of the Vietnamese Mother Goddess religion: the association between Yin and Yang, a primeval cosmology accounting for the origins of all phenomena in the universe.

CONCLUSION

The Mother Goddess religion of the Kinh people, an indigenous religion, originated in the veneration of spirits conceptualized as gods or goddesses. Throughout its long history and development, the religion incorporated religious and cultural elements from Taoism, Buddhism, and the beliefs of indigenous Vietnamese ethnic groups, becoming a kind of popular syncretic religion, sometimes referred to as a kind of Vietnamese "Taoism."

Over time the religion has undergone a process of transformation, adapting to various social and political changes. Nowadays the Mother Goddess religion plays several important roles.[18] The religion reflects the history of the nation by incorporating key historical figures and events into its deities, beliefs, and rituals. And in the domain of Kinh folk beliefs, the ritual practices promote good health and prosperity in this world. Because of these factors, the religion continues to proper and change today.

---

[18] See Taylor, *Goddess on the Rise* and many of the other essays in this volume for a thorough discussion of the role of goddesses in contemporary Vietnam.

TRAN HUNG DAO AND THE MOTHER GODDESS RELIGION

Pham Quynh Phuong[1]

INTRODUCTION

I received a phone call from a stranger in early 2000. After two minutes of silence, a woman's panicked, choking voice said that, through one of my friends, she knew about my master's thesis on the subject of Tran Hung Dao. She pleaded for my help: "I am possessed by Saint Tran [*Duc Thanh Tran*]. I cannot breathe. I don't know anyone who can help. Please help me!" As I was frightened, my first impulse was to hang up. I would later learn that this woman was a twenty-seven-year-old English teacher at a university.

This was the first time I had encountered someone claiming to be possessed by Tran Hung Dao, in fact, to be "stuck with him." I gave Lan (all names in this essay are pseudonyms) the telephone number of another university teacher who could speak with her about Vietnamese spiritual beliefs. Yet, I knew that I had to speak with her again and that she would become a subject of my future research into the cult of Saint Tran. The friend to whom I introduced Lan told me later that "The spirits are training her, and she will be a medium!" Lan appeared tense when we visited her some days later. She told us that she had been experiencing a dreadful ordeal, and that for several days, Tran Hung Dao/Saint Tran came to her every night to "train" her. She had been suffering terrible vomiting and could not take care of her little son.

I returned to see her in 2003 while doing dissertation fieldwork in Hanoi, assuming excitedly that she must now be religiously experienced with Saint Tran. By now he would have been training her for three years. To my initial disappointment, however, I learned that she was by then worshipping many spirits, and that she had switched to the Mother Goddess Lieu Hanh as her main god. She said incarnation by

[1] I would like to thank the Harvard-Yenching Institute for a doctoral scholarship and La Trobe University for financial support of my fieldwork. I am grateful to Joel Kahn, Christopher Eipper, Wendy Mee, Laurel Kendall, Do Thien, Jennie Lynch, Jill Forshee, and Nguyen Thi Hien for their comments on the content of, or my use of English in, this essay. I am especially indebted to my interlocutors who have given me an insight into their religious practices. Without their help, this research would have been impossible.

Saint Tran exhausted her. His energy was too great. When he descended into her body, she felt "extremely heavy" (*nang khung khiep*). She found that worshipping the Mother Goddess was easier and lighter for her (*nhe nhang hon*). Moreover, she received "blessed gifts" (*loc*) from the Mother Goddess, much more so than when she worshipped Saint Tran.

In this essay, I aim to explore the relationship between Tran Hung Dao and the Mother Goddess religion (*Dao Mau*), which in the past was also called the "Three Palaces religion" (*Dao Tam Phu*) and "Assembly of Spirits" (*Chu Vi*) and today is called the "Four Palaces religion" (*Dao Tu Phu*). I will raise several questions: Why has Tran Hung Dao, a national hero with impeccable nationalist credentials, become the saint (*thanh*) of a particular cult, the Saint Tran cult, which aims to cure illness and exorcise evil spirits? Why has this cult been incorporated into the Mother Goddess religion? How has the cult come to appear in spirit possession rituals in a performative way?[2] In what specific ways has Tran Hung Dao been integrated into the Mother Goddess pantheon? And what does this adaptation of Saint Tran mean to spirit mediums, especially women?

I have observed many spirit possession rituals performed by male and female mediums in which Saint Tran has been a spirit in the Mother Goddess system. He usually appears after the three mother goddesses (*Mau*).[3] In my interviews with a number of spirit mediums conducted in 2003, I discovered a great diversity of experiences and eclectic innovation in their practices involving the Mother Goddess and Tran Hung Dao. Mediums switch back and forth between the Mother Goddess and Saint Tran and usually end up worshipping both. For many spirit mediums, Mother Goddess spirits and Saint Tran Hung Dao's family both influence their lives, but depending on the medium's destiny or spirit root (*can*), one or the other will be more important to her or him. This is worth noting because in early studies of spirit possession (during the first half of the twentieth century), the Saint Tran cult and the Mother Goddess cult (*Chu Vi* cult) are treated as quite separate—with frequent distinctions between female mediums (*dong cot*) of *Chu Vi* and male mediums (*thanh dong*) of Saint Tran Hung Dao.[4] These early studies also show that because the main activities of the Saint Tran cult were expelling ghosts and evil spirits, the cult received higher esteem because of the "unimpeachable moral behavior" of its

---

[2] By "performative," I do not mean that the spirit mediums playact, but, rather, that they indicate the characteristic of the spirit's appearance in relation to other kinds of possessions—which can be frightening and thrilling.

[3] First Mother (*Mau De nhat*), Second Mother (*Mau De nhi*), and Third Mother (*Mau De tam*) are believed to descend into a spirit medium's body under the red veil (*hau trang bong*), although they never visibly appear (*toa bong*). For those possessed by Saint Tran, Saint Tran is the first spirit to appear in a possession ritual after the mediums indicate that the three mother goddesses have descended under the red veil. For those not possessed by Saint Tran, the First Mandarin (*Quan De nhat*) will appear first.

[4] P. Giran, *Magie and Religion Annamites* (Paris: Librairie maritime et coloniale, Rue Jacob 17, 1912); Phan Ke Binh, *Viet Nam Phong Tuc* [Vietnamese Customs] (1915; repr., Ho Chi Minh City: Nha Xuat Ban Thanh pho Ho Chi Minh, 1992); Nguyen Van Khoan, "Essai sur le Dinh et le culture du génie tutélaire des villages au Tonkin" [Essays on the Dinh and the Cult of Village Guardian Spirits in Tonkin], *Bulletin de l'École Française d'Extrême-Orient (BEFEO)* 30 (1930): 107-39; Nguyen Van Huyen, *The Ancient Civilisation of Vietnam* (1944; repr., Hanoi: The Gioi Publishers, 2002); Georges Boudarel, "Kiep Bac," *Vietnamese Studies* 1 (2001): 62-67, originally published 1942; M. Durand, *Technique et panthéon des médiums viêtnamiens (Dông)* (Paris: École Française d'Extrême-Orient, 1959).

members.[5] In contrast, female mediums of *Chu Vi* were looked down on as "crazy mediums," accused of sexual wantonness that was considered immoral.[6]

If these ethnographic studies (by Vietnamese and French scholars) are credible and reflect actual religious activity in Vietnamese society at that time, then the Saint Tran cult was a domain of male practitioners or sorcerers, whereas the Mother Goddess cult (or *Chu Vi* cult) was the domain of female mediums, at least until the 1950s.[7] One might argue that even though early scholars wrote about these religious cults as if they were separate, mixing might already have occurred. Nevertheless, in the early and mid-twentieth century, women's involvement as ritual priests in the Saint Tran cult was not common. Instead, they appeared as victims of evil spirits who needed help from male mediums of Saint Tran. The intermingling of the two spirit possessions cults today and the active involvement of female mediums in this kind of ritual are novel and of considerable interest.

In this essay I suggest that the intermingling of Saint Tran worship and Mother Goddess worship, manifested by the incorporation of Saint Tran into the Mother Goddess pantheon and Saint Tran spirit possession performed by female mediums of the Mother Goddess cult, has arisen much more explicitly at a time of heightened religious resurgence, which is in part a response to the level of social change occurring in contemporary Vietnam. The opening up of Vietnam to a market economy has been accompanied by a degree of religious freedom and cultural transformation, as well as economic, political, and social uncertainty. Personal and private factors, as well as social, cultural, and political ones, account for these developments. Three important elements deserve detailed consideration. First, I will argue that although the worship of Saint Tran reflects Vietnamese historical consciousness, in which respect for great heroes is explicit, its meaning extends beyond that of Saint Tran's status as a national hero. The resurgence of the Saint Tran cult, as well as the appearance of Saint Tran in the Mother Goddess pantheon, needs to be understood with reference to a political climate in which the veneration of Tran Hung Dao holds a high level of legitimacy. Second, I will try to explain the relatively novel occurrence of female mediums claiming possession by Tran Hung Dao. I will argue that by claiming to be possessed by Saint Tran, female mediums empower themselves in a society in which women's choices are still limited and inequality with men persists. Last, but not least, my investigation of the intermingling of the Saint Tran cult and Mother Goddess worship shows their importance in people's attempts to address their financial and health concerns.

In the next section, I present a short overview of Tran Hung Dao as a historical figure and his popularity as a deity in contemporary life. Using literature from the early twentieth century, I then move on to explore the relationship between Tran Hung Dao and the Mother Goddess religion. In doing so, my aim is to demonstrate how the integration of Saint Tran into the *Tu Phu* pantheon of the Mother Goddess religion became part of a modernization process in which this national hero found a new place in people's consciousness.

---

[5] P. Giran, *Magie and Religion Annamites.*

[6] Nguyen Khac Kham, "Vietnamese Spirit Mediumship: A Tentative Reinterpretation of its Basic Terminology," *Vietnam Forum* 1 (1983): 24-30; Phan Ke Binh, *Viet Nam Phong Tuc*; Do Thien, *Vietnamese Supernaturalism: Views from the Southern Region* (New York, NY: RoutledgeCurzon, 2003).

[7] Durand, *Technique et panthéon des médiums viêtnamiens (Dông).*

FROM TRAN HUNG DAO TO THE SAINT TRAN CULT

Among the many national heroes in the history of Vietnamese resistance to foreign invasion, Tran Hung Dao ("Tran Hung Dao" is the honorary title for Tran Quoc Tuan) is the most prominent. Tran Hung Dao devoted his life to serving the four kings of the Tran dynasty (1226-1400) and led the fight to free the country from the Mongol and Chinese invaders, engraving this time in Vietnamese memory as a seminal period in the making of the nation. Nationalist historians and military theorists find his life and work[8] to be great sources for understanding "Vietnamese patriotism" (*chu nghia yeu nuoc Viet nam*) and traditional military methods, and they extol him as a great personality,[9] a military genius (*thien tai quan su*), and a brilliant politician.[10]

Many Vietnamese regard Tran Hung Dao as Saint or Holy Sage Tran (*Duc Thanh Tran*),[11] a powerful spirit and originally a heavenly person sent down to the earth to help the Vietnamese expel foreign aggressors.[12] As Tran Hung Dao was historically a military hero who defeated the purportedly most brutal and powerful army encountered by the Vietnamese up to that time, the Vietnamese people mythologize him as a magical force who can subdue any kind of evil spirit. He possesses supernatural powers and a noble personality beyond that of an ordinary person. Different classes of people—rich and poor, intellectuals and illiterates, traders and farmers, political leaders and commoners—all venerate the popular Tran Hung Dao in both secular and religious ways. The representation of Tran Hung Dao (like that of many other deities) means different things to different people. Considered an exorcist, magician, the ancestor of naval forces (*Thanh to Hai quan*), protector god,

---

[8] *Hich tuong si* [Proclamation for Soldiers], *Binh thu yeu luoc* [Essential Elements of the Art of War], and *Van Kiep tong bi truyen thu* [Van Kiep Esoteric Book] are attributed to Tran Hung Dao. However, some modern historians suspect that these works were written by later generations.

[9] Phan Huy Le, "Hung Dao Dai Vuong Tran Quoc Tuan—mot nhan cach lon" [Hung Dao Dai Vuong Tran Quoc Tuan—A Great Personality] in *Mot chang duong nghien cuu lich su (1995-2000)* [A Period of History Studies] (Hanoi: Nha Xuat Ban Chinh tri Quoc gia, 2000), pp. 399-415; Tran Quoc Vuong, *Nhung guong mat tri thuc* [Intellectual Figures], vol. 1 (Hanoi: Nha Xuat Ban Van hoa Thong tin, 1998).

[10] Le Dinh Sy et al., *Tran Hung Dao—nha quan su thien tai* [Tran Hung Dao—A Military Genius] (Hanoi: Nha Xuat Ban Chinh tri Quoc gia, 2002).

[11] Vietnamese people distinguish between spirits, deities (*than*), and saints or holy sages (*thanh*). If *than* can be human or natural spirits, *thanh* are often human deities (or deified humans) and great merit or high virtue attaches to them. Thus, *thanh* are likely to be ranked higher than *than*.

[12] The most popular myth of Tran Hung Dao tells that he was a green or pure youthful angel (*Thanh Tien dong tu*) who was sent to the earth by the Jade Emperor (*Ngoc Hoang*) to help Vietnam expel foreign aggressors. See also J. M. de Groot on Chinese religion, in which he points out that the Universal is composed of two souls: Yang and Yin; Yang is the celestial sphere and Yin the earth. Heaven is the greatest yang power. See J. M. de Groot, "The War against Spectre," in *The Religious System of China*, vol. 6 (Taipei: Ch'eng-wen Publishing Co., 1967). In popular Vietnamese myth, many heroes, such as Saint Giong, Tran Hung Dao, and Ho Chi Minh, are heavenly people.

protector of children[13] and women, the god of land (*than giu dat*), and Holy Father (*Cha*), Tran Hung Dao is also a military hero according to the historical biographies of his cults. Mr. Thieu, a fifty-one-year-old veteran and master medium of the Tran family (*Nha Tran*), told me that:

> Tran Hung Dao is Saint Tran [*Duc Thanh Tran*]. He is the most powerful of spirits. He manages all three worlds: heaven, this world of us living, and hell. Don't you know that he's controlling the world of the spirits and death? Yes, he still has his own army just as he did when he was alive.

Beyond the two state-patronized, main temples located in Tran Hung Dao's homeland (Bao Loc in Nam Dinh province) and his fiefdom and battle site (Kiep Bac in Hai Duong province), people worship Saint Tran at other sites throughout the country. His sacred space spreads from the north to the south, from the deltas to the uplands. Expatriate Vietnamese communities in Thailand, China, and California also worship Tran Hung Dao. There are countless temples and shrines dedicated to Saint Tran in villages, urban communities, clan houses, and private homes. Of these private shrines, as Toan Anh noted in the 1960s: "people go there occasionally, on the first and fifteenth days of a lunar month, or when they want to supplicate something. Sometimes these shrines are very crowded, no less than public temples."[14] This observation reflects the popularity of the cult almost half a century ago, and it still applies today.

As an independent religious phenomenon, the Saint Tran cult falls under the category of "folk belief" (*tin nguong dan gian*) of Vietnamese folklorists (in comparison with the category of "religion" [*ton giao*]).[15] Categorized as a "folk religion" (*ton giao dan gian*) or "traditional religion" (*ton giao truyen thong*) by religious researchers, the cult occupies a lower level when compared to "high" or "world" religions like Buddhism, Confucianism, Taoism, Catholicism, and Islam.[16] According to policy makers of the Vietnamese government's Religious Committee (*Ban Ton giao chinh phu*), "Tran Hung Dao religion" (*Dao Tran Hung Dao*) is one of fifty "new religions" (*ton giao moi*), "new religious phenomena" (*hien tuong ton giao moi*), or "new religious movements" (*phong trao ton giao moi*) that have emerged since the 1980s.[17] Both the general tables of religions of the Vietnamese Fatherland Front and the Central Public Relations Committee of the Government regard Tran Hung Dao as a newly developing religion. If several "new religious movements" such as

---

[13] There is a popular custom called "contractual sale" (*ban khoan*) in which a child is sold symbolically to Saint Tran until the child is thirteen years old. Saint Tran is believed to possess the power to protect children.

[14] Toan Anh, *Nep cu-Tin nguong Viet nam* [Old Vietnamese Customs and Religious Beliefs] (1968; repr., Ho Chi Minh City: Nha Xuat Ban Thanh pho Ho Chi Minh, 1991), p. 231. Pagination is to the 1991 edition.

[15] Ngo Duc Thinh, *Tin nguong va van hoa tin nguong o Vietnam* [Religious Beliefs and the Culture of Religious Beliefs in Vietnam] (Hanoi: Nha Xuat Ban Khoa hoc xa hoi, 2001).

[16] Dang Nghiem Van, *Nhung van de ton giao hien nay* [Religious Issues Today] (Hanoi: Nha Xuat Ban Khoa hoc xa hoi, 1994).

[17] Do Quang Hung, "Hien tuong Ton giao moi—May van de ly luan thuc tien" [New Religious Phenomena—Some Theoretical and Practical Issues], *Tap chi Nghien cuu Ton giao* 5 (2001): 3-12.

"Ho Chi Minh Jade Buddha" (*Ngoc Phat Ho Chi Minh*) or Uncle Ho religion[18] are graded in the category close to Buddhism (*gan voi Phat giao*), Tran Hung Dao religion is classified in the category close to folk beliefs (*loai gan voi tin nguong dan gian*).[19]

The Vietnamese saying—"A general when alive, a deity after death" (*Sinh vi danh tuong, tu vi than*)—applies to many military heroes in Vietnamese history. Yet no other national heroes share Tran Hung Dao's status among the people. Only Saint Tran has influenced people's lives at both a macro- and micro-level. Literature on the Saint Tran cult has often classified it as an "inner/indigenous religion" (*Noi Dao*), in which Tran Hung Dao is the supreme deity.[20] Tran Hung Dao's family enjoys veneration historically like no other. All of his family members have become spirits and appear in spirit possession rituals. His two daughters are known as the First Royal Damsel (*Vuong Co de nhat*) and the Second Royal Damsel (*Vuong Co de nhi*). His third son (*Duc Ong De tam*), Tran Quoc Tang, is worshipped separately at Cua Ong temple in Quang Ninh province, and his son-in-law, Saint Pham Ngu Lao (*Duc Thanh Pham*), his close servants Yet Kieu and Da Tuong, his soldiers, and the young girl at Suot gate (*Co be cua Suot*) and the boy-attendant at Suot gate (*Cau be cua Suot*) are worshipped in many temples.[21]

Saint Tran's supernatural efficacy is believed to culminate at a special point of time—the festival of the lunar month of August, when he is worshipped as Holy Father—in counterpoint to the Mother Goddess Lieu Hanh, who, according to legend, is said to have died in the lunar month of March (see Ngo Duc Thinh's essay, this volume). In the northern delta, there is a saying, "August is Father's death anniversary, March is Mother's death anniversary" (*Thang Tam gio Cha, thang Ba gio Me*). Who "Father" is believed to refer to in this saying differs in different areas of Vietnam.[22] He is either Father King of Eight Oceans (*Vua Cha Bat Hai*) in Thai Binh province or Saint Tran (*Duc Thanh Tran*). Since Saint Tran and Father King Bat Hai each have death anniversaries in August, people generally consider both as "Holy Father." Thus, March and August are the most hectic months on the lunar calendar for spirit mediums of Saint Tran and the Mother Goddess.

---

[18] Although they are classified as "new religions," these groups have little to do with religion. They mostly teach morality.

[19] Do Quang Hung, "Hien tuong Ton giao moi—May van de ly luan thuc tien," pp. 3-12.

[20] Durand, *Technique et panthéon des médiums viêtnamiens (Dông)*; Tran Van Giau, *Su phat trien cua tu tuong o Viet nam tu the ky XIX den Cach mang thang Tam* [Ideological Development in Vietnam from the Nineteenth Century to the August Revolution] (Hanoi: Nha Xuat Ban Khoa hoc xa hoi, 1973).

[21] "*Cua Suot*" refers to the sea gate at Quang Ninh province. *Co Be* and *Cau Be cua Suot* are understood differently by mediums as Saint Tran's generals or his children.

[22] When doing fieldwork in different cities and provinces of Hanoi, Ho Chi Minh City, Thai Binh, Nam Dinh, Hai Duong, and Ha Tay, I found that people's opinions of who "Father" refers to were incredibly diverse. Generally speaking, throughout Vietnam Saint Tran Hung Dao is regarded as the Holy Father (*Cha*), although many disciples of *Tu Phu* mediumship consider Father King Bat Hai (*Vua Cha Bat Hai*, a natural deity, who is an incarnation of a holy snake) in Thai Binh province to be the Holy Father. In the area of Phu Giay, Nam Dinh province, "Father" could also refer to Ly Bi. Others believe that "Father" refers to Father King Emperor of Jade (*Vua Cha Ngoc Hoang*). Scholars tend to explain the counterpoint of Mother-Father and March-August as a principle of yin-yang, feminine-masculine. Many male spirits therefore can be put under the category of "Father." See Nguyen Minh San, "Quanh hinh tuong tam linh Cha-Me dan toc [Understanding of the Spiritual Symbol of the National Father-Mother], *Tap chi Van hoa Nghe thuat* 8 (1996): 21-25.

There are different kinds of rituals[23] conducted for Tran Hung Dao today, but according to early studies, Saint Tran cult rituals were usually exorcisms to expel an evil spirit (Pham Nhan) who harassed women. Male mediums were sorcerers considered capable of exorcising the evil.[24] During his visit to the Kiep Bac pilgrimage site in September 1942, Georges Boudarel observed:

> In the central ground, the incantation of an infertile woman begins. The most aged man plies her with questions to exorcise her, waves red and green banners in front of her, while gongs are beaten to attract the genie's attention. The woman is in a trance. She turns on herself while sitting up. She looks like she is being hypnotized. Then suddenly, she has seen Pham Nhan's evil spirit: she turns over and over, striking her head on the ground as if she wants to fight against the evil spirit who tortures her. Finally, she stands up and runs madly towards the river, which seems to fascinate her. Then, she throws herself in it to "drown the evil spirit." Her parents save her completely unconscious. The spirit has at last been chased away. The trance ends.[25]

Boudarel's observation is similar to that of French and Vietnamese scholars like Phan Ke Binh, Toan Anh, Nguyen Van Huyen, and Maurice Durand who consider exorcism to be the main activity of both the Saint Tran cult and its most sacred Kiep Bac temple. These studies also reveal that, although the majority of believers were female victims of evil spirits, the spirit mediums or sorcerers known as *thanh dong* were usually men.[26] In his book on Vietnamese customs published in 1915, Phan Ke

---

[23] My fieldwork has revealed diverse forms of ritual. There are some so-called Taoists in the Tam Dao mountains who claim to be initiated by Saint Tran. Several public temples dedicated to Saint Tran Hung Dao in Hanoi worship him in a Buddhist manner and do not allow spirit possession. In contrast, spirit possession rituals take place ebulliently in many private temples; some of these practices are more theatrical (performative) and/or thrilling than others.

[24] In the index to *Viet Dien U linh tap* [Spiritual Powers of the Viet Pantheon], written in the eighteenth century, a story of Pham Nhan and Tran Hung Dao was added. The story tells of Ba Linh, a pseudonym of Nguyen Nhan, who is usually called Pham Nhan. Ba Linh's father was a trader from Kang T'ung in China. He came to the south (Vietnam) to trade and got married to a woman of An Bai village, Dong Trieu province, in northeast Vietnam. Ba Linh was born there, but when he grew up, he followed his father back to China to study. Since he studied well, he earned a doctorate in the Yuan dynasty. He was also a highly able sorcerer who could make himself invisible. He usually treated women in the palace who were sick but then underhandedly went into the seraglio to have secret sexual relations with them. When the king discovered these secrets, he seized Ba Linh and intended to behead him. This occurred just as the Mongol-Yuan army was about to invade Dai Viet (Vietnam). Pham Nhan volunteered to be a guide for the invasion of Vietnam in order to atone for his sins. In the Bach Dang River defeat, Hung Dao Vuong arrested Nhan. Nhan asked Hung Dao Vuong to let him die in his mother's An Bai village. Pham Nhan asked Tran Hung Dao: "After I die, what will Your Majesty feed me?" Tran Hung Dao angrily answered: "May you eat women's blood!" Since then, after Nhan's death, his soul has wandered around the country, following any woman who is about to give birth or who has just given birth and making her sick and beyond treatment. But if her relatives go to Tran Hung Dao's temple and ask for an old sedge mat in the temple, stretch it out for the patient to lie on, and then dissolve incense ash taken from the temple for the patient to drink, she will recover quickly. Ly Te Xuyen, *Viet Dien U linh tap* [Spiritual Powers of the Viet Pantheon] (Saigon: Khai Tri Bookshop, 1960).

[25] Boudarel, "Kiep Bac," p. 64.

[26] In "Vietnamese Spirit Mediumship: A Tentative Reinterpretation of Its Basic Terminology," Nguyen Khac Kham stated that, based on Chinese and Vietnamese dictionaries, *"thanh dong"*

Binh (1875-1921), one of the first Vietnamese scholars to become interested in spirit possession, stated that the appellation *thanh dong* means people who worship Saint Tran.[27] Possessed by Tran Hung Dao, *thanh dong* therefore embody his power to dispel the evil spirit Pham Nhan from tortured believers. This is also a feature of the Saint Tran cult that distinguishes it from the *Chu Vi* cult, which is called the Mother Goddess religion (*Dao Mau*) by folklorists today.[28]

THE SAINT TRAN AND *CHU VI* CULTS

Importantly, both religious forms, the Saint Tran cult and the *Chu Vi* cult, originated in the Red River Delta in the north of Vietnam. The holy land of the *Chu Vi* cult is in Phu Giay in Nam Dinh province. The center of Saint Tran worship is at Bao Loc temple (Nam Dinh province) and Kiep Bac temple (Hai Duong province). Although the earthly biographies of many spirits of *Chu Vi* remain unclear and relate to nature (some of them historicized), the spirits of the Tran family (*Nha Tran*) are connected to historical figures of the Tran dynasty, one of the most prosperous dynasties in Vietnamese history.

The distinction between the Saint Tran cult and the *Chu Vi* cult first appears in scholarly literature in the first half of the twentieth century. In his work on village communal houses (*dinh*) and tutelary deities (*thanh hoang*), Nguyen Van Khoan stated:

> There are three main kinds of worship, defined by people['s] aspiration: the worship of *Chu Vi* [assembly of spirits], the worship of the generals of Tran Hung Dao, and the worship of souls of the nether world and devils. Those who specialize in worshipping *Chu Vi* are female mediums [*ba dong*], those who specialize in worshipping Tran Hung Dao's generals are male mediums [*ong dong*] and ritual priests [*thay phap*], and those who specialize in worshipping the nether world's souls are amulet makers [*thay bua*] or sorcerers [*thay phu thuy*].[29]

Regarding the work of mediums of Saint Tran and his generals, Nguyen Van Huyen, a member of l'École Française d'Extrême-Orient (EFEO) and the first minister of education after the 1945 Revolution, wrote in 1944:

> They treat patients, distribute favors in violent scenes of ecstasy in the course of which they thrust two big puncheons of about 50 cm long into their cheeks and they make cuts to their tongues. The blood that gushes from these wounds is collected on the amulets that the faithful and the patients will carry or swallow. Hung Dao and his assistants Pham Ngu Lao, Yet Kieu, Da Tuong, etc., continue

---

does not mean a young and green-dressed medium like many others had believed, but "a pure, virtuous medium for Saint Tran Hung Dao, a contrast with one of the lesser esteemed mediums for the Chu Vi cult, or a '*dong cot.*'"

[27] Phan Ke Binh, *Viet Nam Phong Tuc.*

[28] Ngo Duc Thinh, *Dao Mau o Viet Nam* [The Mother Goddess Religion in Vietnam] (Hanoi: Nha Xuat Ban Van Hoa-Thong Tin, 1996).

[29] Nguyen Van Khoan, "Essai sur le Dinh et le culture du génie tutélaire des villages au Tonkin."

today to combat the malevolent spirits that trouble the life of men and women in many places.[30]

Paul Giran was perhaps the earliest scholar who attempted to distinguish between the Saint Tran and the *Chu Vi* cults from a socially and morally hierarchical perspective. Employing a Western evolutionary view in his study of magic and religion at the beginning of the twentieth century, Giran claimed that there was an evolutionary progression of spirit cults in Vietnam, in which magic was the lowest form. Giran believed that the *Chu Vi* cult was a form just a bit higher than magic and that the important difference between the cults was to be found in the higher morality of the Saint Tran cult. Thus, he believed that the Saint Tran cult was superior to the Three Palaces (*dao Tam Phu*) or *Chu Vi* cult. According to Giran, the superiority of the Saint Tran cult over *Chu Vi* manifested in several ways. The Saint Tran cult belonged to a higher-ranked social group (men), whereas the other belonged to a lower social group (women). In terms of the spirits of the two cults, many subaltern spirits of mother goddesses in *Chu Vi* could make trouble for people. Giran wrote that some adherents of the *Chu Vi* cult, as victims of those spirits, had to invite Saint Tran to expel these spirits from their bodies. Saint Tran tortured these maleficent spirits and forced them to promise to stop causing trouble. The superior moral standing of the Saint Tran cult vis-à-vis the *Chu Vi* cult also manifested in the belief that anyone who abandoned *Chu Vi* and switched to worshipping Saint Tran would become seriously ill. However, magnanimous Saint Tran never appeared to punish people who switched to worship *Chu Vi*.[31]

A tone of disdain toward female mediums of the *Chu Vi* cult echoes in a number of works, with female mediums being accused of having reckless sexual desire. Ta Chi Dai Truong, citing a poem written in the nineteenth century by Tran Te Xuong (1870-1907), asserted that "spirit possession [*len dong*] now has the meaning of satisfying sexual desire. Disciples of spirit possession [*dong bong*] in this period were people who belonged to the marginalized class in a society where sexual passion was constrained."[32] In a different way, Phan Ke Binh found the spirit possession of female mediums was an excuse for imitating the French women's dances, thereby signifying the decline of Vietnamese morale under the French conquest.

These statements by pioneer scholars allow us to distinguish the two cults. They seem to have some contrasting attributes: masculine–feminine, exorcism–playfulness, high morality–low morality, high esteem–low esteem, and superior–inferior. The gender contrast noted in these early works on spirit possession manifests the power division tacitly accepted by both sexes.

Although the two cults have had a close relationship, in the old literature scholars separated them. Both French and Vietnamese scholars have perpetuated this division, from Paul Giran and Phan Ke Binh in the 1910s to Maurice Durand in the 1950s. One can still see this division reflected in the late 1990s. What has allowed the Vietnamese government policy makers and religious researchers to regard the Saint Tran cult, already noted a century ago in the literature, as a "new religious movement" is its efflorescence in the last two decades. The resurgence of religious

---

[30] Nguyen Van Huyen, *The Ancient Civilisation of Vietnam*, p. 258.

[31] Giran, *Magie and Religion Annamites*, p. 293.

[32] Ta Chi Dai Truong, *Than, Nguoi va dat Viet* [Viet Deities, People and Land] (Westminster, CA: Van Nghe, 1989), p. 311.

activities after the Renovation (*doi moi*) policy has brought about many dynamic changes to the cults of Saint Tran and *Chu Vi*. Such changes manifest saliently in the adoption of Saint Tran into the Mother Goddess religion. From a separate religious form that exorcised evil spirits from female patients using male mediums, Saint Tran has now become a part of the *Tu Phu* pantheon, enjoying the veneration of females who make up the greater number of mediums in Vietnamese society.

SAINT TRAN JOINS MOTHER GODDESS *LEN DONG*

I came with an acquaintance to Tien Nuong palace (*phu Tien Nuong*, the name of the private shrine) for one of my informant's *len dong* rituals one day near the end of 2002. Constructed on the third floor of a house in a busy working area of Hanoi, the shrine contained a large, central altar dedicated to the spirits of *Tu Phu*, Buddha, and Ho Chi Minh. A smaller altar for Saint Tran, his family and generals sat to the right, and another altar for the Mother of Forests and Mountains sat to the left.

Mrs. Thu, the shrine's owner, told me that, as a master medium, she possessed the spirit's root (*can*) to serve every spirit—both mother goddesses and Father (Tran Hung Dao), as well as many other spirits, such as the Buddha Kwan Yin and the Taoist divinity Thai Thuong Lao Quan. Before the spirit possession ritual, she had to conduct rites in front of the main altar to petition the Buddha and the deities. There were always three kinds of food to offer to the three main subjects: offerings for the assembly of spirits of the four palaces (*Cong dong Tu Phu*), for the Mother of Forests (*Phu Thuong Ngan*), and for Saint Tran (*Duc Thanh Tran*). The offering to Saint Tran was usually chicken or pork meat (sometimes pork head) with sticky rice, while the offering to the Mother of Forests and Mountains included seafood (shrimp, crab, and snail) and forest specialties such as bamboo shoots. Mrs. Thu also conducted a rite with food for wandering souls (*cung co hon*) to ensure that her ceremony would go smoothly.[33]

Mrs. Thu sat in front of the altar with four women surrounding her, acting as her assistants in the ceremony. These women called themselves "the four highest-ranking court officials" (*tu tru trieu dinh*). When Mrs. Thu conducted her ceremonies, she often chose these women because they were very close to her and had more free time than other followers. They came from different jobs and living conditions, but they assisted Mrs. Thu for the same reasons: to serve the spirits, to help their master organize ceremonies for her followers, to profit from *loc* (blessed gifts, which included offerings such as fruits, drinks, small change, and sweets)[34] from their group-mates' ceremonies, and to have "fun" (*cho vui*).

After her salutations to the audience, Mrs. Thu started her possession by covering her head with a red veil. Shaking her head under the veil and giving a sign with her fingers, Mrs. Thu indicated that the three mother goddesses (the Mothers of

---

[33] My interlocutors explained that there are two worlds, the world of the living and the world of the dead and spirits. The nether world, however, is not cut off from the world of the living. Spirits and the deceased are not inert. They involve themselves in the life of the living. Wandering souls of the deceased who cannot find their way home (because, for example, they died suddenly in an accident or have no family to offer food to them) are believed to become hungry ghosts and malevolent. Offering food to wandering souls before a ceremony is, thus, to prevent their possible intrusion during the ceremony.

[34] Alexander Soucy examined the notion of *loc* in his thesis: "Buddha's Blessing: Gender and Buddhist Practice in Hanoi" (PhD dissertation, Australian National University, 1999).

Heaven, Water, and Mountains and Forest) had entered into her body and then left without appearing (showing their faces—*trang bong*).[35] After these three incarnations (*gia*), she went into a trance with the descent of Saint Tran. She threw off the red veil while raising her forefinger, and we knew that this was Saint Tran's incarnation. Her assistants then started to change her dress and serve her. In a red robe, she received a sheaf of incense, a cup of wine, and a sword. After standing up and kneeling in front of the altar three times, she danced with the sword for a while, manifesting the physiognomy of a general. She sat down on a chair[36] and listened while her husband, who was kneeling behind her, extolled her (as the manifestation of Saint Tran) and requested attention, blessings, and gifts from "Saint Tran."

With a pleased expression in her role as Saint Tran, Mrs. Thu said:

> The owner of this shrine has a true heart, filial and meek, so now I appear here. I am very happy. This shrine will help people everywhere. My name, Saint Tran, has gone down in history. I appear in five continents. All your wishes will be satisfied. I will bless you. Hey, where is the beat of the drum and the music? Hey, my soldiers, pray to Saint Tran, I will calm you. Hey, play three drum rolls and nine drumbeats for me!

She slapped a pillow next to her to show her emphasis and excitement to the singers (*cung van*), who were singing to glorify Saint Tran's feats in battle. After that, she covered her head with the red veil, indicating that Saint Tran was leaving and a new spirit was descending. This time, Saint Tran's second daughter appeared,[37] and all Mrs. Thu's assistants swiftly changed her clothes, dressing her in a green robe. She repeated several actions—purifying by incense, drinking, dancing with flags and swords, expressing appreciation of the singers by giving them money, and blessing[38] herself as the medium (serving the spirit [*hau Thanh*]), as well as her assistants, the singers, and all participants. Two other incarnations of *Nha Tran* spirits followed: the young prince at Suot sea gate or the youngest son of Tran Hung Dao (*Cau be cua Suot*) and the young lady at Suot sea gate or the youngest daughter of Tran Hung Dao (*Co be cua Suot*), according to Mrs. Thu. After the appearance of *Nha Tran*'s spirits, many manifestations of the *Tu Phu*'s spirits appeared in the following order: great mandarins (*Quan Lon*), ladies (*Chau*), princes (*Ong Hoang*), princesses (*Co*), and young princes (*Cau*). Spanning nearly five hours, the ritual ended with an incarnation of the Youngest Prince (*Cau Be*). In the role of *Cau Be*, Mrs. Thu gesticulated excitedly as she danced, speaking with a lisp and simulating the gestures of a young boy. Distributing many blessed gifts (*loc*) to participants in the

---

[35] According to spirit mediums, since mother goddesses are very sacred (*thieng*), they never show their faces but instead incarnate under the red veil (*trang bong*), in contrast to other spirits that do appear (*toa bong*).

[36] A chair is used only for spirits of *nha Tran*, not for spirits of *Tu Phu*.

[37] Mrs. Thu explained that Tran Hung Dao's first daughter never appears because she became a nun (*di tu*) and a civil mandarin (*quan van*). Compared with military mandarins (*quan vo*), civil mandarins rarely descend (*giang dong*).

[38] From my observation, every spirit says the same thing: they recognize the medium's attempts and bless the participants and people (*ban khen cho bach gia tram ho*). A follower of Mrs. Thu told me that she and her fellow mediums had to learn from their master what to say when spirits incarnated in their bodies because "those words are greeting words and it is a tradition that we should follow."

rousing atmosphere of applause, Mrs. Thu was ecstatic with happiness. After throwing off the red veil, and with a satisfied smile, she thanked all who had attended her ritual.

I observed in many *len dong* rituals that Tran Hung Dao, his children, and his generals appear after the three mother goddesses (who only descend under the red veil). In these rituals, Saint Tran appears with a calm manner, which is similar to the way the First Mandarin (*Quan De Nhat*) of the *Tu Phu* system appears, who also wears a red robe—in contrast to the thrilling and frightening manner typical of exorcist rituals of the Saint Tran cult. Tran Hung Dao and his subordinates are grouped under the term "Tran family" (*Nha Tran*) or "Tran dynasty" (*Tran Trieu*), while the other spirits of the Mother Goddess system belong to the four palaces (*Tu Phu*), in which the Mother Goddess Lieu Hanh is supreme. "Serving spirits of the Tran family" (*hau Nha Tran*)—a counterpart of "serving spirits of the four palaces" (*hau Tu Phu*)—is a familiar phrase among spirit mediums. Those who possess the spirit root (*can*) of *Nha Tran* serve Saint Tran and his family, and those who possess the *can* of *Tu Phu* serve spirits of the mother goddesses. Those who carry both types of *can*, calling themselves "servants to both realms" (*lam toi doi nuoc*), experience possession by the spirits of the two systems.

SERVANTS TO BOTH REALMS (*LAM TOI DOI NUOC*)

I was eager to learn how mediums know whether they embody the *can* of *Nha Tran* or of *Tu Phu*, or of particular spirits of both those systems. Some mediums explained to me that they read people's faces or characters to determine what *can* they possessed. Those believed to embody the *can* of Saint Tran are usually hot tempered (*nong tinh*) or straightforward. The quality of a person's voice can also indicate their *can*. For example, those with Saint Tran's *can* speak with hoarse voices, whereas the voices of those with *Tu Phu*'s *can* are likely to be strident. Confused by my informants' intricate explanations, I sought answers from Mrs. Thu. This master medium had been responsible for more than one hundred ceremonies to initiate new spirit mediums (ceremonies called "opening the palace" [*mo phu*]). I asked her, "Do I have *can*? What is my *can*?" Mrs. Thu pulled out a notebook from beneath the shrine's altar, asked my age, then checked the notebook. She said, "Here it is. In your previous life [*kiep truoc*], you owed 5,000 *quan* [the currency used in the old time] and fifteen prayer books. You have to pay into the treasury number four, to the spirit named *Menh Ty quan*. You have to plant three trees, buy three votive shoes, and set free one duck [*phong sinh*]." She checked another page, read aloud two lines of verse, then told me: "Your *can* is close to *Nha Tran* and *Quan Tam Phu* [the Third Mandarin of the *Tu Phu* system]! But your destiny is not heavy [*nang can*]; you are compatible [*co duyen*] to spirits of *Nha Tran*." I turned out to be a potential medium of both religious systems—*Nha Tran* and *Tu Phu*. Mrs. Thu encouraged me, "Once you are in a trance, you will know what a spirit is [*biet the nao la ong Thanh*]." After that, I better understood how mediums came to know about their *can*, as indicated by their compatibility with certain spirits.

The year of one's birth is another important way of determining a person's *can*. One of Mrs. Thu's followers told me that nine out of ten of her friends are mediums because of the *can* they possess as a result of being born in 1962, the year of the tiger. This had made their lives hard and their destinies heavy (*nang can*). It is noteworthy that the Buddhist concept of "karma" is very popular among Vietnamese spirit mediums. They believe that in their previous lives they were indebted to the spirits of the four palaces or Tran dynasty, or that they did not improve or rectify themselves (*tu*) properly. Consequently, in this life they must better themselves by serving/paying off spirits of Saint Tran (*tra no Thanh*) or the four palaces (*tra no Tu Phu*). Some of my informants explained that the mother goddesses and Saint Tran were related in a manner similar to the coexistence of two essential systems of government for a country: civilian (*van*) and military (*vo*). Here the mother goddesses are civil mandarins, whereas Saint Tran is a military mandarin. Other informants asked me, "Can you not pray to your father and your mother? Of course you have to worship Saint Tran and the mother goddesses. They are our Father and Mother." As they struggle with hardships in their lives, spirit mediums view their good or bad fortune as the outcome of their relationship with spirits of *Nha Tran* or *Tu Phu*. If serving one spirit system does not bring the mediums what they expect, they are likely to seek help from the other. Master medium Thu explained to me why it is necessary for mediums of *Tu Phu* to serve Saint Tran:

> Saint Tran has special power. He puts down in [the] nether world and this world. He helps to strengthen your destiny; he gives you reputation, appearance, talent, and fortune, which will make you completely different from ordinary spirit mediums. Spirits of [the] Mother Goddess religion also give you those things, but for some people, if their destinies are too heavy, or their families have some fierce things such as a tremor under the ancestors' graves [as cause of mishaps] or a member in their families is stuck with a soul or ghost, serving Saint Tran is necessary. After being possessed by Saint Tran, they can see a quick magical response.

Tensions exist between spirit mediums who serve *Nha Tran* and those who serve *Tu Phu*. Mediums of Saint Tran often criticize mediums of *Tu Phu*. A woman accompanying me on a pilgrimage group to a Saint Tran temple said, "Mediums [*dong*] of [the] Saint Tran family are earnest [*nghiem tuc*]; only people whose roots [are] of one in the Tran family can be initiated, and then they must work to help other people, not like *dong* of the *Tu Phu*." Whispering, as she was afraid of vexing other mediums in the group who served only the mother goddess, she added, "*Dong* of *Tu Phu* are very capricious [*linh tinh*] and snobbish [*dua doi*]. I only serve *Nha Tran*." A sixty-three-year-old medium, a trader in Hanoi's largest wholesale market (the Dong Xuan market), complained to me that nowadays mediums' actions in the *len dong* ritual were topsy-turvy (*lung tung*). According to her, the distribution of money as *loc* to audiences by many mediums was wrong and unacceptable because "serving Saint Tran must be august and imposing since Saint Tran is incarnated to work, not to distribute gifts to participants like spirits of mother goddesses [*Ngai ve lam viec chu lam gi co chuyen phat loc*]."

This tension reveals personal struggles not only concerning a medium's decision to be on this side or the other or both. It also discloses dilemmas associated with their aspirations and abilities. Mr. Du, the eldest of eight spirit mediums in his Hanoi clan (which follows the tradition of worshipping Saint Tran going back five generations), told me that, in the 1930s and 1940s, only people with *can* performed spirit possession ceremonies, while nowadays spirit possession was out of control, especially *dong* of *Tu Phu*:

Mediums in the Four Palaces religion take a leaf out of others' books. They imitate each other. They want to be initiated for prosperity. But a medium of the Saint Tran family dare not be initiated rashly [*bua bai*] if they don't have *can* because they have to work [*lam viec*] to save people.

Paradoxically, Mr. Du complained that "spirit mediums of Saint Tran do not receive anything financially. We don't have much fortune, which is different from mediums of the *Tu Phu*. They have a lot of *loc*." According to him, mediums of the *Tu Phu* must spend a lot of money on each ceremony (at least four million VND, equal to nearly US$300), which he could not afford. Mediums of Saint Tran spend much less. He smiled with bitterness: "Serving spirits of *Tu Phu* is fun, but only rich people can be mediums of *Tu Phu*."

Remarkably, Mr. Du's three nephews and son, all initiated as spirit mediums of Saint Tran, held an "opening the palace" ceremony (*mo phu*) recently to become mediums of *Tu Phu*. I observed one sumptuous initiation ritual costing US$700. His nephew, Mr. Tuan, a thin man hosting that ritual, told me, "I have to follow my family tradition of worshipping Saint Tran, but if I am a medium of *Tu Phu*, my business will have good fortune [*lam an co loc*]." While we were watching Tuan in trance, his cousin, another medium, whispered that actually Tuan did nothing but gamble. His family depended upon his wife, a trader at the Dong Xuan market. But they had a lot of money. Tuan, with a big satisfied smile after the ritual, giggled: "My wife said she paid for all of this ritual, but if I do not get fatter [*beo len*], she will kick me out of the house."

CONVIVIAL SPIRIT POSSESSION (*HAU VUI*) AND WOMEN'S EMPOWERMENT

Spirit mediums possessing the *can* of both Saint Tran and the mother goddesses frequently use phrases such as "serving spirits in a joyful way" (*hau vui*), "serving spirits for beauty" (*hau lam canh*), and "serving spirits to work" (*hau lam viec*). While *hau lam viec* refers to exorcist rituals that involve frightening activities such as piercing cheeks, strangling necks, and cutting tongues to get blood to apply on amulets, *hau vui* or *hau lam canh* indicates the "performative character" of the rituals. A veteran, Mr. Du's nephew, describes serving spirits of *Nha Tran* as follows:

> I had been a medium of *Tu Phu* before I became a medium of *Nha Tran* as well. My uncle, Mr. Du, opened the palace of *Nha Tran* for me. But he always said to us that he would not believe that we were genuine mediums if we could not get the blood from our tongues [*lay dau man*], strangle necks [*that co*], and pierce cheeks [*xien linh*]. Mediums of *Nha Tran* have to do that.

Despite what "genuine mediums" of Saint Tran say about others, mediums of *Tu Phu* still serve Saint Tran during the *len dong* ritual in a joyful or convivial way (*hau vui*). In *len dong*, Saint Tran appears like a great mandarin of *Tu Phu*. Because Saint Tran and the First Great Mandarin are supposed to wear the red costume, many mediums use the same costume for both of them.

Although spirit mediums who are "servants to both realms" (*lam toi doi nuoc*) serve spirits of both *Nha Tran* and *Tu Phu*, who is allowed to be possessed by whom is a matter of controversy. When asked this question, my informants gave me different answers. Interestingly, female mediums were likely to claim, bluntly, to be possessed by Saint Tran, whereas male mediums seemed more hesitant to profess this.

I met male mediums who became suspicious when Saint Tran was said to be incarnated into an ordinary medium. A twenty-year-old male medium from a village in Hung Yen province explained that Saint Tran is invited only on special occasions, such as initiation rituals, exorcist rituals to expel ghosts, or the opening ceremony of a new shrine, and that only the head mediums of the shrines (*thu nhang dong den*) and master mediums (*dong thay*) are allowed to be possessed by Saint Tran. He and other normal mediums could incarnate only lower spirits, from Saint Tran's second daughter (*Vuong co de nhi*) and those below her. All the male members of the clan shared this opinion. For them, Saint Tran is too powerful for mundane people; all the male mediums of this clan are therefore possessed in trances by Saint Tran family members, such as Saint Tran's son, son-in-law, and servants—but not by Saint Tran himself. As Mr. Du put it, "Saint Tran is a great hero. He is a general like general Vo Nguyen Giap. I do not dare to be possessed by him."

In contrast, many female mediums told me of experiencing Tran Hung Dao's incarnation. Mrs. Thong, a trader at the Dong Xuan market in Hanoi, said that her experience of the Mother Goddess spirits was very different from what occurred when Saint Tran descended into her, "I feel very intense and cold in my head and body [*cam thay rat nang va ret*]." Unlike the majority of spirit mediums, Lan, the thirty-year-old English lecturer mentioned in the introduction of this essay, does not need a spirit possession ritual to enter a trance. Burning incense is the only condition needed for her to "consult" Saint Tran or the Mother Goddess Lieu Hanh. I myself was able to engage in several "dialogues" with "Saint Tran" through Lan.[39] Lan told me after a dialogue, "You know, his energy was extremely heavy [*nang luong cua Ngai manh khung khiep*]. I think that is why he can ward off evil spirits and ghosts."

Spirit mediums generally must serve spirits of the Mother Goddess cult for three years before serving spirits of Saint Tran's family because these years help their "fates to be steady" (*ban menh vung*) before receiving Saint Tran's energy. Their bodies need training to prepare them for possession by Saint Tran; otherwise they will faint away (*xiu*) or suffer possession by ghosts (*tau hoa nhap ma*).

All of Mrs. Thu's disciples share these views. Among the more than one hundred female adherents, most respectfully call her "master" (*thay*)—including many of her old colleagues. Not only Mrs. Thu and her family (her husband and two children are also spirit mediums), but also all her followers experience incarnation by Saint Tran in their rituals. Mrs. Thu told me that she encouraged her followers to invite Saint Tran to incarnate in their bodies so that their destinies would be fortified (*lam cho ban menh vung len*), even if they do not possess the *can* of Saint Tran's family. In her words and in the experiences of her followers, "even though you are mediums of Mother Goddess [spirits] only, after you serve *Nha Tran*, your life will completely change. You will not be afraid of anything anymore." Mrs. Bich, one of her close followers, recently retired from a job in the Ministry of Defense and expressed her gratitude to Mrs. Thu, her master. According to her, master mediums of other shrines do not allow their followers to experience incarnation by Saint Tran because

---

[39] Lan is believed to be able to communicate or call spirits to descend into her body in a controllable way. She invited "Saint Tran" and the "Mother Goddess" to incarnate into her body to talk to me. She burned incense and closed her eyes for a few minutes, then proclaimed: "I am Saint Tran. What do you want to ask me?" Then we started our dialogue.

"They are afraid that if [the] destiny [*ban menh*] of their followers is stronger, they will betray their masters [*ho so de tu se quay lai phan thay*]."

Saint Tran possesses a female medium in a *len dong* ritual, 2003, Hanoi. After performing several ritual actions as a mandarin of *Tu Phu*, the medium sits down, enjoys the liturgical music, and listens to her disciple, who is also her husband, extol Saint Tran.
Photo by Pham Quynh Phuong.

Importantly, these comments reveal how incarnating Saint Tran can lead his adherents to become stronger, safer, and more confident. In other words, by claiming to be possessed by Saint Tran, spirit mediums empower themselves in a specific way. Mrs. Thu's life serves as an example: She was born in a province in the Red River Delta in 1959. She joined the army when she was eighteen years old and studied at the Hanoi Law University afterward. She married at age twenty-three and worked as a secretary in a district court in Hanoi. She had three children. She was disciplined after she broke the family-planning policy by having two children too close in age. She believes that everything went wrong after she married and entered a life of miserable poverty. Many times she wanted to commit suicide because she felt hopeless about her future. With little money from her job at the district court, she had to care for two unhealthy children and suffered from her husband's abuse. She developed a psychiatric illness. Her followers told me that she used to climb trees and sing nonsensically. Then she was diagnosed with cancer and experienced a period of great hardship and pain. Finally a female spirit medium came to visit and told Mrs. Thu that she was not physically but spiritually ill (*benh am*) and encouraged her to undertake the initiation ceremony to become a spirit medium. This was a momentous day in her life. A few years later, she resigned from her job at the district court to become a master medium and set up her private shrine. Many of her old colleagues have become her followers. Formerly suffering great anguish, Mrs. Thu has become a powerful woman in her family and among her followers. She has drawn all her family (her husband, three children, her parents-in-law, and her brothers and sisters) into the hectic, daily activities of spirit possessions, which take place on the third floor of her house.

Mrs. Thu and her followers do not worship Saint Tran only but also many other spirits. Moreover, they would not admit to seeking power of any kind. Their central claim that they incarnate Saint Tran, are in contact with him, or are chosen by him might nevertheless suggest otherwise. A narrative of empowerment emerges from the image of Tran Hung Dao itself. As a prestigious national hero and a powerful symbol of nationalism, he is associated with strength and power. As mediums teach their followers and encourage adherents to become new mediums, they speak of potential power. Mrs. Thu encouraged me, "Your life will completely change if you are a medium of Saint Tran. Your destiny will be secured and your voice will carry 'weight' [*co suc nang*]."

The power that mediums achieve sometimes manifests initially in their great impact on their partners. Formerly Thu's husband was a tough man with a rigid preconception of spirit possession, and he used to mock and desecrate what Mrs. Thu undertook as "superstition" (*me tin*). However, he eventually became a medium and is now attached to his wife's religious activities and gives her full respect. This might demonstrate how women (whether consciously or unconsciously) employ spirit possession "as a means of insinuating their interests and demands in the face of male constraint,"[40] and that such possession can be a "weapon" of women.[41] Although the empowerment gained through spirit possession applies to both men and women, women in particular can find their strength by claiming to experience the incarnation of Saint Tran.

Thu's power also appears in the relationship she enjoys with her followers, who regard her as a "guide" and "master" and mimic what she does in their own ceremonies. Many of her old colleagues who work at legislative offices and universities have become her followers. Empowerment, in this sense, has been achieved both individually and collectively.

The appellations applied to cult practitioners have changed significantly since the previously mentioned studies of spirit possession by French and Vietnamese scholars. Currently mediums of both the Saint Tran and Mother Goddess cults are said to practice "*Thanh dong*." Many mediums would take offense if they were referred to as "*dong cot*." All my medium informants determinedly called themselves "*thanh dong*" or "*dong*," never "*dong cot*."[42] By adopting the appellation "*thanh dong*" (a term originally applied only to men), female mediums have overcome the disdain with which they were regarded and have enhanced their power and status in a community of mediums that has grown significantly in recent years. Because the exorcist rituals typical of the Saint Tran cult are too violent for female mediums to perform, many are happy to perform them in a new, less frightening, and more convivial manner, which they call "*hau vui*." This, in turn, facilitates the mingling of the Saint Tran cult and Mother Goddess worship.

---

[40] I. M. Lewis, *Ecstatic Religion: An Anthropological Study of Spirit Possession and Shamanism* (Middlesex, MD, and Victoria: Penguin Books, 1971), p. 79.

[41] D. Bargen, *A Woman's Weapon: Spirit Possession in the Tale of Genji* (Honolulu, HI: University of Hawai'i Press, 1997).

[42] "*Dong*" and "*cot*" both refer to a spirit medium. Durand supposes that "*cot*" is a Sino-Vietnamese word that means "corpse" or "skeleton" (Durand, *Technique et panthéon des médiums viêtnamiens*). Nguyen Khac Kham's opinion is that "*dong*" refers to mediums in general and thus can be used for either sex, whereas "*cot*" refers to a medium of the dead (necromancer). The phrase "*dong cot*" designates a female medium or a medium for spirits of the *Chu Vi* cult (Nguyen Khac Kham, "Vietnamese Spirit Mediumship").

SAINT TRAN AND MOTHER GODDESS TEMPLES

Most Mother Goddess temples now contain Saint Tran altars called *Tran Trieu* (Tran dynasty). Moreover, Saint Tran and the Mother Goddess altars have also penetrated into many Buddhist pagodas. When I visited the Hanoi Management Board of Vestiges and Relics in 2003 to find out the number of extant Tran Hung Dao temples, I was disappointed to see the data remained the same as six years previously. Data recorded in the 1980s indicated fifty temples, pagodas, and shrines in Hanoi where people worshipped Tran Hung Dao separately or combined with the mother goddesses. Yet, the number of new shrines or temples dedicated to Saint Tran has increased substantially in the last two decades. However, a research worker at the management board told me that they could not account for the total number of Tran Hung Dao worship sites due to lack of money and because almost every pagoda contained an altar to Tran Hung Dao and the mother goddesses. If I wanted to know the answer to my question, he said, I should have asked about the number of pagodas!

It is significant that despite the adoption of Saint Tran in the holy land of the Mother Goddess religion in Phu Giay, Nam Dinh province—the homeland of the supreme Mother Lieu Hanh—the mother goddesses do not find a place in the most sacred site of Tran Hung Dao worship, that is, in Kiep Bac temple, Hai Duong province, where Tran Hung Dao's wife is seen as *Mau* (Mother) instead.[43] At the lower level of private shrines, however, mixing appears.

Although Saint Tran has been incorporated into the *Tu Phu* pantheon, the reasons for, and the position of, Saint Tran in Mother Goddess temples vary. Generally speaking, the adaptation of Saint Tran into Mother Goddess temples reflects a historicizing tendency. This is also true of the spirits in the Mother Goddess pantheon, as many Mother Goddess spirits have been supplied with "historical biographies." Vietnamese people are proud of their history, and a great national hero like Tran Hung Dao attracts devotion. Yet while the state's establishment and promotion of the cult reflect a nationalist dimension, ordinary people's veneration of Tran Hung Dao and their identification of him as a saint are inspired by more than his heroic deeds. His reputation as a powerful spirit who specializes in expelling ghosts and evil spirits gains him a popular standing.[44] Moreover, if we take a deeper look, there are also other aspects behind the veneration of Saint Tran.

WEALTH GIVES BIRTH TO RITUAL FORM (*PHU QUI SINH LE NGHIA*)

Lan, the English teacher, affirmed that Saint Tran should be worshipped separately and that inclusion of him in Mother Goddess temples was wrong: "Saint Tran and the mother goddesses belong to different systems." The fact that people put his altar in Mother Goddess temples revealed their "pragmatic attitude" (*thuc dung*),

---

[43] This is partly because Tran Hung Dao is a national hero. Kiep Bac temple receives regular visits of the most important government leaders. When asked why the mother goddesses are not worshipped at Kiep Bac temple, local authorities said that because Mother Lieu Hanh was the supreme goddess of a "superstitious religion," she could not be integrated into Tran Hung Dao's temple.

[44] In contemporary Vietnam, the belief in "yin illness" (*benh am*) caused by the intrusion of ghosts and evil spirits has been popular. Because he is credited with defeating the capricious spirit Pham Nhan, Tran Hung Dao has been promoted to be the supreme god in the field of exorcism.

she believed, since they did not have enough space and money to put them in separate temples. With the revival of religious activities and the emergence of a middle class, the offering of statues (*cung tuong*) has become popular among adherents. Many of the *nouveaux-riche* buy statues and offer them to temples or pagodas to obtain blessings from spirits, to thank the spirits for their help, or to acquire fame. Temple keepers in Kiep Bac temple complained that nowadays many new, urban middle-class people want to donate not money, but statues or religious paraphernalia to the temple. So many Tran Hung Dao statues were donated that the temple keepers had to put them in storage, but they still had to burn incense to maintain the "statues' souls." In a well-known Taoist temple in Hanoi, a new table was recently set up in a cramped space to worship Saint Tran—thanks to a woman who dreamt of a spirit who asked her to donate a statue to the temple. When she learned that the temple had almost every statue except Tran Hung Dao's, she offered the statue of him. People could not refuse, even though too many altars already cramped their temple.

An altar of Tran Hung Dao was also included in the late 1990s in Phu Giay temple, the holy land of Mother Goddess worship. Mr. Duc, the temple keeper, whom I have known for ten years, commented:

> I know this is not correct to have Saint Tran because he has never been here, but now people worship him everywhere. Because we did not have his altar here, so people had to go far away. Now they can go to pray to Mother [Lieu Hanh], then go next door to pray to Father. This is because of people's needs and for their convenience.

Interestingly, although Mr. Duc believes that "Father" is King Bat Hai or Ly Nam De, not Tran Hung Dao, he emphasizes the "convenience" of this arrangement. Another hidden reason that might apply to every temple is that the more altars there are in temples, the more money is collected from donation boxes placed nearby.

LEGITIMIZATION AND HIGHER STATUS

I met Mr. Du, the oldest medium of a clan following a tradition of worshipping Saint Tran, in a large house where he lives with his children near West Lake in Hanoi. Born in 1917, he witnessed most of the local events of the twentieth century. He was, in his words, "seized by spirits" (*bat dong noi*) to become a spirit medium when he was twenty-nine years old and has been serving Saint Tran for nearly sixty years. He recalled:

> As a young medium [*thanh dong*], I was invited to go everywhere in Kiep Bac, Cua Ong, Yen Tu, Huong pagoda, Yen Bai, to carry out rituals to help people. Before 1945, we performed spirit possession ceremonies freely without any inhibition. After the Land Reform in the 1950s, they prohibited them with extreme strictness [*cam ghe lam*]. My brother, Mr. Duyen, was arrested to undergo reeducation for a week since he owned this shrine. He had to do self-criticism, and since then we had to practice underground. We did not dare to serve the spirits [*hau dong*] publicly anymore. But it was lucky that our shrine remained unscathed while many other people, they themselves had to damage their shrines to keep away from trouble. They were too scared. Our shrine

remained untouched because we were worshipping Saint Tran, the most famous national hero who fought Yuan [China]. Who dared destroy his temple?

Mr. Du's confidence reveals a past in which Saint Tran appeared as a protective shield for the shrine. The Decree 56-CP of the Cabinet Council of the Government (*Hoi dong Chinh phu*), issued on March 18, 1975, linked regulations on organizing festivals, weddings, and funerals and recognized some traditional festivals related to national heroes like the Hung kings, the Trung sisters, and Tran Hung Dao, admitting that they were worthy of preservation provided that all "superstitious elements" were eliminated in order to "enhance the content of educational thought" (*nang cao noi dung giao duc tu tuong*). The decree also stated that it was compulsory to eradicate "superstitious festivals" like the Phu Giay and Dong Bang festivals. The Phu Giay festival, the biggest festival dedicated to the supreme Mother Goddess Lieu Hanh, was therefore banned until the mid-1990s. Local people in the Dong Bang temple in Thai Binh province (another sacred site for disciples of the Mother Goddess religion), where King Bat Hai (a sacred snake) was originally worshipped, set up an altar for Tran Hung Dao. They then printed a brochure indicating that the temple had mainly venerated Tran Hung Dao since the fourteenth century because he used to pass through the village. This helped them to avoid a serious attack from the authorities. By creating a story in which King Bat Hai appeared in Tran Hung Dao's dreams, giving him hints on how to defeat enemies, local people found a way to connect their spirit to the great national hero and the nation's history. Luckily, the anniversary of King Bat Hai coincided with that of Tran Hung Dao in August of the lunar calendar. Consequently, the temple was officially recognized in 1986. Thus, for two decades people have regarded Dong Bang temple as Tran Hung Dao's temple.

In 2003, when I visited this temple, to my surprise there was hardly anyone who acknowledged Tran Hung Dao; they spoke only of King Bat Hai. Because I insisted, some men on the temple's management board (*Ban quan ly di tich*) showed me an altar on the right of the big statue of King Bat Hai. The altar had several incense bowls but no statues. A man admitted that the altar was for the assembly of male spirits (*cong dong duc ong*) in general, not for Tran Hung Dao. But because Tran Hung Dao is a male spirit, of course he was there! (*cung tho chung o do*) Obviously, in the atmosphere of a more relaxed attitude toward religion by the state, local people feel less pressure to disguise their deity and their religious activities, such as conducting spirit possession rituals.

Charles Keyes, Laurel Kendall, and Helen Hardacre have pointed out that many modern states in East and Southeast Asia, including Vietnam, have found it difficult to formulate a settled policy toward religious rituals. From the standpoint of modernization, it is necessary for government officials to deemphasize ritual practices. But from the standpoint of nation building, the promotion of selected practices, and even the invention of new rites, is essential.[45] Vietnam's patriotic tradition ensured that the cult of Saint Tran was preserved and kept relatively intact, whereas religions less conducive to nationalism, like Mother Goddess worship, were restrained. Many of the national heroes who are worshipped in temples are officially

---

[45] Charles Keyes et al., "Introduction: Contested Visions of Community in East and Southeast Asia," in *Asian Visions of Authority: Religion and the Modern States of East and Southeast Asia*, ed. Charles Keyes, Laurel Kendall, and Helen Hardacre (Honolulu: University of Hawai'i Press, 1994), pp. 1-16.

recognized generals. There have been no attempts to delegitimize the cults associated with such national heroes, even though ritual activities such as the spirit possession rituals associated with them have been suppressed.[46]

Dong Bang temple, where Bat Hai Dai Vuong (King of Eight Oceans) and Tran Hung Dao are co-worshipped, Thai Binh province, 2003. Photo by Pham Quynh Phuong.

The state has clearly faced a dilemma, which has created a space for common mediums to legitimize their shrines by including Tran Hung Dao, thereby promoting their shrines to a higher rank. Tran Hung Dao/Saint Tran, "a typical Vietnamese" (*con nguoi tieu bieu*), the most powerful symbol of Vietnamese patriotism, has helped Vietnamese citizens to sanction individual ritual needs, legitimizing what the authorities formerly considered to be illegal. Since national heroes are favorites of the people, and worshipping "heroes and people who have merit to the nation" (*anh hung, co cong voi dat nuoc*) is one of the many criteria by which the state recognizes and chooses to financially support a temple, many local people even go so far as to make up spirit stories/legends in which their deities appear as historical or natural heroes in the history of national resistance. In this way, they attempt to obtain state approval.

In an article published in the *Van Nghe* newspaper, Vu The Khoi claims that, based on his analysis of the original Sino (Han) writing, the royal honor-conferring diploma (*sac phong*) written by King Thieu Tri in 1846, was not conferred on Tran Hung Dao in Son Hai temple (one of the biggest temples dedicated to Tran Hung Dao in Hanoi), as alleged. According to Vu The Khoi, the title "*Dai nguyen soai Tong quoc chinh Thai su, Thuong phu quoc cong*" on the royal diploma initially referred to Trinh Tung (1599) and Trinh Trang (1626), but not Tran Hung Dao. The temple's owner, unintentionally or perhaps purposely, assigned this title to Tran Hung Dao, which attracted the interest of historians to "the oldest temple worshipping the national hero, Tran Hung Dao, in Hanoi."[47]

Adherents fabricate stories of spirits (*than tich*) in order both to have their temple recognized by the state and to satisfy the popular aspiration to have a cult associated

[46] Shaun K. Malarney, "The Emerging Cult of Ho Chi Minh? A Report on Religious Innovation in Contemporary Northern Vietnam," *Asian Cultural Studies* 3 (1996): 122.

[47] Vu The Khoi, "Coi chung sac phong rom" [Be Aware of Fake Royal Honor-conferring Diploma], *Bao Van Nghe*, February 9, 2001.

with the history of national resistance. In the *Xua-Nay* magazine, Dinh Khac Thuan points out that Bach Lien village, in Ha Tay province, originally worshipped Great King Cao Hien (*Cao Hien dai vuong*), a figure with an unclear biography. Symptomatic of the "disease" of fetishizing spirits who have great merit in the eyes of the nation (*benh "sinh" su tich nhan than co cong voi nuoc*), people of this village have included Tran Hung Dao as a main god and therefore, according to Dinh Khac Thuan, have distorted history (*lam meo mo lich su*).[48]

The problem will not be easily resolved. State policy continues to privilege temples worshipping national heroes. In the latest resolution of the seventh conference of the ninth Central Committee of the Vietnamese Communist Party (*Ban chap hanh Trung uong Dang khoa 9*) in 2003, apart from reaffirming that "religion and belief are a spiritual need of a part of the population that has existed and will continue to exist in the process of building Socialism," the resolution proposes to "preserve and promote positive values in the tradition of ancestor worship, venerating people who have great merit for the country and the people" [*ton vinh nhung nguoi co cong voi To quoc va nhan dan*] while it "strictly forbids using religion and belief to carry out superstition" [*nghiem cam loi dung tin nguong, ton giao de hoat dong me tin di doan*].[49] That the Mother Goddess religion welcomed the great national hero Tran Hung Dao is, in this context, quite easy to understand.

THE GODS OF SECURITY AND PROSPERITY

In the domain of popular religious activities, concern for peace of mind, good health, and financial security are perennial. After a long period of economic hardship and state-restricted religious activity, the 1986 Renovation Policy issued by the Vietnamese Communist Party marked a significant change in economic and social life, as well as in religious practices. The market economy has created an auspicious environment for the development of small businesses and also harsh competition for those involved in it. With the intensification of market relations, even spirits that were often associated with mere exorcism and protecting health (like Saint Tran) have been reinterpreted and incorporated into rituals designed to increase and protect material well-being.

The concept of supernatural responsiveness reflects human agency to the extent that people judge the worth of different spirits based on their responsiveness to human concerns. A male master medium who organized a pilgrimage trip to Lang Son (that I took part in) told me that a Saint Tran altar was essential for every shrine—not only Mother Goddess temples, but also Buddhist pagodas—to protect the shrines from harassment by evil spirits. Clearly, in popular belief, Tran Hung Dao is an ideal guardian spirit because he is a military hero. In many private houses, Tran Hung Dao's amulets hang above the ancestor's altar, on doors, or are hidden under pillows to expel ghosts and evils spirits.[50] In most of the Mother Goddess temples, Tran Hung Dao's altars are situated on the left. Some mediums explained that Saint Tran altars were located nearest to the door in temples so that the deity

---

[48] Dinh Khac Thuan, "Than lang va viec sao luc than tich" [Village Spirits and the Recording of Spirit Stories], *Tap chi Xua & Nay* 135 (2003): 16-17.

[49] *Bao Hanoi moi*, March 21, 2003.

[50] Many people believe that carrying Saint Tran's amulets helps to avoid accidents and helps babies to sleep and not to cry.

could stop evil spirits who attempted to enter. Conversely, in Mrs. Thu's shrine, the Saint Tran altar is on the right. Mrs. Thu explained this to me: "Saint Tran is the right hand of Mother [*canh tay phai cua Mau*]."

If followers regard Saint Tran as a protector deity specializing in health and security, they believe the Mother Goddess spirits of prosperity bring good fortune to people.[51] The Mother Goddess altars spread and entered into every pagoda even earlier than did the Saint Tran altars. I have heard this comment many times: "If a pagoda has no Mother Goddess altar, it has no prosperity" [*Chua nao khong co ban tho Mau thi khong co loc*]. Thus, Buddhist pagodas, the popular religious structures in Vietnamese villages and the most tranquil of places, also reflect the dynamics of a modern commercializing society.

Rather than talking about *len dong* as relieving their suffering or altering their destiny, many mediums frankly admitted to me that they wanted to serve spirits (*hau Thanh*), and serve as many they could afford, because they felt happy and enjoyed blessed gifts (*loc*) following every trance. I am convinced that many mediums work hard to earn money in order to spend generously in a *len dong* ritual, believing that the more they spend, the more they gain.[52] They then use a part of the profits earned from doing business (profits that they believe to be a result of their previous *len dong* ritual) to go into trance again. For these men and women, mediumship involves both relief and pressure. This is especially so for urban people more exposed to the uncertainty of the market economy. The mother goddesses have become spirits of prosperity who support those facing the risks associated with this modern economy. Saint Tran, who can ensure health and security, has become the mother goddesses' counterpart.

CONCLUSION

In this essay I have attempted to show the multidimensional nature of the relationship between Tran Hung Dao and the Mother Goddess religion from the perspectives of spirit mediums who serve either *Nha Tran* or the mother goddesses and those who worship both. The incorporation of Saint Tran into the Mother Goddess pantheon suggests the formation of a syncretic consciousness in which resistance to foreign aggressors and reverence for national heroes play an important role. Many personal, social, cultural, and political factors have led to the appearance of Tran Hung Dao in the Mother Goddess temples, and I have tried to show that we must be attentive to the subtle intricacies of these religious activities in Vietnam.

---

[51] One intriguing feature of the Lieu Hanh cult is the significance of the locations where, according to legend, she appeared and her temples were set up. The places where Lieu Hanh appeared are connected with the development of various commodities and with entrepreneurship. In legends, the apparition of Lieu Hanh often took the form of a beautiful innkeeper or a vendor along the important traffic routes. It suggests a relation between the cult and the commercial economy that took form and developed in Vietnam during the seventeenth and eighteenth centuries. The movement of Lieu Hanh around the country suggests a symbol for the new emerging merchant class in Vietnam. See Pham Quynh Phuong, "Theo buoc chan cua Van Cat than nu" [Following the Steps of the Goddess of Van Cat Village], *Tap chi Van hoa dan gian* 4 (2001): 44-53.

[52] A religious master explained to me that, when mediums distribute money in a *len dong* ritual, they are trying to spread their own suffering or unluckiness. The more people who receive money, the less sin the mediums incur.

My informants often express contradictory opinions that reveal the changing nature of the Saint Tran cult and the Mother Goddess religion in recent decades. From an independent cult whose rituals were performed mainly by male mediums to exorcise ghosts and evil spirits (a practice that persists in some factions of the medium community), the Saint Tran cult has transformed itself, becoming part of the Mother Goddess religion, with female mediums who appear in *len dong* rituals in a performative way. Adherents invoke him, not only as a protector god who can exterminate ghosts and evil spirits and cure their diseases, but also as a protective shield to legitimize and promote their shrines and elevate their shrines' social status. Reflecting the belief that Saint Tran and the mother goddesses—as the protector god and the goddesses of wealth—possess ultimate authority over the fates of supplicants, they now appear, more often than not, together in temples. Coupled with the Mother Goddess Lieu Hanh, who is often regarded as the goddess of trading and material well-being, Saint Tran appears as the god of bodily well-being. One of the sacred functions of spirits is to intervene in the mundane world. If this has become more obvious since Renovation, it reflects the growing material concerns of religious practitioners operating within a market economy.

The mutual benefits of this relationship are apparent: the Mother Goddess religion benefits from the prestige and protection (from the state) provided by Saint Tran. The Saint Tran cult, in turn, by adapting to the Mother Goddess system, has increased its following, especially among the Mother Goddess cult's predominantly female adherents. Saint Tran and the mother goddesses, as the holy father and the holy mothers, have developed into parallel spiritual supports for those trying to cope with the difficulties of contemporary life.

"HOT-TEMPERED" WOMEN AND "EFFEMINATE" MEN: THE PERFORMANCE OF MUSIC AND GENDER IN VIETNAMESE MEDIUMSHIP

Barley Norton[1]

Research on "gender" in Vietnam has proliferated since the 1990s. Many recent gender projects have assessed the effects of the political, social, and economic changes since the Renovation policy (*doi moi*) was implemented in 1986, and these studies have provided valuable insights concerning the relations between womanhood, sexuality, the state, work, the family, and the household in the Renovation era.[2] Less attention, however, has been paid to the influence of "cultural practices"—for example, practices relating to ritual, religion, theater, music, and dance—on gender ideologies and constructions of gender in Vietnam.[3]

[1] Field research in Vietnam was conducted with financial support from the Humanities Research Board of the British Academy and the School of Oriental and African Studies, and the Arts and Humanities Research Council. I gratefully acknowledge the support of these institutions. I would also like sincerely to thank my Vietnamese music teachers—Pham Van Ty, Dang Cong Hung, and Le Ba Cao—and all the mediums and other ritual participants who generously contributed to the research.

[2] See Jayne Werner and Danièle Bélanger, eds., *Gender, Household, State: Doi Moi in Viet Nam* (Ithaca, NY: Cornell Southeast Asia Program Publications, 2002); Tine Gammeltoft, *Women's Bodies, Women's Worries: Health and Family Planning in a Vietnamese Rural Community* (Surrey: Curzon Press, 1999); Pham Van Bich, *Vietnamese Family in Change* (Surrey: Curzon Press, 1999); Le Thi and Do Thi Binh, *Ten Years of Progress of Vietnamese Women, from 1985 to 1995* (Hanoi: Phunu Publishing House, 1997); Kathleen Barry, ed., *Vietnam's Women in Transition* (Basingstoke: MacMillan, 1996).

[3] A few anthropologists have recently examined gender issues in relation to religious and ritual practices in Vietnam. See Shaun Malarney, "Return to the Past? The Dynamics of Contemporary Religious and Ritual Transformation," in *Postwar Vietnam: Dynamics of a Transforming Society*, ed. Hy V. Luong (New York, NY, and Oxford: Rowman & Littlefield, 2003), pp. 225-56; Philip Taylor, *Goddess on the Rise: Pilgrimage and Popular Religion in Vietnam* (Honolulu, HI: University of Hawai'i Press, 2004); Alexander D. Soucy, "The Buddha's

This essay addresses the gendered implications of Vietnamese mediumship, a set of cultural practices rooted in the "system of religious beliefs" (*he thong tin nguong*) commonly referred to as the Four Palace religion (*Dao Tu Phu*) or Mother Goddess religion (*Dao Mau*). Through examining mediumship music and the practices of mediums, both during spirit possession and in everyday life, I aim to demonstrate how music constructs the gender identities of spirits and how the gender identities of mediums are performatively negotiated.

During sixteen months' fieldwork research in northern Vietnam in 1996-97, 1998, and 2002, I attended numerous mediumship rituals, *len dong*, in public temples (*den, phu, mieu*) and private temples in individuals' homes (*dien*) dedicated to the spirit pantheon of the Mother Goddess religion. During rituals, which can last several hours, a medium is possessed in turn by a sequence of spirits from the pantheon. Assistants sit around the medium; their role is to attend to the medium's every need during possession and to help facilitate interaction between the possessee and other ritual participants. Except during large festivals, the medium invites his/her "disciples" (*con nhang de tu*) to participate in the ritual. Throughout *len dong*, a band of musicians, known as *cung van*, perform songs of the *chau van* music genre.[4] For each spirit possession, the band performs a sequence of songs—which I refer to as a songscape—appropriate to the identity of each spirit and the ritual actions of the medium.[5] In northern Vietnam, the main instruments used to accompany *chau van* songs are the moon lute (*dan nguyet*) and a set of percussion instruments, which usually include bamboo clappers (*phach*), a small-headed drum (*trong*), and a small cymbal (*canh*) (see figure 1). The ensemble may also be augmented to include other, nonessential instruments such as the sixteen-stringed zither (*dan tranh*), two-stringed fiddle (*dan nhi*), bamboo flute (*sao*), and knobless small gong (*thanh la*).

GENDER AND RITUAL ROLE

Vietnamese mediumship is predominantly the domain of women: the majority of mediums, as well as those who attend rituals, are women. However, male mediums make up a significant minority, and *chau van* bands conventionally consist of male musicians. Despite the tendency for men and women to assume different ritual roles, followers of the Mother Goddess religion were unwilling to see the matter in strictly gendered terms; after all, both men and women are able to become mediums and musicians.[6]

Blessing: Gender and Buddhist Practice in Hanoi" (PhD dissertation, Australian National University, 1999).

[4] *Chau van* (literally, "serving literature") may also be referred to as *hat van* (literally, "singing literature"). *Hat* (literally, "sing") can also be used as a classifier for *chau van*, that is, *hat chau van*. There are different styles of *chau van* in the northern, central, and southern regions in Vietnam. The discussion of *chau van* in this essay refers to the style in northern Vietnam where I conducted my fieldwork. The main Vietnamese sources on *chau van* in northern Vietnam are Ngo Duc Thinh, ed., *Hat Van* (Ha Noi: Nha Xuat Ban Van Hoa Dan Toc, 1992); Bui Dinh Thao and Nguyen Quang Hai, *Hat Chau Van* (Ha Noi: Nha Xuat Ban Am Nhac, 1996); Thanh Ha, *Am Nhac Hat Van* [The Music of Hat Van] (Ha Noi: Nha Xuat Ban Am Nhac, 1996).

[5] See Barley Norton, "Vietnamese Mediumship Rituals: The Musical Construction of the Spirits," *The World of Music* 42,2 (2000): 75-97.

[6] Similarly, Jane Atkinson found that "to examine Wana shamanship with questions of gender in mind conflicts decidedly with a Wana perspective on the matter ... When asked to explain why most shamans were men, people resisted the suggestion that gender was a qualification

Figure 1. A *chau van* band performing at Dau Temple, Hanoi, 1998. The musician Pham Van Ty is playing the moon lute. Photo by Barley Norton.

First let us consider the issue of why more women than men participate in mediumship practices. The ritual participants I spoke to were generally resistant to the idea that the Mother Goddess religion should be considered to be a "women's religion" or only of interest to women. Nonetheless, when I pressed them about the reasons why more women than men became mediums and participated in mediumship rituals, they gave a variety of responses, which may be summarized as follows: 1) the fate of women was such that they are "seized" (*bat*) by the spirits more than men; 2) women suffer "madness" (*dien*) more than men; 3) women are interested in "spiritual matters" (*duy tam*), whereas men are concerned with "material matters" (*duy vat*); 4) women, rather than men, are drawn to the mother spirits, in particular the most famous mother spirit, Lieu Hanh; 5) women "carry the weight" of the family, so if anybody in the family needs the protection of spirits, one of the female members must become a medium; 6) only "effeminate" men (*dong co*) may become mediums, and because there are more women than "effeminate" men in society, it follows that there would be more female than male mediums; 7) it is the spirits that "choose" (*chon*) people to become mediums, so the spirits are responsible for the ratio between male and female mediums.

The first four responses listed above do not so much provide reasons why women are drawn to mediumship as make the case that women have a "natural" propensity to be interested in the Mother Goddess religion and thus to become

for shamanship or other ritual activities." Jane M. Atkinson, *The Art and Politics of Wana Shamanship* (Berkeley, CA: University of California Press, 1989), pp. 280-81.

mediums. The fifth and sixth responses edge toward sociological explanations in terms of family responsibilities and the constitution of society at large but still highlight cultural notions of gender. The seventh response emphasizes spiritual agency, rather than human volition, as the primary factor in determining whether men or women become mediums.

Societies in which the majority of religious adherents who experience possession are female bring to mind Ioan Lewis's theory that oppressed groups in society, most notably women, establish marginal possession "cults" as a form of protest against established power asymmetries and that male ecstatics dominate the official institutionalized religions. Lewis interprets female possession as merely a strategy, either consciously or unconsciously employed, that gives "women an opportunity to gain ends (material and non-material)."[7] Criticism of Lewis's interpretation has focused on the oppositions he sets up between male/female, marginal/institutionalized, center/periphery. Janice Boddy has argued that Lewis's emphasis on women's peripheral and subordinate status "is a classic but unhappily androcentric portrayal of women, who are forever seen as reacting to men rather than acting for themselves within a specific cultural context."[8] Similarly, Laurel Kendall has argued that women's rituals are not peripheral to Korean society, and Karen Fjelstad has suggested that Lewis's formulation promotes a male-centered view of female possession that is not shared by women.[9] Scholarly work on how shamanism, official priesthoods, politics, and state power have intertwined in different historical contexts also makes it difficult to maintain rigid oppositions between marginal/institutionalized, and so forth.[10]

Since the 1950s, the Vietnamese Communist Party has condemned mediumship as part of a wide-ranging antisuperstition campaign, and it is only since the Renovation policy was implemented that there has been a relaxation in this campaign and a strong resurgence in mediumship practices.[11] Although Party ideologues and others opposed to spirit possession continue to brand mediumship as marginal (and in need of eradication), this was not the view of ritual participants or the many Vietnamese I met who had never been involved in mediumship. Indeed, to assert that spirit possession is marginal seems untenable given the large number of followers of the Mother Goddess religion in contemporary Vietnam.[12] Mediumship is

---

[7] I. M. Lewis, *Ecstatic Religion: A Study of Shamanism and Spirit Possession* (London: Routledge, 1989 [1971]), p. 77.

[8] Janice Boddy, *Wombs and Alien Spirits: Women, Men, and the Zâr Cult in Northern Sudan* (Madison, WI: University of Wisconsin Press, 1989), p. 140.

[9] Laurel Kendall, *Shamans, Housewives, and Other Restless Spirits: Women in Korean Ritual Life* (Honolulu, HI: University of Hawai'i Press, 1985); Karen Fjelstad, "Tu Phu Cong Dong: Vietnamese Women and Spirit Possession in the San Francisco Bay Area" (PhD dissertation, University of Hawai'i, 1995).

[10] See Nicholas Thomas and Caroline Humphrey, *Shamanism, History, and the State* (Ann Arbor, MI: University of Michigan Press, 1994).

[11] See Barley Norton, "'The Moon Remembers Uncle Ho': The Politics of Music and Mediumship in Northern Vietnam," *British Journal of Ethnomusicology* 11,1 (2002): 71-100.

[12] The Institute for Religious Studies estimated the number of mediums in Hanoi in 1986 as one for every four thousand inhabitants; see Dang Nghiem Van, *Ethnological and Religious Problems in Vietnam* (Hanoi: Social Sciences Publishing House, 1998). How this figure is arrived at is not available for scrutiny, and its accuracy is dubious. However, it does indicate the prevalence of mediums *before* the *len dong* boom in the Renovation era, and the number of mediums in Vietnam today is undoubtedly much higher than in 1986.

not institutionalized in the manner of, for example, Vietnamese Buddhism, but mediums are afforded varying degrees of status and prestige, which further problematizes the issue of marginality. It would also be inappropriate to describe temples as a predominantly female domain simply because the majority of ritual participants are women; public temples are often infused with male prestige.

During fieldwork it became apparent that male mediums have a disproportionate status and wealth compared with their number. The most renowned and wealthy medium in northern Vietnam, who has renovated several important temples in Hanoi and in the countryside, is male. I also met many other male "temple-mediums" (*dong den*) who "look after" (*trong nom*) public temples. These male mediums usually preside over famous temples in prominent locations, which are the most popular temples and receive generous donations from disciples. For instance, many of the main temples in the center of Hanoi and at the famous pilgrimage site of Phu Giay in Nam Dinh province are run by male temple-mediums. Some public temples do have female temple-mediums, yet these temples tend to be minor ones that are less popular with disciples and therefore less opulent. By contrast with the comparatively large number of male mediums who preside over public temples, most female mediums construct private temples in their homes. The social differentiation between women's place in the domestic realm and men's authority in the public domain is therefore reflected within mediumship.

There is a common perception, which is most prevalent among male mediums and their disciples, that men are "better" (*gioi hon*) than women at the "big job" (*viec lon*) of looking after large temples. To cite one example, a male temple-medium in Hanoi told me that men had more "talent" (*tai nang*), "ability" (*nang khieu*), and "understanding" (*hieu biet*) of religious beliefs than women, and he added that temples kept by men were "decorated more beautifully" (*trang tri dep hon*) and were "more magnificent" (*nguy nga hon*) compared with those kept by women. Although such an assertion of male superiority was challenged by many of the female mediums with whom I raised the issue, it is indicative of a quite widely held view that has no doubt played a part in male mediums' assuming prominent positions at public temples.

A degree of male prestige is also accorded to *chau van* bands. Professional musicians have traditionally been accorded a low status in Vietnamese society, and singers, especially female singers, have often been associated with "immoral life-styles."[13] To what extent these attitudes remain present in contemporary Vietnamese society is debatable, but within the context of mediumship, adherents to the Mother Goddess religion were respectful of the knowledge and expertise of professional *chau van* musicians. As well as performing during *len dong*, some musicians also carry out other prestigious ritual roles, such as reciting prayers before a ritual and writing prayers using Chinese or Sino-Vietnamese characters. Musicians who are specialists

---

[13] As Le Tuan Hung has noted, laws discriminated against professional musicians prior to the eighteenth century. For example, they were not permitted to take civil examinations, and professional female singers have often been associated with prostitution. See Le Tuan Hung, *Dan Tranh Music in Vietnam: Traditions and Innovations* (Melbourne: Australia Asian Foundation, 1998). See also Barley Norton, "Singing the Past: Vietnamese *Ca Tru*, Memory, and Mode," *Asian Music* 36,2 (2005): 27-56.

in other aspects of ritual life are referred to as "spirit priests" (*thay cung*).[14] Women's access to education was severely restricted until the second half of the twentieth century, so traditionally women rarely gained the skills to read and write prayers in Chinese/Sino-Vietnamese characters, and in contemporary Vietnam, spirit priests are still predominantly male.

Gender associations with particular instruments have also played a part in preventing women from becoming *chau van* musicians.[15] The main instrument used in *chau van*, the moon lute, was in the past known as the instrument "held by noblemen" (*quan tu cam*), and it is still extremely rare to find a female moon-lute player in Vietnam today. As one musician commented, the moon lute is not considered suitable for women because it is not "soft" (*em diu*) and its shape is not "feminine" (*nu tinh*), unlike instruments frequently played by women such as the pear-shaped lute (*ty ba*) and the sixteen-stringed zither (*dan tranh*). Since the *len dong* boom in the Renovation era, a few women have begun to sing *chau van*, yet many mediums said they preferred male singers because they were able to "flatter" (*ninh*) the spirits better than female singers.

THE MUSICAL PERFORMANCE OF GENDER

When possessed by spirits, mediums traverse genders: when a medium of one gender is possessed by spirits of the other gender, s/he adopts the spirit's gender (see figure 2).[16] The medium's clothes, mannerisms, way of speaking, ritual acts, and way of dancing differ for each spirit, but they are all influenced by the gender of the spirit. The music performed also evokes the gender of the spirit incarnated. In this section, I will discuss some of the most prominent gender-specific traits of spirits that mediums adopt and the role of music in the construction of the spirits' gender identities.

Male spirits wear mandarin tunics (*ao bao*) and a tiara-like hat (*khan xep*). They smoke cigarettes, drink alcohol, and dance with swords, spears, and sticks with bells. Male spirits—especially mandarin spirits—are described as "strict" (*nghiem tuc*) and "prestigious" (*uy tin*). Female lowland spirits wear women's tunics (*ao dai*) and a tiara-like hat often adorned with flowers (*khan hoa*).[17] Female mountain spirits wear clothes influenced by the clothes worn by women belonging to ethnic minority

---

[14] The term "*thay cung*" is also used for ritual specialists who are not musicians. For further discussion of spirit priests, see Shaun K. Malarney, *Culture, Ritual, and Revolution in Vietnam* (New York, NY, and London: RoutledgeCurzon, 2002), pp. 97-98.

[15] The gender associations that pertain to musical instruments have been widely documented. See, for instance, Veronica Doubleday, "The Frame Drum in the Middle East: Women, Instruments, and Power," *Ethnomusicology* 43,1 (1999): 101-34.

[16] The term "traverse" has been adopted from Anne Bolin, "Traversing Gender: Cultural Context and Gender Practices," in *Gender Reversals and Gender Cultures: Anthropological and Historical Perspectives*, ed. Sabrina Ramet (London: Routledge, 1996), pp. 22-51.

[17] For details of the spirit pantheon of the Mother Goddess religion, see Ngo Duc Thinh's essay, "The Mother Goddess Religion: Its History, Pantheon, and Practices," in this volume. The division of female spirits into lowland and mountain spirits is based on whether or not spirits belong to the Mountains and Forest Palace (*nhac phu*) in the "yin" spirit world (*coi am*) and whether spirits have associations with mountainous or lowland regions in the "yang" human world (*duong tran*). For further discussion of the spirit pantheon, see Barley Norton, "Music and Possession in Vietnam" (PhD dissertation, SOAS, University of London, 2000).

groups. Female spirits do not smoke cigarettes, and they drink nonalcoholic drinks; female mountain spirits chew betel. The dances of female spirits use fans, ropes lit on fire, and rowing oars. The mannerisms of female spirits are "soft" (*em diu*) and "graceful" (*duyen dang*). When male mediums are possessed by female spirits, they often use a falsetto voice. The young prince spirits (*cau*) and child spirits (for example, the Young Princess [*Co Be*]) conform to many of the traits of "male" and "female" behavior while also behaving like children. Young prince spirits, for instance, smoke cigarettes, drink alcohol, and dance with sticks with bells, but they are less serious than other male spirits and are often "naughty" (*nghich*). When possessed by child spirits, mediums often speak with the voice of a child and sometimes mispronounce words as a child might (for example, by not pronouncing consonants).

Figure 2. A male medium possessed by a female spirit, the Second Princess Cam Duong. The male medium is dressed in women's clothes and is performing a graceful dance with a large hat. Photo by Barley Norton.

An important aspect of gender traversing is that mediums must perform the actions of male and female spirits "beautifully" (*dep*). During *len dong*, and especially in the case of transgender possession, disciples often exclaim how beautiful the medium is when dressed in the spirits' magnificent clothes or when dancing. "Doing the work of the spirits beautifully" (*lam viec thanh dep*) is not just an optional extra; it is central to being an effective and respected medium.

Recent ethnomusicological writing on gender has highlighted the power of musical performance to actively engender individuals through the lived experience of the event and to shape cultural ideas about masculinity and femininity.[18] In relation to *len dong*, musical performance enforces the gender positionalities during possession and the gendered characteristics of the spirits. This is achieved in two main ways: through the use of distinctive song texts for each spirit, which include descriptions relating to the gender characteristics of the spirits, and the gendered division of the repertoire.

The texts of *chau van* songs tell of the legends, great deeds, and miraculous powers of the spirits. They praise their talents, virtue, and generosity. They describe their beauty, character, appearance, and gestures. Although song texts for both male and female spirits use rich, devotional language imbued with old Sino-Vietnamese terminology, the characteristics and deeds of spirits are highly gendered. Many of the texts for male spirits extol stereotypical masculine characteristics, such as strength and prowess in the art of war, and in some cases, scholarly and artistic activities like painting and poetry, which are associated with the historically "male" tradition of civil examinations. In marked contrast to the texts for male spirits, those dedicated to female spirits often describe stereotypical feminine characteristics, such as gracefulness and physical beauty. Such descriptions of female spirits are somewhat reminiscent of the Confucian precept of the "four virtues" (*tu duc*). According to this precept, women are "virtuous" if they achieve an idealized standard in the areas of labor (*cong*), physical appearance (*dung*), appropriate speech (*ngon*), and proper behavior (*hanh*).

Female spirits are also linked to nature and the environment more than are male spirits, thereby seeming to confirm the classic male/female, culture/nature dichotomies.[19] This is most pronounced for female mountain spirits like the Second Lady (*Chau De Nhi*) and the Young Princess (*Co Be*), who are depicted joyfully strolling in the mountains and forests, but lowland female spirits are also often strongly associated with the natural world. For instance, the Third Princess (*Co Bo*) is best known for her "rowing dance" (*mua cheo*), and the songs for the spirit describe the beautiful scene as she rows down the river.[20] Comparison of the following song

---

[18] For example, see Jane C. Sugarman, *Engendering Song: Singing and Subjectivity at Prespa Albanian Weddings* (Chicago, IL, and London: University of Chicago Press, 1997); Pirkko Moisala and Beverley Diamond, eds., *Music and Gender* (Urbana, IL, and Chicago, IL: University of Illinois Press, 2000); Tullia Magrini, ed., *Music and Gender: Perspectives from the Mediterranean* (Chicago, IL, and London: University of Chicago Press, 2003).

[19] On the male/female, culture/nature dichotomies, see Sherry Ortner, "Is Female to Male as Nature Is to Culture?" in *Woman, Culture, and Society*, ed. Michelle Zimbalist Rosaldo and Louise Lamphere (Stanford, CA: Stanford University Press, 1974), pp. 67-87.

[20] Most of the spirits in the pantheon belong to one of four "palaces" in the celestial world, hence the term "Four Palace religion" (*Dao Tu Phu*). The four palaces are the Water Palace (*Thoai Phu*), the Sky Palace (*Thien Phu*), Mountains and Forest Palace (*Nhac Phu*), and the Earth Palace (*Dia Phu*). See Ngo Duc Thinh's essay, "The Mother Goddess Religion," in this volume for more details. The Third Princess belongs to the Water Palace and is more strongly

texts for the Fifth Mandarin (*Quan Lon Tuan Tranh*), the Tenth Prince (*Ong Hoang Muoi*), and the Third Princess highlights many of the distinctions outlined above.[21]

The Fifth Mandarin

He gives orders to the soldiers
The great mandarin in his divine carriage
First he protects families
Then he destroys evil foes
The world knows he has the power to save humanity
…
The Trieu Da enemy tried to invade
The court ordered soldiers to be deployed
The boats crossing the Tranh River filled the sky
Suddenly a violent storm erupted
…
The Tranh River! O, the Tranh River!
The reflection of the moon dances on the Tranh River
For thousands of years the sacred spirit has been a glorious hero
Whoever crosses the Tranh River, remember the brilliant warrior

The Tenth Prince

In Central Vietnam there are many famous rumors about the Tenth Prince
He leads the army that defeats enemies, he keeps the precious rivers safe
The Chinese enemies of the Thanh dynasty are defeated
…
Vietnam's Tenth Prince
In the art of war he has no equal
He has the intelligence and wisdom of a genius
He writes excellent poems
…
A fan inscribed with a poem
No other poems compare to those of the Tenth Prince
Poems flow from the Tenth Prince's pen
Such success and prestige
From the writer's hand, peace is brought to the world
Everybody sings the ancient song of peace

The Third Princess

The princess parts her silky hair which shimmers like the shadow of a willow tree

---

associated with rivers and water than male spirits, like the Third Mandarin, who also belong to the Water Palace.

[21] All translations throughout the essay are my own.

Her perfect eyebrows are curved like a willow tree
She has the sparkling eyes of a phoenix which reflect like mirrors
She has beautiful ivory skin, rosy cheeks, and lips like autumn moons
With such fresh youth, she is in her prime
Her three-colored headscarf is tied with a pin
She gracefully gathers mulberries and prunes the cinnamon tree
She politely receives a rose branch, orchid, and hibiscus
...
The princess has such a graceful neck
She wears lovely makeup
The lady sits at the join of the river and waterfall
Up- and down-stream, the boats are grateful for the princess's protection
...
Shout out the rowing call
So that the princess holds the oars
Traveling everywhere
The princess is drifting in all four directions
The wind in the pine trees and the clouds
The lady rescues mortals

The texts of the Fifth Mandarin and the Tenth Prince link them to the long history of Vietnamese resistance to Chinese domination. In some of the stories of the Fifth Mandarin, the spirit appears in the form of a snake and destroys Chinese military ships, creating a violent storm on the Tranh River in Hai Hung province. The name "Trieu Da," which appears in the text, was adopted by a Qin Chinese general whose family ruled the northern Vietnamese area before it became integrated as a province of China in 111 BCE. Like the Fifth Mandarin and many other prestigious male spirits, the Tenth Prince also is known as a fearsome warrior. In the song texts, the Tenth Prince is associated with the defeat of Chinese Thanh dynasty troops who were sent to Vietnam in the late eighteenth century. As well as being a warrior, the prince is a renowned scholar and poet and is known for his womanizing and fondness for rice wine.

The flowery descriptions of the Third Princess's grace and appearance in the song text quoted above are typical of the poems dedicated to female spirits. Such idealized portrayals of physical beauty undoubtedly attract the attention of disciples, but female spirits are worshipped for other reasons too. In the case of the Third Princess, many mediums develop a close relationship with the princess because of her ability to cure illness with "incense water" (*nuoc thai*). Similarly, many religious followers are attracted to female spirits who are renowned for their fortune-telling powers, such as the Ninth Princess (*Co Chin*).

In the *chau van* musical system there is a complex relationship between songs and individual spirits: with a few notable exceptions, individual songs are not performed exclusively for one particular spirit, but rather a particular song or group of songs may be performed for one or more groups of spirits. In general terms, the main gendered divisions of the repertoire are: 1) the use of different melodies for the dances performed by male and female spirits; 2) the use of the "Con" and "Phu" groups of melodies for the female and male lowland spirits respectfully.[22]

It is evident from the vibrancy of mediums' dances and the excited reaction they usually receive from ritual participants, especially when the medium is possessed by a spirit of the opposite gender, that dancing is one of the main ways that mediums articulate the character and gender of spirits. Ritual participants consider the music and the dances of female spirits to be more "fun" (*vui*) and "lively" (*linh hoat/soi noi*) compared with the "majestic" (*oai nghiem*) dances of male spirits. This is most apparent when comparing the dances of female mountain spirits with the "martial dances" (*mua vo*) of mandarin spirits. The usual melody played for male spirit dances is the "Luu Thuy" melody, a stately melody associated with the grandeur of the imperial court in Hue. Alternatively, a rhythm called "Trong Chien" (literally, "War Drums") may be performed for some martial dances. As the name "War Drums" suggests, the driving rhythms of "Trong Chien"—which consist of loud tremolo rolls on the drum and cymbals—evoke the atmosphere of war and therefore emphasize the military prowess of the mandarin spirits. For female mountain spirits, the "Xa Mua Moi" melody is always used, whereas for the dances of lowland female spirits the "Nhip Mot" melody is usually performed. Both of these melodies use the "one-beat rhythm" (*nhip mot*), which is heavily accented and is considered to be the liveliest rhythm used in *chau van*. (In its basic form, the one-beat rhythm consists of a quarter note followed by an eighth-note rest followed by an accented eighth note). The use of the one-beat rhythm "incites" (*kich dong*) mediums possessed by female spirits to dance in a more lively way than the majestic way they dance when possessed by prestigious male spirits.

The second gendered division of the repertoire—the distinction between the "Con" and the "Phu" groups of melodies—only applies to lowland male and female spirits. The "Con" and "Phu" melodies are performed once the medium has finished dancing and has returned to sit in front of the temple altar. Each "Con" and "Phu" melody has its own different aesthetic, but generalizing at the level of the group, the "Phu" melodies imbue "masculinity" (*nam tinh*), "authority" (*uy nghi*), and "seriousness" (*nghiem tuc*), and the "Con" melodies imbue "femininity" (*nu tinh*), "smoothness" (*muot ma*), and "lyricism" (*tru tinh*). Other melodies that are divided according to the gender of spirits include "Van" and "Ham," which are performed for lowland female spirits, and "Kieu Duong," which is performed for male spirits.

Status and age also have a bearing on the division of melodies on gender lines. The "Phu" melodies and "Kieu Duong" are particularly associated with mandarin spirits, who are the male spirits highest in the hierarchy of the spirit pantheon. The songscapes of prince spirits sometimes include "Phu" melodies, but many bands favor alternative melodies, such as "Nhip Mot," which are less "serious" than the "Phu" melodies and therefore more in keeping with the lower status of prince spirits compared to mandarin spirits. "Phu" melodies are never played for the young prince

---

[22] The "Con" group of melodies includes "Con Day Lech," "Con Xuan," "Con Luyen," "Con Luyen Tam Tang," "Con Oan," and "Con Hue," and the most commonly performed songs of the "Phu" group are "Phu Noi," "Phu Binh," "Phu Chuoc Ruou," and "Phu Van Dan." "Con Hue" is the only melody in the "Con" group that is performed for a male spirit, the Tenth Prince. The reason for this exception is that "Con Hue" is influenced by the music from central Vietnam in the region around Hue, and it is performed for the Tenth Prince in order to evoke the spirit's home province of Nghe An in central Vietnam.

spirits because they are children and therefore cannot assume the same gender position as adult male spirits.

The gender of spirits is distinguished through the use of different songs, but what are the musical differences between these melodies? Are there specific musical features, which may be designated as masculine and feminine? Figure 3 lists a number of musical traits that differentiate the male songs (that is, "Kieu Duong" and the "Phu" melodies) and female songs (that is, "Ham," "Van," and the "Con" melodies).[23]

Figure 3: Musical Traits of "Male" and "Female" Songs

Songs for female spirits	Songs for male spirits
Two-beat rhythm (consisting of a quarter note, an eighth-note rest, followed by an eighth note and two quarter notes)	Three-beat rhythm (consisting of a qua: note, a quarter-note rest, and two qua: notes)
Verses made up of short vocal phrases	Verses made up of long vocal phrases
Minimal melisma	Extended melisma
Little syncopation	Highly syncopated
Each verse of a song concludes with the same phrase sung to vocables	Verses do not usually end with a repea phrase sung to vocables
Full instrumental accompaniment to the vocal line	Sparse instrumental accompaniment to vocal line
May be sung in unison by more than one person	Solo voice

Although the musical traits outlined above point out the main differences between "male" and "female" melodies, it is difficult to link these to culturally defined conceptions of masculinity and femininity. For instance, there is nothing inherent in the two-beat or the three-beat rhythms that is feminine or masculine respectively, and the two-beat rhythm is, in any case, used by other melodies that are performed for both male and female spirits. *Chau van* musicians did, however, consider the three-beat rhythm to be less "tight" (*chat che*) than the two-beat rhythm, thus enabling greater flexibility in the rhythm of the vocal line and more syncopation. As a result of the greater rhythmic flexibility of melodies sung to the three-beat rhythm, two or more singers are unable to sing the songs for male spirits in unison as is possible for the songs for female spirits, and the instrumental accompaniment for male songs is sparser. The greater independence of the vocal line of songs for male spirits could be suggestive of authority, but *chau van* musicians did not make such an assertion. According to musicians, the songs for female spirits are more lyrical and hence more feminine than the songs for male spirits due to the short

---

[23] There is no obvious distinction in the modes and ornaments used by the songs for male and for female spirits.

phrases sung to vocables at the end of verses and the absence of long, drawn-out melisma.

"Effeminate" Men and "Hot-Tempered" Women

> Gender ought not to be construed as a stable identity or locus of agency from which various acts follow; rather, gender is an identity tenuously constituted in time, instituted in an exterior space through a *stylized repetition of acts*.[24]

The ability of mediums to perform stereotypical gender roles of male and female (and young) spirits beautifully is recognized by followers of the Mother Goddess religion to be part of their "destined aptitude" (*can so*); in other words, it is central to a medium's calling. The phrase *"dong co bong cau,"* which was often used by mediums and disciples, illustrates this point. The literal meaning of this phrase—"'princess spirit' mediums, young prince spirits"—emphasizes that mediums may be possessed by spirits of the opposite gender, by both princess spirits and young prince spirits.[25]

The first part of the expression, *"dong co,"* is also used on its own as a description of male mediums: it refers to men who are "effeminate."[26] Three mediums (two female and one male) described *dong co* in the following way:

> Effeminate male mediums have the character and voice of a woman. Some people [men as well as women] have women's blood ... and a woman's voice.

> When a man has the "destined aptitude of the Ninth Princess Spirit" [*can Co Chin*], then when that spirit is incarnated, the character of the man is naturally different: he has a sharp tongue, the voice of a woman, and chews betel like a woman. He is still a man, but because of the aptitude of a princess, the female spirit helps his destiny, and he becomes a *dong co* ... who is very graceful ... They [*dong co*] wear women's clothes on the outside and inside ... Many people hug them and call them women.

> If male mediums have the "destined aptitude of princess or lady spirits" [*can co hay can chau*], then they have a "strong femininity" [*nang ve nu tinh*] ... That is a natural phenomenon ... They are men, but their "appearance and mannerisms are weak" [*dang dieu eo la*], and they speak like women.

The term *"dong co"* is resonant with two meanings: it refers to the ability of male mediums to dress and behave like women while possessed, and to their effeminacy. Their being effeminate is not just confined to *len dong* rituals; rather it is part of male mediums' gender identity in their everyday lives.

---

[24] Judith Butler, *Gender Trouble: Feminism and the Subversion of Identity* (London: Routledge, 1990), p. 140.

[25] *"Dong"* means medium and *"co"* refers to the princess spirits of the pantheon. *"Dong co"* is not to be confused with *"co dong,"* which is a term for female mediums who are not elderly. The *"co"* in *"co dong"* is a personal pronoun: it does not refer to the princess spirits.

[26] In everyday speech, *"dong co"* is also used to describe "effeminate" men who are not mediums.

The book *Hat Chau Van* mentions that, as well as male and female mediums, there are also "transsexual" (*ai nam ai nu*) mediums.[27] I never met a transsexual medium during fieldwork, but such a possibility opens up a third category and perhaps different gender identities. While the primary meaning of the term "*ai nam ai nu*" refers to a physical condition, it is often used figuratively with a similar sense to "*dong co.*" As one musician who regularly performed at rituals remarked: "male mediums are *ai nam ai nu*: their voice, bearing, and behavior is like a woman's."

The expression "*bong cau*" may be applied to female mediums in a somewhat similar way to the use of "*dong co*" or "*ai nam ai nu*" for male mediums. "*Bong cau*" (literally, "young prince spirits")—and occasionally "*dong cau*" (literally, "'prince spirit' mediums")—were used by ritual participants to describe female mediums who have a strong affinity for male spirits, but these terms are not heavily loaded with the connotation that these mediums have a "masculine" character. Some female mediums who were noted for having the destined aptitude of a mandarin or prince spirit said they had a "strong masculinity" (*nang ve nam tinh*), but they more commonly described themselves as having particular character traits, such as being "hot tempered" (*nong tinh*), "hot gutted" (that is, ill at ease) (*nong ruot*), or "difficult" (*kho chiu*). These characteristics were not necessarily explicitly linked to male spirits in the way that the behavior of male mediums was associated with characteristics of female spirits. But they were considered part of a medium's unique character, and a female medium with a strong destined aptitude for a male spirit may have a particularly hot-tempered character. So even though female mediums are not usually thought of as being "masculine" or behaving like men, they are "difficult" women and "unfeminine" in the sense that they do not conform to stereotypical women's roles or behavior. Being possessed by spirits helps to soothe their hot-temperedness: female mediums said they felt "more relaxed" (*thoai mai hon*) and were "easier to bear" (*de chiu hon*) after possession.

The quote from Judith Butler's book *Gender Trouble* at the beginning of this section provokes some interesting questions regarding Vietnamese mediumship. To what extent do ritual acts constitute a medium's gender identity? Does the repetition of ritual acts during *len dong* destabilize or subvert established gender categories? It has been argued in the case of Vietnamese mediumship that men and women transgress dominant gender identities.[28] Understood from such a perspective, *len dong* is a space in which male mediums may assume "feminine" gender positions (as well as "masculine" ones) and female mediums can come to terms with "unfeminine" aspects of their personality, such as being hot tempered (as well as displaying stereotypical "feminine" aspects such as being graceful).

The ritual acts of mediums, however, are not to be misconstrued as an example of how gender identity may be performatively constructed or deconstructed at will.[29]

---

[27] Bui Dinh Thao and Nguyen Quang Hai, *Hat Chau Van* (Ha Noi: Nha Xuat Ban Am Nhac, 1996), p. 31. Although "*ai nam ai nu*" literally means "love man love woman," it does not suggest bisexuality. Rather, it refers to the physical condition of being transsexual. The term "*nua nam nua nu*," which means "half man half woman," is also occasionally used as an alternative to "*ai nam ai nu.*"

[28] For a comparable discussion of spirit possession and transgendering in Africa, see Janice Boddy, *Wombs and Alien Spirits.*

[29] In her second book, *Bodies That Matter* (New York, NY: Routledge, 1993), Butler has argued against the most voluntarist interpretations of the concept of performativity that were prompted by her book *Gender Trouble.*

In fact, Butler suggests in relation to drag that although gender performativity has the potential to subvert established categories (by disrupting the relationship between anatomical sex identity and gender identity), it also reiterates ideal, normative corporeal styles. Being a medium in Vietnam does enable the creation of divergent gender identities, but only within the culturally prescribed limits established by the gender identities of spirits. In many ways, the spirits confirm normative gender identities (prestigious mandarins, graceful ladies, and so on). Mediums therefore construct their own gender identities with reference to pregiven stereotypes and assume identities that are also culturally sanctioned (for example, being "effeminate," "unfeminine").

FEMALE MEDIUMS AND "FAMILY HAPPINESS"

Many female mediums linked worshipping the spirits with ensuring peace, harmony, safety, and prosperity for their families. Male mediums did not link their activities with their own family situations as female mediums did, although they shared the conviction that "serving the spirits" (that is, holding a *len dong*) would ensure prosperity, health, and happiness. When asked about the aim of holding *len dong* rituals, one female medium said: "Firstly, when I serve the spirits, I am very happy, I like it. Secondly, when I return home after a *len dong*, living is easier and more prosperous, and the children study well." Another said that the function of *len dong* was "to have money and gifts and for my family to be safe and prosperous," and she also commented that the spirits would "fulfill the wishes" (*toai nguyen*) of her family. This comment suggests that the practice of distributing money and gifts during rituals, which might be interpreted as an egalitarian act of sharing, is associated with family prosperity and well-being. "Family happiness" (*hanh phuc gia dinh*) is also central to many of the crises that female mediums experience prior to initiation. Examples of afflictions that lead to initiation include the death of newborn babies, an inability to care for children, and illness, which are very real instances of a rupture in family well-being and a breakdown in the prescribed role of women as procreators/nurturers. After initiation, these crises are resolved through the protection, assistance, and the "pity" (*thuong*) of spirits. (See also the essays by both Kirsten Endres,[30] and Karen Fjelstad and Lisa Maiffret[31] in this volume.)

The ways in which "serving the spirits" is linked to family happiness is particular to female mediums. However, the notion of family happiness is much more widespread. As Tine Gammeltoft has discussed, maintaining good family relations is a preoccupation of Vietnamese women in general, and the ideal of a "happy family" is propagated by government documents and popular culture.[32] Vietnamese women's studies researchers have also endeavored to promote the notion of family happiness in order to improve gender equality within the family and "overcome the vestiges of old and backward views and customs."[33]

---

[30] Kirsten Endres, "Spirit Performance and the Ritual Construction of Personal Identity in Modern Vietnam," this volume.

[31] Karen Fjelstad and Lisa Maiffret, "Gifts from the Spirits: Spirit Possession and Personal Transformation among Silicon Valley Spirit Mediums," this volume.

[32] Tine Gammeltoft, *Women's Bodies, Women's Worries*, pp. 72-76.

[33] Kathleen Barry, "Introduction," in *Vietnam's Women in Transition*, ed. K. Barry. Barry points out that family happiness in Vietnam is a "largely uncritiqued assumption" in which "there is

Despite female mediums' desire to ensure family happiness through seeking the benevolence of spirits, being a medium, in some cases, has precisely the opposite effect. Many female mediums conceal their ritual practices from their disapproving husbands. According to these mediums, their husbands objected because they thought that holding *len dong* was "superstitious" (*me tin di doan*) or a waste of money. Some mediums also said their husbands were concerned that they might have "affairs" (*ngoai tinh*) with *chau van* musicians, and during fieldwork I did hear rumors of such affairs. So, contrary to female mediums' expressed intention to foster family harmony, many risk marital antagonism due to their ritual practices.

During one ritual that I attended, a female medium, whom I will call Thanh, referred to an incident of marital discord provoked by her participation in *len dong* rituals. When possessed by the Seventh Princess (*Co Bay*), Thanh uttered the following words "transmitted" (*truyen*) by the spirit:

> Your husband said that "tongues have no bones and there are many twisty roads," so the Third Princess scolded and punished.

After the ritual Thanh mentioned that her husband had recently criticized her religious practices because he did not "believe" (*tin*) in the spirits. The phrase "the tongue has no bones and there are many twisty roads" is a reference to his criticisms. When Thanh was possessed by the Third Princess (*Co Bo*), the spirit punished her by making her so cold that she had to stop the ritual temporarily. After a ten-minute break, the ritual continued with the incarnation of the Ninth Princess (*Co Chin*). When possessed by the Ninth Princess, Thanh implored her mother-in-law, who was present at the ritual, to make her husband respect the spirits:

> If that husband is still dishonest, then why should I forgive?

> The person who gave birth [to Thanh's husband] must know the way to admonish him; then I will forgive.

Thanh's utterances while possessed provide a specific example of how mediumship may serve to undermine the authority conventionally ascribed to husbands. The following proverbs, which were often mentioned by female mediums, confirm that mediumship has the potential to invert traditional power asymmetries:

> Being a medium comes first; having a husband who is a king comes second.
> (*Thu nhat ngoi dong; thu hai chong vua.*)

> Marrying a wife who is a medium comes first; marrying a husband who is a king comes second.
> (*Thu nhat lay vo dong; thu nhi lay chong vua.*)

These proverbs openly challenge patriarchal authority by asserting that female mediums are more important than patriarchal figures (husbands and kings) and

---

a belief that something within the family must be fixed as if there were some prior, natural state to which it will or can return." Ibid., p. 13.

overturn one of the Confucian "three obediences," namely, a woman's subservience to her husband.

On one occasion when a medium called Van mentioned the first proverb quoted above, she said that after a *len dong*, she was so happy that she did not care about anything else, not even whether her husband became king. Van went on to suggest that women's traditional role of attending to every need of the family, especially the needs of the male members of the family, is reversed during rituals. To extend the two proverbs quoted above, *len dong* rituals provide a space where mediums are treated like husbands and kings.

Such claims do, however, have to be balanced with a consideration of the pantheon of spirits and of mediums' relations with the spirits. Even though over half the pantheon is made up of female spirits (and the mother spirits have the highest ranking), the pantheon of spirits is hierarchical.[34] Mediums are also the "servants" of the spirits: they are "chosen," "ordered," and "forced" by the spirits to be initiated and have to "obey" them while possessed. So could it be that female mediums are simply replacing human "masters" with spiritual ones? Certainly, the scope for challenging patriarchal authority during rituals and the egalitarian nature of distributing gifts while possessed must be understood within the context of the hierarchical nature of the spirit pantheon and mediums' underlying submission to spiritual authority.

MALE MEDIUMS AND SEXUALITY

The term *"dong co"* refers to the effeminate gender identity of male mediums rather than their sexuality, yet many also said they were "homosexual" (*dong tinh luyen ai*). Some male mediums said that their involvement in mediumship precluded marriage, as the following statement by one male medium demonstrates:

> When I was possessed by the spirits ... [the spirits] said I should not marry, and that if I did an ordinary job, I would be taken back to the heavens; [the spirits said] that if I went out on the road, I would get run over by a car. My mouth spoke out like that [that is, the spirits spoke "through" my mouth]. So I had to become a religious person and do good work.

Despite instances of abstinence from marriage, it is not uncommon for male mediums to marry. During fieldwork I did meet some married male mediums who privately admitted they had sex with men, including other mediums (and some also made sexual advances toward me). Female ritual participants were aware of this situation, as the following comment by a female medium illustrates:

> [*Dong co*] like relations with men, including those *dong co* who have wives ... The *dong co* who have wives haven't made it public yet, but generally they have "sentiment" [*tinh cam*] for men.

---

[34] Maurice Durand even goes as far as to say that the hierarchical nature of the pantheon of spirits is influenced by "the organization of the Chinese empire." Maurice Durand, *Technique et panthéon des médiums viêtnamiens (Dông)* (Paris: École Français d'Extrême-Orient, 1959), p. 32.

A newspaper article published in 1997, which condemns *len dong*, refers to mediums' assistants as "genuine homosexuals" (*dan pe-de chinh hieu*).[35] But homosexuality is not recognized by Vietnamese law and is not often part of public discourse. The awareness of many followers of the Mother Goddess religion that male mediums had homosexual relationships (even if they were married and had children) would seem to suggest that *len dong* is one site where, even if not explicitly, a different sexual orientation is acknowledged. However, although ritual participants were tacitly aware of the homosexuality of most *dong co*, they were resistant to the suggestion that homosexuality was relevant to mediumship. For instance, when I asked a female medium whether *len dong* rituals provided men with an opportunity to "show" (*boc lo*) their homosexuality, she replied: "you cannot combine *len dong* with homosexuality. Homosexuality is outside, you cannot enter it into *len dong*; they are separate." Similarly, when I asked homosexual male mediums whether mediumship gave them an opportunity to "express" (*dien dat*) or "show" (*boc lo*) their homosexuality, their responses were invariably negative. Such statements are in keeping with the lack of public acknowledgment of homosexuality, but they also reflect the strongly held view among ritual participants that sexual orientation is unconnected to the divine calling to become a medium and the practices of mediumship. The following response in an interview I conducted with a male medium called Tien was typical:

BN: Are all male mediums homosexual?

Tien: It is not necessarily the case, it depends on the person, some are and some aren't ... Just like in the general population, some people like girls and some like boys. You cannot distinguish [between mediums and the general population] ... It is the spirits who choose people to become mediums.

In this way, issues relating to sexuality are bypassed as irrelevant to mediumship, and instead the agency of spirits is emphasized. To suggest, therefore, that the motivation for men to become mediums is dominated by a homoerotic drive would undermine spiritual efficacy, and it would also ignore the existence of the minority of male mediums who do not engage in homosexual activity.

LEN DONG: SOCIAL REALITY OR CULTURAL FANTASY?

In her gender analysis of Temiar ritual and music in Malaysia, Marina Roseman has observed a series of "symbolic inversions":

Halaa [Temiar mediums] are predominantly male, their spirit guides are predominantly female. Men, ranging extensively through the jungle during subsistence activities, are transformed into the earth-bound students of female

---

[35] Quoted from Ngoc Quang, "*Len dong: mot te nan me tin can len an*" ["*Len dong*: A Social Evil in Need of Condemnation"] *Lao Dong* newspaper, 1997 (exact date unknown).

spirit guides during ritual singing sessions. Women, restricted daily to swidden and settlement, are the wandering teachers of the spirit realm.[36]

In rare cases when *halaa* are female, they connect with male spirit-guides. Roseman describes such gender inversions in terms of conjuncture: "The male element incorporated by females (and the female element by males) represents a dynamic conjunction of opposites, which overcomes boundaries and generates the 'transformation' ... of Temiar trance."[37]

The performance of stereotypical male and female roles during *len dong* might usefully be thought of in terms of a dynamic conjunction of opposites. However, for Roseman, ritual inversions are primarily symbolic and have little effect on everyday life: "Ritual, with its intricate inversions and transformations, often describes cultural fantasies, rather than social realities."[38] In the case of *len dong*, I would argue that there are stronger links between social realities and ritual performance than is suggested by Roseman in relation to Temiar rituals. Female mediums' hot-temperedness and male mediums' effeminate behavior are not just confined to ritual performance. Rather, aspects of mediums' characters—which are present in their everyday lives—find expression, negotiation, and (partial) resolution through possession. This is most obvious when considering initiation crises since illness and/or misfortune lessen after initiation. Disciples are also concerned with practical matters during *len dong*: receiving the gifts, advice, and protection of the spirits is informed by, and affects, economic and social realities.

Male mediums do not dress in women's clothes outside of *len dong* rituals (nor do female mediums wear men's clothes when not possessed), and they are not noted for carrying out tasks that are normally done by women (for example, cooking, going to the market). Nevertheless, they are perceived as behaving like women in their everyday lives through their effeminate demeanor, and this is expressed during possession. Also, most men involved in mediumship manage to earn a living either by being temple mediums or through fortune-telling/healing.[39] Being *dong co* is therefore not restricted to rituals: it permeates everyday life. Male mediums assume a variant gender positionality and are often afforded new possibilities for supporting themselves financially.

The interpenetration of ritual and everyday life is no less apparent for female mediums. After the exuberance of possession—which gives ample opportunity for the expression of hot-temperedness (for example, through the sometimes truculent behavior of mandarin spirits)—their difficult temperaments are eased, and they feel happy and relaxed. Some female mediums generate an income through fortune-

---

[36] Marina Roseman, "Inversion and Conjuncture: Male and Female Performance among the Temiar of Peninsular Malaysia," in *Women and Music in Cross-Cultural Perspective*, ed. Ellen Koskoff (Westport, CT: Greenwood Press, 1987), p. 144.

[37] Ibid., pp. 145-46.

[38] Ibid., p. 148.

[39] It is the medium who pays for the expenses of a ritual (such as providing a meal for the disciples and paying for the gifts distributed to ritual participants during possession), so mediums do not make money out of holding *len dong*. However, disciples give some gifts and a small amount of money when they request a medium for a healing or fortune-telling session. Fortune-telling/healing mediums can therefore earn a living through such sessions. Temple mediums are able to support their role as temple guardians through the donations they receive from followers of the Mother Goddess religion and from other mediums.

telling or healing, but, unlike male mediums, the majority have regular jobs (for example, selling goods or working on the land or in government offices).

Apart from the possibility of earning a living through healing and fortune-telling, there are other practical ways in which the social realities of female mediums are affected by their religious practices. At temples all over Vietnam, there are many *len dong* festivals, which give mediums (and disciples) the opportunity to travel frequently to different parts of the country and to enlarge their sphere of social interaction. The comments of one "husbandless" medium called Khoat who did not go to festivals, illustrate some of the constraints that are sometimes placed on women's movement:

> I don't go willy-nilly to many different festivals like other mediums. I am on my own, that is, I don't have a husband ... so if I went out to different places, went on the back of someone's motorbike or did this or that, people would think this and that about me, and that I wasn't going to places to worship. So my parents don't allow me to go. I just worship at home.

Khoat's parents did not consent to their daughter's traveling long distances because she was no longer with her husband and they were worried about gossip. But, as suggested by Khoat above, most mediums managed to overcome such obstacles and traveled freely. To make a comparison with the Temiar of Malaysia: Temiar (female) spirit-guides wander in the spirit realm; Vietnamese (female) mediums wander in the human world.

Like many female mediums, Khoat worshipped in a private temple adjacent to the house in which she lived. The tendency for female mediums to have their own temples, either in, or adjacent to, their homes, has been noted as a restriction to the domestic rather than the public sphere. However, temples do afford mediums with a space that is separate from normal domestic activities and that is under their control. During the many visits I made to meet the medium Thanh, neither her young children nor husband ever entered her temple. Whenever Thanh made trips away from the village, she always locked her temple but not the family house; the temple, rather than the house, was a space to which no one else had access without Thanh's permission.

Thanh has a reputation as a fortune-telling medium, so people from the surrounding area often come to her temple for consultations. Thanh's "private" temple is therefore to a certain extent "public," as strangers often visit her temple. This, in turn, has greatly expanded Thanh's social sphere. So, while it is the case that temples presided over by male and female mediums do tend to be in the public and domestic spheres, respectively—which seemingly confirms gender-based power asymmetries—private temples are distinct from, and more public than, other domestic spaces.

Conclusion

This essay has discussed Vietnamese mediumship from a gendered perspective. Musical performance has been highlighted as crucial to the traversing of gender during *len dong*. The gender characteristics of spirits are articulated, not only through the ritual dress and actions of mediums, but also through the use of distinctive *chau van* melodies and song texts for male and female spirits, which embody "masculine" and "feminine" characteristics. Musical performance enables mediums to dance and carry out ritual actions appropriate to the gender identity of the incarnated spirit. In the *chau van* musical system, the gender of spirits is musically constructed; music is constitutive of the gender identities performed during *len dong*.

Gender traversing during possession by spirits enables both male and female mediums to transgress lines of gender. Established gender identities are, to a certain extent, destabilized through such ritual acts: male mediums assume an "effeminate" gender identity and female mediums deal with aspects of their personalities such as being "difficult" and "hot tempered," which are, according to widely propagated stereotypes, "unfeminine." Mediumship therefore enables—indeed, requires—men and women to behave in ways that are outside of conventionally prescribed gender roles. Mediumship provides female mediums with possibilities of challenging "patriarchy" and provides a space for women to be treated like "husbands and kings." However, the gender positionality of mediums is still made in relation to stereotypical, normative gender boundaries: male spirits exhibit idealized masculine traits, such as being "prestigious" and "serious," and female spirits present idealized versions of "soft" and "graceful" women.

Vietnamese mediumship defies reduction to a single, unitary interpretation. Rather, it is complex and contradictory: the egalitarianism of distributing money and gifts during rituals has to be measured against the mediums' subservience to the spirits and the hierarchical nature of the pantheon of spirits; female mediums' increased access to the public domain should be balanced with the fact that many of them preside over private temples in the domestic realm; and female mediums' concerns with family happiness needs to be understood in the context of some of them going against their husbands' wills by becoming mediums and presenting other challenges to male authority. Ritual acts therefore do not constitute a voluntaristic construction or destabilizing of gender identities. Rather they afford mediums—within clearly defined limits—a degree of flexibility to negotiate the conventional gender identities ascribed to men and women. Such negotiation is not merely confined to the ritual domain: it also affects mediums' everyday lives.

Spirit Performance and the Ritual Construction of Personal Identity in Modern Vietnam

Kirsten W. Endres[1]

In his classic treatise on Vietnamese religion, the French missionary Leopold Cadière metaphorically compared the Vietnamese belief system with the tropical forest of the Annamite cordillera:

> [A]ll around you are huge trunks that plunge their roots into unknown depths and support a vault of green foliage; branches that bend towards the ground and take roots; lianas stretching from tree to tree that do not seem to have a beginning or an end, inextricable shrubs ... large, bizarre flowers that cover the ground or adorn the crown of a tree ... rough, black, slippery bark that makes you shiver; dead branches on a carpet of humus, of putrefaction; everywhere an abundance of fluids, an intense vitality that engulfs you.[2]

In the aftermath of French colonial rule, the Vietnamese revolution zealously attempted to defoliate these treetops and clear the mossy undergrowth of so-called "depraved customs" (*hu tuc*) and harmful "superstitions" (*me tin di doan*). The Party-led antisuperstition campaign aimed at abandoning all ideas and practices that engaged supernatural forces in dealing with human agonies and anxieties.[3] Spirit possession rituals related to the *Tu Phu* religion clearly belonged to this category.

[1] I carried out my fieldwork in Hanoi between 2001 and 2003. I am grateful to the mediums who confided their life-stories to me and invited me to their performances, both of which I truly enjoyed. My thanks also go to Huong and Binh, who assisted my fieldwork, for all their help in conducting and transcribing interviews. Finally, I wish to thank Susan Bayly and John Kleinen for their insightful comments on earlier drafts of this essay.

[2] Leopold Cadière, *Croyances et Pratiques Religieuses des Viêtnamiens* (Saigon: Imprimerie Nouvelle d'Extrême Orient, 1958), p. 1.

[3] Shaun Malarney, *Culture, Ritual, and Revolution in Vietnam* (New York, NY, and London: RoutledgeCurzon, 2002).

Their prohibition, however, was only effective to the point that spirit mediums henceforth performed in secret.[4] When the country was united under North Vietnamese leadership in 1975, local communities started to push for the revivification of their ritual traditions. With the onset of the economic reforms known as *doi moi*, it finally became clear that the forest of Vietnamese religion(s) had ultimately withstood the Party's secularizing campaign—and maybe even sprouted some new blossoms.[5] Far from being an old-fashioned belief practiced by elderly village ladies, spirit possession rituals are rapidly gaining in popularity even among the young urban crowd. Master mediums (*dong thay*, also *ong/ba dong*)[6] in Hanoi enjoy an ever-growing clientele of devoted followers,[7] and famous temples dedicated to the *Tu Phu* pantheon[8] receive a constant stream of pilgrims during the festive season.

As Nguyen Thi Hien has pointed out, the initiation into the practice of spirit possession often relates to critical moments in human life.[9] An illness that cannot be medically cured, a streak of bad luck in business or personal affairs, or haunting dreams may indicate the spirits' calling. With the help of an experienced master medium or a fortune-teller (*thay boi*), the underlying cause of these misfortunes is identified. It is important to note that a person qualifies as a practitioner not because of his or her free will to follow the *Tu Phu* religion but because that person has a "spirit root" (*can*), meaning that he or she is fated for mediumship. The underlying notion is that a medium owes (the spirits of) the four palaces a debt from a previous incarnation (*kiep truoc*) that can only be repaid by entering into the spirits' service and becoming a medium.

Since practice theory and performance-oriented approaches have gained currency in providing a framework for analyzing ritual enactments, various authors have addressed rituals as "creative strategies by which human beings continually

---

[4] Barley Norton, "'The Moon Remembers Uncle Ho': The Politics of Music and Mediumship in Northern Vietnam," *British Journal of Ethnomusicology* 11,1 (2002): 71-100.

[5] Malarney, *Culture, Ritual*, pp. 189-207.

[6] In most publications on Vietnamese mediumship, the term "*ong dong/ba dong*" is used as a generic term for male/female mediums, for example, Maurice Durand, *Technique et panthéon des médiums viêtnamiens (Dông)* (Paris: École Française d'Extrême-Orient, 1959); Barley Norton, "Music and Possession in Vietnam" (PhD dissertation, SOAS, University of London, 2000). However, practitioners maintain that the term should only be applied to master mediums who have acquired enough knowledge and expertise to initiate followers into the practice of *len dong* (spirit possession ritual). In contrast, a range of terms is used to designate a person who simply practices mediumship. He or she is referred to as a "follower" or "disciple" (*con nhang de tu*) of a master medium, a "novice medium" (*thanh dong*), a "chair (for the spirits) of the four palaces" (*ghe cua bon phu*), a "person having the fate of a medium" (*nguoi co dong*), or simply "a servant" (*nguoi hau*).

[7] For a detailed account of the relationship between master mediums and their followers, see Larsson and Endres's essay, "'Children of the Spirits, Followers of a Master': Spirit Mediums in Post-Renovation Vietnam," in this volume.

[8] See Ngo Duc Thinh's essay, "The Mother Goddess Religion: Its History, Pantheon, and Practices," in this volume.

[9] Nguyen Thi Hien, "The Religion of the Four Palaces: Mediumship and Therapy in Viet Culture" (PhD dissertation, Indiana University, 2002).

reproduce and reshape their social and cultural environments."[10] Influenced by Victor Turner's treatment of ritual as a genre of social action that "confront[s] problems and contradictions of the social process,"[11] these approaches have moved on to exploring the role that performativity plays in the actual social construction and transformation of human reality.[12] Taking up this approach, this essay will show how male and female practitioners of Vietnamese spirit mediumship constitute their personal identities and their relationship to the world through the ritual embodiment of divine entities belonging to the pantheon of the *Tu Phu* religion. Through the lens of individual life-stories, I will explore how becoming part of a group network of mediumship practitioners (*hoi dong bong*) enables practitioners to cope ritually with their existential realities in a rapidly changing modern society.[13]

FATE HAS BEEN UNKIND: MS. HUONG'S STORY

Each time I visit Ms. Huong[14] in her tiny but spotless Hanoi dwelling, she treats me with an abundance of seasonal fruit and always points out at great length that she had washed each of them several times with boiled water and wiped them again with paper tissue before serving. One of her dominant themes is her obsession with cleanliness. In her opinion, Hanoi has become filthy and unsafe since all the "country bumpkins" (*nguoi nha que*) have started to flock to the city to participate in and contribute to the city's buoyant economic life. In her eloquent narratives, Ms. Huong presents herself as a cultivated and generous, though quick-tempered, woman who has been condemned by fate to suffer hardship, injustice, and resentment from kin. In great detail, she recounts incidents of parental maltreatment during her childhood, stories of seduction and jealousy, Party-state arbitrariness, and her daughters' disrespect. Born in 1937 into a petit-bourgeois family in Hanoi, she had to suffer her mother's scolding and physical abuse throughout her childhood and adolescence. Moreover, her father was an inveterate gambler who often became violent after losing money or property. When she was sixteen, a friend suggested that she have her fortune told, and although she claims not to have had much faith in

---

[10] Catherine Bell, *Ritual Theory, Ritual Practice* (New York, NY, and Oxford: Oxford University Press, 1992), p. 76; see also Stanley J. Tambiah, "A Performative Approach to Ritual," *Proceedings of the British Academy* 65 (1979): 116-42; Victor Turner, *The Anthropology of Performance* (New York, NY: PAJ Publications, 1986); and Bruce Kapferer, *The Feast of the Sorcerer: Practices of Consciousness and Power* (Chicago, IL, and London: University of Chicago Press, 1997).

[11] Turner, *The Anthropology of Performance*, p. 94.

[12] Edward L Schieffelin, "Problematizing Performance," in *Ritual, Performance, Media*, ed. Felicia Hughes-Freeland (London: Routledge, 1998), pp. 194-207; Ursula Rao and Klaus Peter Köpping, "Einleitung: Die 'performative Wende'; Leben-Ritual—Theater," in *Im Rausch des Rituals*, ed. K. P. Köpping and U. Rao (Hamburg: LIT Verlag, 2000), pp. 1-32.

[13] Janice Boddy, "Spirit Possession Revisited: Beyond Instrumentality," *Annual Review of Anthropology* 23 (1994): 407-34; see also Nguyen Kim Hien, "Len dong, mot sinh hoat tam linh mang tinh tri lieu? [Len Dong, a Spiritual Practice Bearing Therapy Features?]," *Van Hoa Dan Gian* 4,76 (2001): 69-78; for a related portrayal of Silicon Valley spirit mediums, see Fjelstad and Maiffret's essay, "Gifts from the Spirits: Spirit Possession and Personal Transformation among Silicon Valley Spirit Mediums," in this volume.

[14] All informants' names have been changed or abbreviated in order to protect their privacy. All of the interviews with Ms. Huong took place in Hanoi, August 2002.

the practice, she agreed. The blind man who gave her the reading told her that she was fated to become a medium and that she would go mad if she refused to accept this as her destiny. Ms. Huong admits that she didn't quite understand what he was talking about, although she had seen mediums performing in a neighborhood temple and very much liked watching their performances. At that time, however, she was still a schoolgirl, so there was nothing to do to follow up on her fortune-teller's pronouncement. She decided to wait until she had reached adulthood and had made her own money. Then, she said, she would eventually become a medium. But waiting was not always easy:

> At night I often had strange dreams; I dreamt of leeches and centipedes squirming and crawling all around me and clinging to my legs and of snakes wrapping themselves around my body. I dreamt I was flying across a river and falling down. I was scared to death; I didn't dare to move or open my eyes until I realized I was only dreaming. That is how the spirits signaled to me that they had "seized my body" [*bat xac*].

In her dreams she also saw the spirits, and afterwards she usually fell ill. Furthermore, she says "the spirits made me very hot tempered; I got very easily angry." Mediums often characterize themselves as "hot tempered" (*nong tinh*) or "hard to please" (*kho tinh*).[15] As Barley Norton has observed, these characteristics are considered part of a medium's fate, and a female medium with a strong male spirit root may have a particularly hot-tempered character. Ms. Huong attributes her personality to four different spirit roots. Her following narration affords an insight into the strategies employed by *len dong* ritual practitioners in dealing with different experiences of the self:[16]

> When I am very stern and hot tempered, this is because of my spirit root of the Seventh Prince [*Ong Hoang Bay*]; he also gambles, but he is fortunate [*co loc*]. Then I have the spirit root of the Third Princess [*Co Bo*], who ... also has a bad quality of character: she decided never to forgive, so when I hate someone, I hate that person till death. People say that I like eating fruit because my fate is linked to the Little Princess [*Co Be*], who lives in the forest, and the Little Princess also likes playing with toys—I have many dolls and soft toys upstairs; I like toys very much. If somebody says, "You are old, but you still like playing with toys," I get very angry and scold, "Get lost!" ... The Little Princess is also very sharp tongued—in fact I never start an argument with anyone, but if someone starts an argument with me, I don't give way even one inch; the Little Princess behaves capriciously, but if anyone yields an inch, then I will yield a mile. The Little Princess gets easily offended and sulky, and I am like this, too. Then I also have the spirit root of the Third Prince [*Ong Hoang Bo*]; he is lascivious, and he likes elegance and beauty. When I was young, my eyes were not sunken as they are

---

[15] Norton, "Music and Possession in Vietnam," p. 72; see also Norton's essay, "'Hot-Tempered' Women and 'Effeminate' Men: The Performance of Music and Gender in Vietnamese Mediumship," in this volume.

[16] Boddy, "Spirit Possession Revisited," p. 423.

now, and everybody said I was lascivious; in fact I was not lascivious, my eyes were said to be lascivious.

In fact Ms. Huong's unconventional character is strikingly at odds with most of the traditional norms and virtues of Vietnamese femininity. Her first marriage took place at the age of twenty and broke up after less than one year while she was pregnant with her first daughter. The reason for the rupture was that her husband was jealous of her former suitor, a French intellectual who had become a member of the Viet Minh (Vietnam's communist-led revolutionary nationalist front, founded in 1942) in 1950. Ms. Huong says she had come close to marrying him but gave up the idea after much anguished deliberation:

I was afraid that if I married a foreigner, the children would not know how to worship their ancestors and that [after death] my soul would be hungry [*so hon minh doi*]; I was also afraid the children would not live with emotion [*tinh cam*], so this is why I decided to marry a Vietnamese.

During her illegal trading activities as a vendor of perfume essences, she met the man who fathered her second daughter, and she gave birth to this daughter when she was twenty-three. The relationship was equally short lived and ended—again for reasons of jealousy—shortly after the baby was born. In 1966, at the age of twenty-nine, Ms. Huong was convicted "out of the blue" and without trial on the grounds that she had been associating with "hoodlums" (*luu manh*).[17] She spent five grueling years in a prison camp in Thai Nguyen. In the years that followed her return to Hanoi, she struggled to make a living to support herself and her two daughters by selling refreshments and by trading in market goods.

Her road into mediumship was obstructed by wartime conditions and the prohibition of *len dong* rituals. She remembers that in 1977, she was watching a woman performing a *len dong* ritual. During the embodiment of the Tenth Prince, the medium suddenly flung the prince's bell-baton (a wooden club adorned with bells) at her and said: "Child, if you do not present yourself to the spirits, you will lose almost everything!" She felt this confirmed once again her fate as a mediumship practitioner, and she started preparing for her initiation ceremony (*mo phu*, literally, "palace opening"). When her daughter went to Saigon in 1979 to visit relatives who had left Hanoi after 1954, she brought back ritual robes and accessories that in those days were not yet available in Hanoi. However, it was not until 1981 that Ms. Huong finally had the "opening of the palace" ceremony organized. The rich fellow traders she had invited to witness her entry into the spirits' service foresaw the transformation that she would experience after her initiation since they were whispering to each other, "From now on she will stop quarrelling!" Ms. Huong says: "Before, if anything struck me as messy, I would curse at the top of my voice, but after the palace-opening ceremony, I was very gentle; whenever someone started an argument, I just ignored it."

Today, she lives alone and regrets that her former lovers are too old to take her out to a dance hall. She is vexed with her two daughters, the younger of whom fled

---

[17] Ms. Huong is very vague about the reasons for her arrest; according to her she was denounced by a zealous communist block warden for no reason.

the country (and maybe her mother) to Canada in the 1980s but apparently does not send home enough money to satisfy Ms. Huong's dreams of luxury. The elder daughter just seems to hate her outright, and Ms. Huong claims that her daughter never sets foot inside her mother's home except when she is asking for money. Ms. Huong lives a lonely life and rarely receives visitors, maybe because very few people can cope with her assertive views about status and etiquette. Because of her limited resources, she can afford to perform only two *len dong* rituals per year, which is the minimum requirement of an initiated medium. The nightmares have ceased to haunt her since she entered mediumship: "Only when I am overdue with serving, I would dream again; I would dream of the spirits calling me to serve [them]."

According to Maurice Durand, a French researcher of the colonial period, mediums were in most cases "socially well-established, intelligent, and cultured women" who were, however, suffering from a "problematic emotional life." He identified as the most active protagonists of mediumship practice women who were heartbroken, divorced or widowed, or had remained childless. Those women practiced mediumship in order to find "oblivion, healing, or hope."[18] To a certain degree, Ms. Huong's case supports this characterization: She describes herself as an intelligent and cultured woman and deeply regrets that her educational opportunities had been limited due to her parents' decision and family situation during the revolutionary period. During her childhood, she felt emotionally rejected by her mother ("My mother did not hate the other siblings; she only hated me—she hated me until she died!"), and as a mother of two adult daughters, she feels that her offspring do not show her proper respect and gratitude in terms of emotional and material support. The relationships with her daughters' fathers were short lived and followed by a succession of unstable love affairs, as a consequence of which she had several abortions. From my own observations gained on numerous occasions and in various social settings since I first met her in 2001, I feel safe in concluding that Ms. Huong's emotional life is indeed highly problematic. Although she claims that entering into mediumship has softened her temper, I have often enough witnessed sudden outbursts of rage and quarrelsome crankiness when something went against the grain of her precise ideas and expectations about how she wanted things to be, and this even happened during the very act of performing a *len dong* ritual. However, it appears that as a practicing medium, Ms. Huong does find some sort of "oblivion, healing, or hope": by constituting a destined relationship with the spirit world, she can project the deviant and unruly aspects of her personality onto a multitude of spirit identities and assign the responsibility for their consequences to her fate. As a result, she is no longer haunted by terrifying dreams and maintains that her hot-temperedness has toned down as compared to the time before she entered into mediumship (*ra dong*).

Yet a "problematic emotional life" is not always at the core of being predestined for mediumship. Let me therefore turn to the story of another medium named Hang.

OF DEBTS AND DIVINATIONS: HANG'S STORY

Hang is a charming and dainty thirty-four-year-old woman, a mother of two quick-witted schoolboys, and a dutiful wife of her husband who works as a driver.

---

[18] Durand, *Technique et panthéon*, p. 15, my translation.

Every day she commutes on her motor scooter between Hanoi and a small provincial town sixty kilometers away, where she takes purchase orders and collects money from the local market vendors. In contrast to Ms. Huong, she is a very sociable person who often invites friends over to her apartment on various family occasions, such as birthdays and death anniversaries. She said she had felt the calling of the spirits since her early childhood:

> When I was first seized [by the spirits], I was six years old. I will tell you how it happened: for three months I could not urinate; I didn't eat or drink anything except boiled water; for three months I only drank water and ate some corn, manioc, and potatoes. And during these three months, every day at twelve o'clock I would have a fit of sudden outrage and cry violently. After that I would continue to play as if nothing had happened.[19]

So one noon the spirits felt pity for Hang and informed her that she should see a fortune-teller. She ran home, yelling, "mother, mother, let me go and see a fortune-teller!" but her mother hesitated because she did not believe much in soothsaying. A neighbor finally convinced Hang's mother of the necessity to seek the advice of a fortune-teller (*thay boi*), who revealed that Hang had a medium's fate. As a temporary solution, her mother organized a special ritual to appease the spirits and prevent them from afflicting her child. After this, there were indeed no more incidents until Hang was ten years old:

> One day when I was playing in front of the family altar, suddenly thirty-six spirits possessed me in succession ... In fact I had never before seen a ritual because it was not as easy as nowadays—in those days, the old people served [the spirits] at midnight, otherwise the authorities would come and arrest them. From then on, at the beginning and in the middle of each year, my mother had to organize a petitioning ceremony for me to ask [the spirits] for a delay [of calling me into their service] until I "presented myself as a medium" [*trinh dong*] at the age of twenty.

I first met Hang on her second opening ceremony in a temple in the outskirts of Hanoi in late 2001. Later she told me that until then she had suffered from repeated harsh setbacks in business, one of which happened because she was foolish enough to fall victim to a trading woman from Hai Phong who conned her into lending her her entire business capital of approximately seventeen thousand US dollars and then vanished without a trace, leaving her to start from scratch again. Some years later, she and her husband were seriously injured in two separate accidents. The reason for this continuous streak of bad luck was later revealed to her by a female fortune-telling medium (*dong boi*): Her first master had made a mistake during her first initiation by ordering a medium-size instead of a large-size votive paper horse as an offering presented to the spirits. To make matters worse, one of the horse's legs broke when it was burnt.[20] This is why she had to "re-enlist" into the spirits' service

---

[19] All of the interviews with Hang took place in Hanoi, October 2002.

[20] The burning of paper offerings symbolizes their transition into the other world. On votive paper offerings, see Nguyen Thi Hien's essay, "'A Bit of a Spirit Favor Is Equal to a Load of

with the help of another master, Mr. Duong, who arranged her second palace-opening ceremony. Not long before I met her, she had bought and refurbished an apartment in a ramshackle collective living quarter (*khu tap the*). It seemed to me that she was now able to secure a decent income for her family—every time I visited her at home, I noticed that she had bought new luxury commodities (a second television set, a VCD recorder, new furniture, an air conditioner, and so on), and she held the most splendid ritual performances four times a year rather than the minimum requirement of two rituals a year. The spirits had obviously been generous in bestowing "blessed gifts" (*loc*) upon her. Hang describes the effects of her ritual practice as follows:

> After serving [the spirits], I inevitably feel at ease, my mind is at ease. Generally speaking, [after serving the spirits], I suddenly have something to trust in, I feel at ease, I don't have to worry anymore ... If you ask me like that, I think this is kind of psychological [*tam ly*]. I don't know how it works, but for example like last year, some days after I served [the spirits], I was very fortunate [*co loc*], like I had some good profit when trading. It is usually like that, like after serving the spirits, my work bodes favorably, and I think the fact that this inevitably happens so naturally after serving [the spirits] is also sort of a psychological thing.

Hang embodies the Ninth Princess during a *len dong* ritual held at Chau temple in Gia Lam, 2004. One of the ritual participants presents the princess with a tray of carefully arranged Coca-Cola cans in order to "ask for blessed gifts" (*xin loc*).
Photo by Kirsten W. Endres.

Mundane Gifts': Votive Paper Offerings of *Len Dong* Rituals in Post-Renovation Vietnam," in this volume.

In spite of Hang's own assertions, however, I was soon to find out that she notoriously kept on borrowing money from a lot of people, and I assume that when a creditor demanded the loan back, she took out another to repay her debt. Three years after her second initiation, rumors had it that she went broke—she had disappeared for several weeks, leaving her network of creditors and fellow mediums furiously cursing her and spreading wild gossip about the amount of money she owed. When I met her again a few months later, she told me that her economic failure had been due to her ignorance of the Third Lady's request that she should hold her next performance at the Third Lady's temple in Thanh Hoa province.

Since the onset of the economic reforms in 1986 has sanctioned the accumulation of private wealth, popular religious practice seems increasingly to emphasize the invocation of the spirit world's assumed efficacy in ensuring material well-being and economic success. Goddesses like the Lady of the Realm (*Ba Chua Xu*) in Southern Vietnam or the Lady of the Storehouse (*Ba Chua Kho*) in the Red River Delta have emerged as pop stars of the Vietnamese religious world, with whom people transact for economic and other this-worldly benefits.[21] Likewise, many of the spirits who inhabit the four palaces are believed to be particularly efficacious in bestowing economic wealth upon their faithful devotees, which may be a reason why *len dong* practice is particularly widespread among female traders and market vendors.[22] Hang's tale is therefore a good example of how fated mediums tackle the challenges of the new Vietnamese market-oriented economy. In the hustle and bustle of the Vietnamese marketplace, petty entrepreneurs are particularly vulnerable to sudden economic booms and slumps. The widespread practice of borrowing money from a whole legion of usurers and friends—each of whom lends a rather small sum that is paid back with high interest after a short period of several weeks—even increases the risk of going broke. It might thus be felt that serving the spirits dutifully and properly eases the tensions and anxieties of the struggle for survival in modern Vietnamese society.[23] Furthermore, as in Hang's case, the failure to serve the spirits properly can offer a metaphysical explanation to those who fail to be successful in the new market-oriented economy.

For the average mediumship practitioner like Hang, serving the spirits is a relatively costly affair. The basic equipment of robes and accessories and the palace-opening ritual costs from five to ten million Vietnamese *dong* (approximately three hundred to six hundred US dollars), and a minimum of two *len dong* performances are required each year. The better off a medium is, the more lavish his or her *len dong* performances will be. It is interesting to note that group networks of master mediums and their followers differ considerably in their social and economic backgrounds. Ms. Huong is a disciple of Master Thanh, who owns the most opulent private temple in Hanoi's old quarter and requires his innumerable followers to

---

[21] See Philip Taylor, *Goddess on the Rise: Pilgrimage and Popular Religion in Vietnam* (Honolulu, HI: University of Hawai'i Press, 2004), p. 85; and Le Hong Ly, " Praying for Profits: The Cult of the Lady of the Treasury" (paper presented at the annual meeting of the Association for Asian Studies, Chicago, 2001).

[22] See also Nguyen Thi Hien, "The Religion of the Four Palaces," p. 92.

[23] Le Hong Ly, "Tin nguong len dong tu cai nhin cua nguoi trong cuoc" [The Belief in Mediumship from the Perspective of the Practitioners] (paper presented at the International Workshop on Mother Goddess Worship and at the Phu Giay Festival, Hanoi, March 30-April 2, 2001).

donate vast sums to its support. Thus, his clientele consists mainly of rich traders and entrepreneurs, a network to which Ms. Huong no longer belongs. She therefore criticizes her master for "commercializing religion" (*buon than ban thanh*, literally, "trading in spirits") and prefers to perform in smaller temples. Hang, formerly a disciple of Master Thanh also, now follows Master Duong, another master medium who operates in the old quarter. His reputation has long exceeded that of Master Thanh; some even consider him as the "most competent" (*gioi nhat*) master medium in present-day Vietnam. His sanctuary is not as large and opulent as Master Thanh's temple, but it is still extravagant compared to that of Master Canh, whose followers generally come from more humble social backgrounds. His shrine is the smallest structure of the three mentioned, and it contains only a very basic set of statues and is simple in decor. *Len dong* performances held at his shrine are less lavish and are regularly attended by a core group of faithful disciples. In the following section, I shall present the narrative of one of his followers, a young man from a village in the outskirts of Hanoi.

SORTING OUT THE YIN AND THE YANG: CUONG'S STORY

Cuong was born in 1974 and has only recently been initiated into mediumship. During the difficult postwar period, he grew up as the adopted son of a woman whose husband had "sacrificed his life for the nation"[24] and had left her with a disabled daughter due to his exposure to toxic resin during his time as a worker at Sao Vang rubber factory before he joined the army. Behind his cheerful facade, Cuong hides his grief about the fact that he has never known a father. Although still young, he has taken up many jobs only to realize that none of them really suited him. He finally decided to work his way into the village administration. As a cadre of the communist youth organization in his village, Cuong is fairly well acquainted with Marxist theory and Party regulations. Although the practice of mediumship is no longer prohibited, it is, to some extent, still associated with "superstition" (*me tin di doan*), and Party cadres and commune officials are firmly enjoined not to participate in such activities. Cuong is thus well aware of the fact that if the village authorities were to get wind of his *len dong* practices, his position in the administration would be at high risk. Nevertheless, he felt he had to take that risk in order to gain his inner balance, a balance that he describes from his declared "idealistic" (*duy tam*) point of view as harmonizing the two worlds of Yin and Yang.

> My way into mediumship was like this: in the period when I was rushing around between work and home, I thought, now why am I working like this, it is taking me nowhere, and my mind is never at ease. I had to worry constantly, and that was very hard. A materialistic person would say all depends on oneself, all depends on one's own deeds, but an idealistic person looks at things differently: an idealistic person believes there is a Yang world [*duong*] and a Yin world [*am*]; the Yang is the world of the living, the Yin is the world beyond, the world of the spirits and the deceased. The Yang affairs I could handle, but the Yin affairs were

---

[24] See Shaun Malarney, "'The Fatherland Remembers Your Sacrifice': Commemorating War Dead in Vietnam," in *The Country of Memory: Remaking the Past in Late Socialist Vietnam*, ed. Hue-Tam Ho Tai (Berkeley, CA, and London: University of California Press, 2001), pp. 46-76.

not yet integral, not yet harmonious. I thought that the two sides would not yet harmonize with each other; this is why I felt so wretched and unhappy.[25]

His gloom made him decide to seek the advice of a fortune-teller (*di xem boi*), and his maternal aunt—who has long been a medium—took him to the shrine of Master Canh. During the consultation, Master Canh revealed to Cuong that he had "the fate of a [spirits'] soldier" (*can dong so linh*) and had to become "a chair [for the spirits] to serve [them]" (*phai bac ghe de hau*). Cuong comments, "as an idealistic person I thought if the master is right and I have a medium's fate, then I have to accept to enter mediumship [*ra dong*] because if a person objects to this fate, the spirits would render this person's life miserable."

During a *len dong* ritual held at his private temple in Hanoi (2003), Master Canh sits in front of the altar. The red veil covering his head indicates that he is prepared to receive the next spirit in sequence. As soon as the spirit has "taken seat," Master Canh throws off the veil with a shout and remains seated until the ritual assistants have changed his clothes, dressing him in the appropriate attire. Photograph by Kirsten W. Endres.

A noteworthy aspect of Cuong's narration is his attempt to express his reflections by using the contrasting concepts of "materialism" (*duy vat*) and "idealism" (*duy tam*). In Marxist theory, idealism is regarded as an antiscientific worldview that underpins religion and superstitious practices. Intriguingly, however, the Vietnamese term for "idealism" is a compound word consisting of "*duy*" (-ism) and "*tam*," (heart). The concept of *tam* is often employed by mediums to elaborate on the essential precondition for entering into a relationship with the spirits.[26] As Master Canh puts it: "In front of the altar, the most important thing is that I have heart [*co tam*]. Once I am 'true-hearted' [*that tam*], once my heart is with the spirits [*co tam voi thanh*], then the spirits will see to it that I am steady and kind."[27] As with Ms. Huong and with Hang, entering into mediumship had a positive impact on Cuong's mental well-being, a state that most mediums describe as feeling confident and at ease:

---

[25] All of the interviews with Cuong took place in Hanoi, October 2002.

[26] See Norton, "Music and Possession," p. 59.

[27] All of the interviews with Master Canh took place in Hanoi, November 2002.

After the palace opening, after I started following the spirits, I felt at ease and untroubled; I felt very happy, and I felt that many activities went absolutely smoothly ... Now I can carry out all my plans, I have confidence in myself. So whatever I do, I do it accurately; I am always steady. I am not confused anymore like before, before the palace opening I was about to be ruined, and now suddenly I can sail in smooth waters [*thuan buom xuoi gio*].

Assured of the spirits' benevolence, Cuong feels self-confident because he has found "a foothold in society" (*mot cho dung trong xa hoi*) that corresponds to his level of education, to his economic resources, and to his general situation:

This is because the spirits sort out the yin and the yang; the spirits relieve me from my bad luck. However, this does not mean that I can steer out completely from my bad luck, that I do not have to carry my heavy burden any more, but since the palace opening I feel that the spirits now carry 90 percent of it for me— they would never carry the whole of it because I have to accept my fate up until now, but as a person who has a medium's fate I am protected by the spirits, and the spirits will ease my burden and bestow blessed gifts [*loc*] upon me.

Cuong feels that he has "spirit roots of the princess spirits" (*can dong co*), in particular of the Little Princess spirit (*Co Be*). During a performance, he feels that he gets very absorbed in embodying the Little Princess "who picks flowers and catches butterflies and laughs and dances merrily." He claims that the Little Princess's characteristics, which he describes as "gentle" (*nho nhe*) and "leisurely" (*dung dinh*), also apply to his personality. At the same time, Cuong is well aware that his rather "sweet" nature does barely correspond to the stereotypical Vietnamese ideal of masculinity. As a general observation, male mediums often display feminized patterns of behavior, and the term "*dong co*" is alternately translated as "female medium"[28] or as "nancy boy."[29] As Norton has observed, the term "*dong co*" refers to the feminized gender identity of male mediums rather than to their sexuality.[30] And although many male mediums are in fact homosexual, others—like Cuong—strictly deny that their demeanor indicates any (sexual) interest in other men. Cuong is rather vexed with the fact that public opinion usually perceives his personality as feminized:

[As a child], one learns how to speak, and then later I develop my way of speaking, so how can this be changed later? The language, voice, manner, and bearing are also related to fate, to my spirit roots. They cannot be changed ... we are all like we are from early childhood; we are born like that. But alas! Many people say "this guy behaves effeminately" [*dong co*], meaning womanish [*eo la*] and even transsexual [*ai nam ai nu*] ..., if people talk like that it kind of hurts my self-esteem; sometimes I think that if I could behave as dignified as a normal person, others wouldn't say all these spiteful words, but [being like I am] is my fate, and I have to accept it.

---

[28] Dang Chan Lieu et al., *Thu dien Viet-Anh: Vietnamese-English Dictionary* (Ho Chi Minh City: Ho Chi Minh City Publishers, 1999).

[29] Bui Phung, *Thu dien Viet-Anh: Vietnamese-English Dictionary* (Hanoi: The Gioi, 2000).

[30] Norton, "Music and Possession," p. 75.

Master Canh sees the shift in gender identity toward the opposite pole as a common peculiarity of destined mediums, both male and female. In his opinion, male mediums tend to have more characteristics that are defined as feminine than the average Vietnamese male, and female mediums are most likely prone toward the masculine side. This imbalance corresponds to a disrupted equilibrium between the two cosmic principles Yin and Yang that express the polar quality of all things.[31] Master Canh's theory is that a fated medium can attain a more balanced temperament only through performing *len dong* rituals. In particular, he explains male homosexuality as an overly high level of yin energy that can be attributed to the spirit-root (*can*) of the lady or princess spirits. According to this understanding, *len dong* ritual practice offers what in Western terms would be called a sexual-reorientation therapy that enables male homosexuals to fulfill their filial obligations by leading a "normal" married life and having children. I might mention at this point that Cuong is in fact married and adores his little daughter, and although he explicitly denies that he is gay, I assume his agonizing over his yin and yang sides being in disharmony points to an inner conflict of how to integrate his unresolved homosexual attractions. By tracing his *"dong co"* characteristics to the spirit root of the Little Princess (*Co Be*), Cuong can now enjoy recognition within a group network of fellow mediums who not only appreciate his personality but also comprehend it in different terms than does the average Vietnamese citizen. Since spirit sequences follow standardized patterns of body movement and facial expression from which mediumship practitioners hardly ever deviate, *len dong* performance actually provides rather limited opportunity for the expression of female hot-temperedness, effeminacy, childlike behavior, and petulance.[32] Nevertheless, mediumship practitioners do feel more carefree (*thoai mai*) after these different identities have been embodied and the mediums' own eccentricities (if there are any) have been (temporarily) appeased.

THE RULES OF PROPER PERFORMANCE

Over the past two years, I have attended numerous *len dong* rituals performed by different mediums. Some I found gripping and stimulating to the extent that I felt completely absorbed; others I thought of as rather uninspiring and even disharmonious. However, at one point I started to notice that my personal notion of a "beautiful" or an "awkward" performance did not necessarily correspond to that of other participants. In May 2002, I went on a pilgrimage with Master Canh's group to Dong Bang temple in Thai Binh province, and because of the festival season, the temple was crowded with groups of mediums and their followers performing in front of the different altars. A discussion broke out when some group members watched a young woman performing in a way I thought was particularly entrancing. Responding quite differently, the group members thought of the performance as crazy and foolish. Later I learned that mediums distinguish between "well-behaved and skillful" performances (*dong khon bong ngoan*) on the one hand and "crazy and

---

[31] Karen Fjelstad, "Tu Phu Cong Dong: Vietnamese Women and Spirit Possession in the San Francisco Bay Area" (PhD dissertation, University of Hawai'i, 1995), p. 101.

[32] See, by way of comparison, Norton, "Music and Possession," p. 78.

foolish" performances (*dong dien dong dai*) on the other. According to Master Canh, only a "controlled medium is possessed by the spirits" (*dong tinh la dong thanh*), whereas an "uncontrolled" or "obsessed" medium is "possessed by ghosts" (*dong me la dong vong*).[33] Several questions arise from this discussion: When is a *len dong* ritual credited with authenticity? What are "the rules" of proper performance? To what extent is a *len dong* prescribed according to a fixed set of rules and to what extent are its performative aspects essential for the ritual act to be considered as efficacious?

During their embodiment of the spirits, most mediums are composed and aware of their surroundings (that is, they are not in a state of trance), yet they may also be aware of each spirit's presence in their bodies. Male spirits can cause a feeling of heaviness in the head and/or shoulders, of "hotness in the guts" (*nong ruot*), whereas many of the female spirits cause feelings of lightness.[34] The medium's state of awareness may also vary. For Hang, the only sequence that makes her "forget everything" and fall into a state of trance is the sequence of the Third Princess (*Co Bo*) for whom she is most intensely destined:

> [I]n general I am completely aware during a performance;[35] I know what is going on around me. It is like ... when the spirits descend I only provide a kind of loudspeaker for them, they don't descend completely; if they descended completely, then I would be obsessed [*dong me*]. This only happens when the Third Princess enters me [*op vao*], but like only for five minutes ... that's all; after the princess has passed by I am quickly aware again.

Hang very carefully stresses the point that her mind is aware during the *len dong*, although she admits that there are moments when she feels she is acting outside of her ordinary self. As an example, she mentions that as a nonsmoker she would actually cough her lungs out if she would draw smoke from a cigarette, but when she smokes during her embodiment of the male spirits, it does not cause a problem.[36] Being fully conscious, alert, and in control is also an important prerequisite for correctly assuming the role of a spirit. Facial expressions and bodily movements follow basic rules depending on the category of spirits as well as on the spirit's history and distinguishing characteristics, and the medium has to focus on their proper enactment. According to Cuong,

> Serving in accordance with the spirits' regulations [*hau dung phep thanh*] means that one has to pay attention to each spirit incarnation [*gia*]. As an example, during the embodiment of the mandarin spirits, the medium is not allowed to laugh or to leap around ... Also, if the medium smiles and dances merrily when serving the Third Princess, this is not correct. Why? Because when I enter into

---

[33] See ibid., p. 55, for a discussion of the terms "possession" and "obsession."

[34] Ibid., p. 50.

[35] I should note at this point that the mediums' translated narratives are slightly edited and that mediumship practitioners rather speak of "serving" (*hau*) than of performing or performance.

[36] All male spirits are heavy smokers, and the rules of proper performance require mediums to light quite a few cigarettes during a *len dong*.

the spirits' service, I have to learn about their history. Understanding the legends is an important precondition for a beautiful performance according to the rules.

Within the boundaries of "the spirits' regulations," the medium may also develop his or her individual style. As a new medium, Cuong is eager to perfect his technique by learning from the more experienced:

I also watch many performances of other mediums in order to find out what is interesting and beautiful in their performance. I perform according to my own style, but I also apply some particularly interesting techniques from other mediums to enhance my performance.

But a performance that is technically skillful is not necessarily considered to be beautiful. The importance of a "true heart" (*that tam*) in entering into a relationship with the spirits has already been mentioned briefly above. According to Hang, it is in fact the true heart that constitutes the beauty of ritually enacting this relationship:

When I serve [the spirits], my movements follow the spirits' guidance; I cannot just do what I want ... But if I am close with the spirit, the spirit will let me dance beautifully. And if someone is not "dedicated" [*nhat tam*, literally, "of one heart"], then the performance cannot be beautiful.

Cuong relates his corresponding conception by using the words "soul" (*hon*) or "heart-soul" (*tam hon*) and adds that the bodily movements need the ritual setting to become truly meaningful:

A beautiful performance is when all the participants enjoy it because the medium performs very soulfully. When I put my whole soul into performing, then it looks gentle, composed, and beautiful. The movements of the legs and arms are flowing, and the face looks much different.

Master Canh further elaborates on this issue by referring to an interesting phenomenon that has recently become apparent in the thriving marketplace of Hanoi—not a small number of mediumship practitioners are said to be "show-off mediums" (*dong dua*), who may not even have a medium's fate but mainly want to compete with other mediums in showing off their riches:

Some people perform beautifully, in a fresh and pleasant way; their faces completely differ from their everyday appearance. But a performance can also be very dull; you watch a while and you feel depressed; the person performing may even suddenly look like a ghost, boring and ugly. It is difficult [to explain], but all of these issues revolve around the person's heart. It is not a matter of putting on a luxurious performance with lots of offerings for distribution; some people may be very poor and have a very difficult life, but their performances are nevertheless beautiful; this is because they are very true-hearted and "genuine mediums" [*that dong*].

A "heavy fate" for mediumship alone does not account for ritual mastery. Correct movements and facial expressions are constitutive of proper performance, and a medium would be criticized for not following the "regulations of the spirits" if he or she assumed the wrong facial expression or bodily posture. The risk of performative failure, however, is diminished by the ritual setting: the *chau van* songs (literally, "serving literature") "invite the spirits" and "create a sense of ritual time,"[37] and the "ritual assistants" (*hau dang*) who change the medium into the spirits' ritual robes and hand him or her the ritual accessories are generally experienced mediums themselves and know how to guide a new medium toward performing the right movements at the right time. Mediums also learn from other mediums by either attending their *len dong* rituals or by watching taped performances of famous masters—and I dare to assume that some even practice in front of the mirror at home. But what essentially distinguishes a *len dong* ritual from a theatrical performance is the "ritual commitment"[38] of the actors. The right flow of movements can only be achieved when the medium adopts this ritual stance and wholeheartedly submits him- or herself to the spirits' guidance. Cuong explains: "Maybe in everyday life I can practice all of these movements, but they will never be like that; only when I 'step into serving' do I suddenly feel an inspiration entering me, and then I just move like that."

The ritual commitment of the medium ideally leads to a state of "flow," a term that Victor Turner owes to John MacAloon and Mihaly Czikszentmihalyi and that Turner explains as "the merging of action and awareness, the holistic sensation present when we act with total involvement"; flow induces "a loss of ego, the 'self' that normally acts as broker between ego and alter becomes irrelevant."[39] In other words, if flow is achieved when the spirits "mount the medium" (which is the literal meaning of *len dong*), then the performance is deemed to be authentic and beautiful. Even more significantly, it is a perceptible indication of the spirits' presence that not only transcends the devotees' experience of their ordinary selves but also contributes to the reflection on and transformation of their social realities by creating a different sense of being-in-the-world.

CONCLUDING REMARKS

Whenever I return from a *len dong* performance, I carry home with me a large plastic bag filled with cans of beer and soft drinks, packets of instant noodle soup, a box of green tea, cookies, various kinds of fruit, and crisp bills of small denominations. In the course of the ritual, the medium presents the spirits with these offerings in sufficient quantity according to the number of ritual participants. Transformed into blessed gifts (*loc*), they are redistributed as a token of the spirits' benevolence that extends to the invitees. The amount and quality of the offerings allows—at least to some extent—conclusions to be drawn about the medium's economic status, and a medium's conspicuous display of prosperity contributes to his or her status and social prestige within the group network of followers, fellow mediums, and invitees. As a result, rivalry among mediumship practitioners is quite common. A Vietnamese proverb states, "the jealousy of husband and wife cannot

---

[37] Norton, "'The Moon Remembers Uncle Ho,'" p. 81.

[38] Caroline Humphrey and James Laidlaw, *The Archetypal Actions of Ritual* (Oxford: Oxford University Press, 1994), p. 88.

[39] Turner, *The Anthropology of Performance*, p. 54.

compare with the jealousy of mediums" (*ghen vo ghen chong khong bang ghen dong ghen bong*). Master Canh explains further:

> They are jealous when they think another medium's performance is more beautiful and skillful, when another medium's robes are more beautiful, when the other medium is richer, when they think their master appreciates another disciple more; this is because mediums are a very resentful lot.

With its increasing emphasis on splendor, performance skills, and conspicuous consumption, *len dong* mediumship practice is certainly the most attractive religious arena in modern Vietnam for ritually acting out personal vanities and striving for social status. For the majority of devotees, however, the therapeutic dimension of *len dong* ritual practice forms the most crucial aspect of entering into the spirits' service.[40] As I have illustrated above, destined mediums feel empowered to manage their existential realities with greater ease by—paradoxical as it may seem—submitting themselves to the spirits' seizure. Entering into mediumship seems to provide a symbolic framework that enables spirit mediums to manage successfully their individual personalities as well as their personal lives. Ms. Huong assigns her hot-temperedness and eccentricity to her spirit roots (*can*) and finds mental relief by appeasing the spirits who she believes determine her fate. Hang feels more confident in pursuing her trading activities and her ambitions to carve out a better life for her family and interprets her business failures as a punishment for not obeying the spirits' demands. Cuong can express his feminine characteristics not only during his *len dong* performances but also among his fellow mediums, who share a different understanding of his personality than members of mainstream Vietnamese society. And whereas Cuong eloquently elaborates on the spirits' workings in sorting out the yin and the yang, Hang even makes a vague attempt at rationalizing her experiences by assuming there is a "psychological" effect of mediumship practice. Regular ritual performance reconciles mediumship practitioners with their "heavy fates"—manifesting themselves in bodily or mental afflictions, imbalanced temperaments, misfortune, economic hardship, or lack of self-confidence—and reshapes mediumship practitioners' human reality to become more tolerable. *Len dong* ritual practice thus constitutes a creative strategy for addressing a variety of personal concerns ranging from bodily illness and emotional distress to existential fear and the quest for the meaning of life. From the multifaceted accounts of mediumship practitioners, I conclude that submission to the spirits' seizure and the consequent socialization into the spirits' service effectively resituates mediumship practitioners who find themselves in an increasingly confusing modern world of changing values, conflicting ideas, and economic struggle.

---

[40] See also Nguyen Thi Hien, "The Religion of the Four Palaces," p. 75.

"WE HAVE *LEN DONG* TOO": TRANSNATIONAL ASPECTS OF SPIRIT POSSESSION

Karen Fjelstad[1]

In 1975, at the end of the American war, many Vietnamese left their native country to seek asylum in other parts of the world. Along with their luggage, they brought with them a rich cultural tradition, a long and complex history, and a syncretic blend of religious practices, including the *len dong* ritual. Today *len dong* crosses several international borders, and Vietnamese peoples practice it in the United States, Vietnam, Italy, France, and Australia. Spirit mediums had been holding possession ceremonies in Silicon Valley, south of San Francisco, since the diaspora, but due to government restrictions and a lack of normalized relations with the United States, such rituals in this California region were relatively isolated from Vietnam. Many California mediums had family members or friends who were active spirit mediums in Vietnam but, prior to Renovation (*doi moi*), they were unable to visit those relatives. Moreover, because these mediums could not purchase ritual goods in Vietnam, they had to build temples and hold ceremonies with locally available material goods. Although some spirit mediums had brought ritual goods with them when they left Vietnam, many did not. After *doi moi* was instituted, overseas Vietnamese were allowed to visit Vietnam for short periods of time and today, following normalization of US-Vietnam relations, they are able to establish businesses and purchase homes in Vietnam. Today these mediums travel to Vietnam, where they carry out initiation ceremonies, sponsor possession ceremonies, and purchase the materials necessary for their rituals on a regular basis.

Doi moi has had a profound impact on Silicon Valley mediums. Renovation has led to the formation and maintenance of relationships between mediums in Vietnam and the United States, revitalized the *len dong* ritual, and prompted heated discussions about the role of consumption in religious practice. On the one hand, we see a proliferation of the use of ritual goods and the growing commodification of ritual resources, but on the other, we see a strong reaction to increased materialism.

[1] I would like to thank all of the mediums who have taken me into their homes and temples, generously sharing their ideas, their stories, and their lives. I also thank Nguyen Thi Hien, Laurel Kendall, and Jill Forshee for their comments on either the content or the writing.

One consequence is that "we [ethnographers] are constantly faced with the everyday discrepancies between what people say matters to them and what they actually give their attention to."[2] Although California mediums vehemently deny being materialistic, they are quick to say that the increased materialism of others is a growing problem. Such reactions manifest themselves in competition between temples, accusations of sorcery (*lam bua*), and discussions of competitive mediumship (*dong dua*). Concern with the relationship between spirituality and materialism in Silicon Valley has parallels in Vietnam,[3] and the resultant competition between temples and mediums is threatening to spirit mediums in Silicon Valley. However, as we shall see, Silicon Valley mediums have developed mechanisms for maintaining solidarity.

This essay will explore the impact of *doi moi* on *len dong* spirit possession in Silicon Valley. It will present a local history of *len dong*, observe its role in the lives of California mediums, and discuss the effects of Renovation and the normalization of United States–Vietnam trade relations on spirit possession in Silicon Valley. I will address the following questions: How has the transnational movement of people, goods, and ideas influenced *len dong* in Silicon Valley? Why do Silicon Valley mediums sponsor possession ceremonies in California and in Vietnam? What kinds of relationships develop between overseas Vietnamese and Vietnamese spirit mediums? Finally, how have imported goods influenced possession ceremonies, the construction of temples, and relationships between spirit mediums?

I obtained data for this essay through participant observation of ceremonies and ethnographic interviews with Silicon Valley spirit mediums over a period of sixteen years.[4] The various ceremonies included possession ceremonies held by male or female mediums, initiation ceremonies, and temple-opening ceremonies. Observing ceremonies at six different Silicon Valley temples, I conducted interviews with spirit mediums of various backgrounds—male and female, young and old, Vietnamese and overseas Vietnamese mediums. In addition to collecting data in Silicon Valley, I carried out similar research and methods with spirit mediums in Hanoi and with overseas Vietnamese returning to Vietnam.

A HISTORY OF *LEN DONG* IN SILICON VALLEY

In 1980, Ba Thuong constructed Silicon Valley's first *Tu Phu* (Four Palaces) temple. Ba Thuong had not planned on becoming a temple medium and had not brought ritual goods with her to the United States. As she explained,

> We did not think that anyone would make a temple in the US ... We thought that no one would "serve the spirits" [*hau*], that no one would follow this religion

[2] Daniel Miller, "Why Some Things Matter," in *Material Cultures: Why Some Things Matter*, ed. D. Miller (Chicago, IL: University of Chicago Press, 1998), pp. 12-13.

[3] See Shaun Malarney, *Culture, Ritual, and Revolution in Vietnam* (New York, NY: RoutledgeCurzon, 2002), pp. 216-18.

[4] Karen Fjelstad, "Tu Phu Cong Dong: Vietnamese Women and Spirit Possession in the San Francisco Bay Area" (PhD dissertation, University of Hawai'i, 1995); Holy Mothers and Generals of the Interior" (unpublished manuscript, 2001); and K. Fjelstad and An Thuy Nguyen, "From Silicon Valley to Hanoi: Transnational Aspects of Spirit Possession in Post-Renovation Vietnam" (paper presented to the American Anthropological Association, Chicago, 2003).

here at all. But when we came here the old people wanted it and persuaded anyone who could [build a temple] to do it.

Unable to purchase ready-made ritual items, Ba Thuong constructed the temple with objects she could find or make. She searched for candles, incense, and fabric in San Francisco's Chinatown, and she purchased factory-made dolls to represent the spirits, carefully sewing each spirit's own clothes.

Within a few years of the first temple opening, two more temples were constructed. With its sizeable population of Vietnamese immigrants, Silicon Valley was able to support three different temples. At that time, the population (approximately 100,000) included first- and second-wave immigrants, as well as those who migrated from other states seeking better weather, family reunification, and employment opportunities. First-wave immigrants were those government officials, military leaders, and employees of the United States government who left Vietnam just before the end of the war in 1975. Second-wave immigrants, comprising the vast majority of Vietnamese in America, left the country after 1975. Population profiles of first- and second-wave immigrants illustrate differences in levels of education, religion, occupation, and socioeconomic status. First-wave immigrants tended to be Catholic and highly educated and held white-collar positions in Vietnam, whereas second-wave immigrants were less educated, Buddhist, and were of a lower socioeconomic status in Vietnam.[5] Members of the former group often learned to speak English while living in Vietnam, and because they were among the first to arrive in the United States, they formed the first mutual assistance associations and refugee resettlement centers, eventually becoming leaders and spokespersons in the community. Second-wave immigrants had lower paying jobs, less education, and did not speak English as well. Although a few spirit mediums of the *Tu Phu* religion came to California in 1975, the majority were second-wave immigrants with poor English-language skills.

When Ba Thuong opened the first Silicon Valley temple, she was providing an invaluable service to spirit mediums. Many mediums were sixty-five years old or older and had served the spirits for thirty years or more. They came to the United States from northern, central, and southern Vietnam, where they had sponsored possession ceremonies once or twice each year. However, they would not have been able to continue performing the ritual in the United States without a temple. This was a matter of serious concern, especially for mediums who felt they had to serve in order to maintain health and well-being. For example, Phan, a seventy-seven-year-old medium who emigrated from Vietnam to the United States in 1980, had sponsored yearly possession ceremonies in her home country ever since becoming a medium at the age of thirty. The Young Prince (*Cau Be*) had possessed Phan after she lost an infant in childbirth, causing flu-like symptoms and a loss of interest in life. She tried several different types of treatment, but nothing worked until she turned to *Tu Phu*. Learning that she had the spirit root[6] of the Young Prince, Phan made an agreement with him—she would honor the spirit with yearly ceremonies, and in return, he would stop making her ill. However, when she arrived in Silicon Valley

---

[5] Liem T. Nguyen and Alan B. Henkin, "Vietnamese Refugees in the US," *Journal of Ethnic Studies* 9,4 (1979): 101-116.

[6] Individuals who become spirit mediums are said to have *can*, which means to have the "calling" or the "spirit root."

there were no temples, so she was unable to keep her part of the agreement. She had to find a place to have a possession ceremony; she believed that if she could not, she would die. As it turned out, Phan was one of the first mediums to sponsor possession ceremonies in Silicon Valley.

Some California mediums learned they carried the spirit root during the journey from Vietnam to America. Minh tried to escape Vietnam seven times before finally succeeding. Each time she made the attempt, pirates attacked the boat and harassed and raped many of the women. During her final trip, Minh had a vision of the Third Princess (*Co Bo*). Associated with the Palace of Water, *Co Bo* dances with oars. The Princess told Minh, "When you go, you will meet misfortunes, but I will try to row the boat so that you will reach your destination. Once you get there you must honor and thank me." After Minh arrived in the United States, she attended possession ceremonies to honor *Co Bo* and the other spirits of *Tu Phu*.[7]

Although a medium's health and well-being are reportedly enhanced by a relationship with a spirit, many people resist becoming spirit mediums. In addition to sponsoring yearly rituals, mediums must build altars in their homes, present spirits with daily offerings, and purchase food and spirit gifts for possession ceremonies. For some Silicon Valley mediums, economic hardship and the immediate requirements of survival in a new social and cultural environment were factors delaying initiation. For example, although Minh learned that she possessed the spirit root during the journey from Vietnam, she postponed serving as a medium for more than ten years.

Some people delayed initiation because they were sensitive to the social stigma that sometimes accompanies mediumship. Outsiders to the religion often portray spirit mediums as selfish, deceitful, and materialistic. One of the common criticisms of these mediums is that they are charlatans who are out to accumulate as much wealth as they can. This view of *len dong* is not new; accusations of deceit and charlatanism contributed to Vietnamese government bans on spirit possession. One young man in Hanoi explained to me that all male spirit mediums are thieves. "They don't really believe," he said, "they just go into the temple so they can take all the money when no one is looking ... They all pretend so they can get close to people and steal their money." Because many Silicon Valley mediums experienced this kind of prejudice in Vietnam, they were careful about revealing their religious practices to outsiders. This helps to explain why, until recently, temples only existed in private homes, and there were never any obvious indications—such as signs posted over doors—to show that particular houses were places of worship.

Some Vietnamese in California hold negative views of *len dong*. During my field research in the late 1980s, people often told me that they considered the religion primitive and unscientific, a faith that only attracted those who knew no better. An incautious mention of the subject got me thrown out of the office of a community leader whom I had contacted as a possible resource person. I had told him that I wanted to study traditional Vietnamese health-care practices, and his initial reaction was quite enthusiastic. In fact, he offered me office space, a telephone, and help from his office assistant. I could not believe my luck! A week later, when I returned to begin my research, we sat down to discuss in more detail what I would be doing.

---

[7] See Philip Taylor, *Goddess on the Rise: Pilgrimage and Popular Ritual in Vietnam* (Honolulu, HI: University of Hawai'i Press, 2004), p. 107, for a discussion of other goddesses who "feature as hidden players in the exodus."

Today many temples include visible signs or flags. This Silicon Valley temple displays the flag
of the former government of South Vietnam.

When I spoke the words *"len dong,"* he jumped to his feet behind his desk, his face
turned bright red, and he announced that I could not study such a primitive,
superstitious religion because I would make Vietnamese look bad. My two decades
of ethnographic fieldwork have revealed a quite different picture of *len dong*.[8] Ever
since the first temple opening, *len dong* rituals and the community of spirit mediums
have provided essential services to Silicon Valley Vietnamese. These include health-
and mental-health-care resources, a foundation for social support, the formation of
mutual-assistance associations, and a vehicle for developing and maintaining ethnic
identity.

First and foremost, *len dong* is a health-care resource.[9] Many people attend
possession ceremonies and become mediums in response to illness and misfortune.
In 1995, I studied Silicon Valley possession ceremonies in an attempt to discern
potentially therapeutic practices. I realized that any understanding of *len dong* would
have to consider the social nature of possession ceremonies. A great deal of visiting
goes on at ceremonies. Friends and family members chat with each other, spirits visit
with mortals, and in some cases (for example, when several mediums are possessed

[8] See K. Fjelstad, "Tu Phu Cong Dong: Vietnamese Women and Spirit Possession in the San
Francisco Bay Area," for a discussion of the positive functions of *len dong* for members of the
Silicon Valley Vietnamese community.

[9] See Nguyen Thi Hien, "The Religion of the Four Palaces: Mediumship and Therapy in Viet
Culture" (PhD dissertation, Indiana University, 2002).

at once), spirits visit with each other. Although almost any topic of conversation is open, mediums and participants often discuss their personal lives and concerns with each other and with the spirits. This allows opportunity for the expression of distress in a socially supportive context. Possession ceremonies also strengthen people's confidence, as they learn that their problems will be solved to some degree and are consequently able to imagine a brighter and happier future.

California temples also function as social support groups. A spirit medium usually maintains a particular temple affiliation.[10] Spirit mediums, initiates, and participants meet each other on the weekends, and many talk on the telephone during the week. Their shared interests and experiences form the basis for close friendships and the development of well-defined groups which function as mutual-assistance associations. Participation in these groups often leads to far-reaching consequences for recent immigrants. Members help each other with financial support, translation services, transportation, and childcare. These services were especially important to Silicon Valley spirit mediums in the 1980s because many of these people fell into high-risk categories (for example, seniors, women), rendering them less likely to receive social services from other kinds of groups. Problems of adjustment are normally exacerbated among women and the elderly because they experience more social isolation and less opportunity to develop English-language skills.[11] *Len dong* helped to counteract this problem.

Vietnamese ethnic and cultural identity are important themes of spirit possession ceremonies. The first time I attended a possession ceremony, I felt as if I was in a world unrelated to Silicon Valley, the area where I grew up. I wondered if people there felt comforted because going to the temple was, in some ways, like going to Vietnam. Everything is decorated in primary colors; the air is thick with the scents of incense, fresh flowers, and fish sauce (*nuoc mam*), and several different conversations take place at once, mostly in Vietnamese. The pantheon of *Tu Phu* includes the goddesses as well as Vietnamese culture heroes and heroines who have successfully fought foreigners. Temples in Silicon Valley reflect the significant Vietnamese experience of interacting with foreigners. These reminders of ethnic identity provide added meaning to immigrant communities. The earliest arrivals to Silicon Valley found emotional solace in possession ceremonies that evoked memories of Vietnam and a home they had recently left. For later arrivals, spirit possession ceremonies are important symbols of a culture and tradition they value and want to keep alive.

When initially allowed an opportunity to return to Vietnam, many Vietnamese-Americans refused because they were certain they would be arrested. In 1988, I traveled to Ho Chi Minh City with a group of refugees who were visiting the country of their birth for the first time since the end of the war. The trip proved to be a painful and emotionally draining experience for the returning overseas Vietnamese, as it took place following many years of separation from their families. When the plane entered Vietnamese air space, the entire group fell silent with anticipation. Everyone crowded the windows to get a view of the tributaries of the Mekong River winding through a countryside of rice paddies punctuated with bomb craters. Just before we landed, people began scooping the remains of Air France lunches into

---

[10] See Viveca Larsson and Kirsten W. Endres, "'Children of the Spirits, Followers of a Master': Spirit Mediums in Post-Renovation Vietnam," in this volume.

[11] See Equity Policy Center, *Indochinese Refugees: Special Needs of Women* (Washington, DC: Office of Refugee Resettlement, 1981).

plastic beverage containers—chicken, coconut cake, bits of cheese, chocolates, all mashed together. This food would be given to beggar children at the airport.

The overseas Vietnamese felt helpless and disoriented after arriving. Mistrustful of the government and guilt ridden at seeing their families living in poverty, some said they felt out of place in their native country. Symptoms of emotional distress among the group became common. Cannon fire in celebration of the New Year sent several women diving for cover under the mattress in our hotel because the last time they heard this sound in Vietnam no one had been shooting blanks. Many people thought the police were following them, and some believed their actions were being monitored. This fear was heightened among spirit mediums because they practiced a now outlawed ritual.

I traveled to Vietnam with Ba Sau, a spirit medium living in California, who had left Vietnam as a boat person and was returning home for the first time in almost ten years. As our plane descended into Ho Chi Minh City, she leaned over and whispered into my ear, "Don't mention anything about *len dong*, we will be arrested if you say anything at all. Don't say a word." Even though she had been a spirit medium for more than thirty-five years, Ba Sau did not consider attending *len dong* possession ceremonies in Vietnam because they were illegal. When she returned to Vietnam in 1988, *doi moi* had already been in effect for two years, but as a spirit medium, a southerner, and a refugee, Ba Sau was extremely fearful. Along with many of the other overseas Vietnamese traveling with her, she feared that the police were following her, that her hotel room was bugged, and that she might not be allowed to return to the United States. She was not about to risk going to a possession ceremony.

Although overseas Vietnamese were initially cautious about returning to their home country, things gradually began to change. Fears lessened as more and more people traveled to Vietnam and returned home safely to tell others about their experiences. Several political and economic changes also contributed to the greater comfort and ease of these expatriates who wished to visit their homeland. These changes included the continuation and expansion of *doi moi*, the establishment of US–Vietnam diplomatic relations, reduction of the US trade embargo, and, especially important to mediums, fewer political restrictions of ritual practices within Vietnam. Today some Silicon Valley mediums still fear returning to Vietnam, but others visit on a regular basis.

THE TRANSNATIONAL MOVEMENT OF SPIRIT MEDIUMS AND RITUAL GOODS[12]

A transnational community of spirit mediums is forming as California mediums travel to and from Vietnam, though some of these travelers are more motivated by a desire to visit family than to practice their religion, and many even fear holding ceremonies in Vietnam. For example, Ba Thuong, a temple medium in her seventies, has returned to Vietnam twice since she left the country in 1975. In both cases she returned to visit family, but during the last trip she decided to sponsor a possession ceremony in Hanoi.[13] A practical woman, Ba Thuong emphasized the convenience of

---

[12] Portions of this section were written with An Thuy Nguyen. See Fjelstad and Nguyen, "Transnational Aspects of Spirit Possession in Post-Renovation Vietnam."

[13] Sponsored rituals are possession ceremonies held by an individual medium who has arranged to use the temple, hired ritual personnel, and purchased food and spirit gifts. These

her ceremony—she was there and it was feasible, so she held a *len dong*. "Besides," she said, "it's fun [*vui ve*]!" Not all mediums traveling to Vietnam carry out possession ceremonies. Ba Sau flies to Vietnam almost every year to visit family members. Although she is no longer quite so afraid of holding a possession ceremony there, she is not interested in doing so. Some mediums are still uncomfortable sponsoring such ceremonies in Vietnam. Although *len dong* were illegal at the time of this research, mediums were not necessarily arrested—it depended on the proclivities of the police and local officials. However, many California mediums believed they would be arrested or detained if caught sponsoring a ceremony. One medium even told me "the penalty for having a *len dong* is death."

Many Silicon Valley mediums return to Vietnam for the specific purpose of sponsoring an initiation or a possession ceremony. They are motivated by several reasons, among the most common: 1) Vietnam offers more ritual resources than the United States, 2) it is a way of honoring Vietnamese culture and history, and 3) people in Vietnam are more deeply devoted (*thanh tam*).[14] Several mediums mentioned the lack of ritual specialists and material resources in the United States. People often purchase votive offerings, drums or gongs, and spirit clothing in Vietnam—ritual objects and supplies unavailable or of lesser quality elsewhere. Other mediums lament the lack of ritual specialists or temples in California dedicated to specific spirits. For example, Jenny, a California medium, would have to sponsor an initiation ceremony in Vietnam because Silicon Valley has no temple dedicated to the group of forest spirits who gave her the power to divine and heal (*Chua Boi*). Hoa attended possession ceremonies in California for twenty-three years, but refuses to sponsor a possession ceremony there because of the lack of live music. Music is an essential component of *len dong* rituals; a specific song greets each spirit, and the pattern of possession corresponds to the pace of the music.[15] Until recently, taped songs accompanied spirit possession in Silicon Valley because there were no local musicians. Today Hoa sponsors her possession ceremonies in Vietnam because, as she says, "the music makes the ceremony livelier."[16]

Many spirit mediums say that holding a possession ceremony in Vietnam inspires a sense of history and cultural continuity. As Ong Thang, a temple medium from Ho Chi Minh City, explains, "People want to have ceremonies at the place of their ancestors and their homeland. For example, in Christianity, people still want to make pilgrimages to Rome." Others, particularly the younger generation, view having ceremonies in Vietnam as one way to maintain Vietnamese tradition. As one medium says, "We want to show that people in America have *len dong* too, not just people in Vietnam." Sponsoring a possession ceremony in Vietnam can also be a way of learning more about religion and ritual. Jenny was eager to hold a ceremony in Vietnam at least partly because "there are a lot of older ladies there and they carry a

---

ceremonies contrast with other ceremonies, such as New Year rites, which are conducted by the temple as a group.

[14] Although none of the mediums said the spirits made the decision to go to Vietnam, some mediums felt they had to travel to Vietnam to meet a particular spirit's demands.

[15] See Barley Norton, "Music and Possession in Vietnam" (PhD dissertation, SOAS, University of London, 2002); see also Norton's essay, "'Hot-Tempered' Women and 'Effeminate' Men: The Performance of Music and Gender in Vietnamese Mediumship," in this volume.

[16] At the time of this writing, live possession music was just being introduced to Silicon Valley.

lot of the old, old traditions and the way they call the gods and pray, you can learn a lot from them."

Some California mediums prefer carrying out ceremonies in Vietnam because, they say, people in Vietnam are more *thanh tam* (devoted). When someone is deeply devoted, she surrenders her heart to the spirits and is willing to spend her life serving them. One expresses such devotion through a willingness to spend either time or money at possession ceremonies. A common complaint made by mediums is that people in California come and go as they please and few stay for the duration of a ceremony. By contrast, when Vietnamese are invited to attend a ceremony, "they accept the invitation to come and they sit without moving from the beginning to the very end." Although spirit mediums (and the spirits) maintain an informal sliding scale for monetary donations, some in Silicon Valley say that people in Vietnam are more generous with their money because spirituality plays a greater role in their lives. As one explained, "In America you don't have time for religion. You've got your school, your job, your friends, you just don't have time for religion."

Although Silicon Valley mediums sponsor possession ceremonies in Vietnam, mediums living in Vietnam are less likely to stage ceremonies in California. The cost of an air ticket prohibits most Vietnamese mediums from traveling to the United States, but even those who can afford the plane fare do not sponsor ceremonies in Silicon Valley. One exception is Ong Thang, a medium with his own temples in southern Vietnam. Ong Thang frequently travels to the United States, where he is associated with a Silicon Valley temple that he helped to build. Ong Thang has sponsored possession ceremonies in California, but he says that few Vietnamese mediums would want to do the same, mostly because it is too expensive.

Doi moi and the normalization of trade relations between the United States and Vietnam also opened avenues for the transnational exchange of ritual goods. Silicon Valley mediums import a number of ritual items from Vietnam. These include statues representing the spirits, votive offerings, and plaques inscribed with Han characters that are placed over altars and at the entrances to temples. In addition to these are instruments like drums, gongs, and bells and many types of clothing and accessories, such as fans and hair clips. In a typical ceremony, a medium might *hau* for many spirits. Each time a new spirit possesses her, she must change into a different outfit, so mediums must have many clothes. The music performed during ceremonies in Vietnam is also brought to the United States in the form of cassette tapes. Although there are now musicians specializing in possession music (*cung van*) living in Silicon Valley, those mediums who cannot afford the expense of live musicians use the prerecorded tapes. Of course not all the materials necessary for the California ceremonies are purchased in Vietnam. Offerings like fruits and flowers given to guests during ceremonies typically come from local markets.

For Silicon Valley temples built before *doi moi,* importing items from Vietnam was not an option. Ba Thuong, the medium who established her temple in 1984, spent several months searching for statues in California that could accurately represent members of the pantheon. Unable to purchase them ready-made, Ba Thuong bought dolls and sewed their costumes by hand. After *doi moi,* she went back to Vietnam but returned only with a small bell and a gong. Ba Tuyet's temple provides a sharp contrast. Recently built, almost everything in the temple, including statues, bells, and clothing, was special ordered in Vietnam.

This altar was constructed with locally available goods.

In order to build her Silicon Valley temple, Ba Tuyet formed a partnership with Ong Thang, who traveled to the United States to help her find a propitious location for the temple and a suitable direction for the altar. He then returned to Vietnam to purchase most of the items for the temple. Today the two mediums buy spirit clothes in Vietnam and sell them to Silicon Valley mediums. As previously mentioned, mediums say they purchase religious goods in Vietnam because the items are less expensive, because they cannot find the exact things they want in the United States (especially high-quality objects), and because they are "more familiar" with goods made in Vietnam. For example, although there are drums sold in the United States, Ba Tuyet bought one from Vietnam because, she said, "I am not used to that [the sound of an American drum] so I use this. It is more true to my origin/roots. This drum is an example of Vietnamese history and culture." Other California mediums prefer to buy ritual objects in Vietnam because they are of higher quality. As Hoa explained:

> It's like your mother's birthday. You buy clothing and you want to choose things that are beautiful and high quality to give. In a religion it is the same. I want to offer clothing and votive horses for the spirits. I like to go to Vietnam because these kinds of things are more plentiful. Like if you go to Macy's you can find things but at K-mart you cannot.

REVITALIZATION, CONFLICT, AND COOPERATION

The transnational activities of spirit mediums and distribution of ritual goods have had a great impact on *len dong* spirit possession. First, the religion has been revitalized in Vietnam and the United States. Second, the increased use of ritual goods created a growing concern with materialism and increased discussions about the relationship between spiritualism and materiality. Third, Silicon Valley temples have become more competitive with each other as a result of these developments. At the same time, however, California mediums have developed mechanisms for reducing competition and fostering cooperation.

In 1987, when I first began to study *len dong*, there were three temples in Silicon Valley. A few temples have come and gone over the years, but the overall number of temples has remained fairly constant. Today there are three larger temples and one that is fairly small. What has changed is the number and composition of participants in the religion. Now there are many more mediums—last year alone there were seven initiation ceremonies—and there are more people considering mediumship. Also, during the past two decades, most Silicon Valley mediums were older women. Since the mid-1990s, revitalization has included younger women and men; one temple takes great pride in attracting younger mediums. While some of these initiates are the children and grandchildren of spirit mediums, many have recently been exposed to the religion for the first time.

Ethnographic studies in Vietnam[17] have documented an increase in *len dong* and other kinds of ritual practice. For example, in his description of popular ritual in the Thinh Liet commune, Malarney notes, "The quality and quantity of ritual items has increased; the ritual infrastructure, such as the altars and the buildings that house them has been improved; and the size and cost of feasts has grown significantly."[18] The increase in ritual practice relates to *doi moi* and changes in the political economy of Vietnam. However, the exact relationship between economic and religious behavior is complex. Whereas some individuals turn to religion because they have *less* economic security, others turn to religion because they have *more* economic security. Some ethnographers say *len dong* are increasingly popular among traders because such persons are especially vulnerable to the insecurities of the market.[19] However, as far back as 1997, Hanoi spirit mediums told me that *len dong* were becoming more frequent because people had more money. Ritual activities increase as money becomes more available because, as one woman explained: "Religion is important to Vietnamese people and if they have some extra money, they will spend it on things they think are important."

Increased economic security has stimulated the revitalization of *len dong* spirit possession in California. When Vietnamese refugees first arrived in the United

---

[17] See Hy Van Luong, "Economic Reform and the Intensification of Rituals in Two North Vietnamese Villages," in *The Challenge of Reform in Indochina*, ed. Borje Ljunggren (Boston, MA: Harvard University Press, 1993), pp. 259-291; S. Malarney, *Culture, Ritual, and Revolution in Vietnam*; Nguyen Thi Hien, "The Religion of the Four Palaces: Mediumship and Therapy in Viet Culture."

[18] Malarney, *Culture, Ritual, and Revolution in Vietnam*, p. 217.

[19] See Kirsten W. Endres, "Spirit Performance and the Ritual Construction of Personal Identity in Modern Vietnam," this volume; Le Hong Ly, "Tin nguong len dong tu cai nhin cua nguoi trong cuoc" [The Belief in Mediumship from the Perspective of the Practitioners] (unpublished paper presented at the International Workshop on Mother Goddess Worship and the Phu Giay Festival, Hanoi, 2001).

States, they focused on meeting basic survival needs. Spending much time and energy seeking economic support, dealing with health problems, and learning how to speak a new language, many overseas Vietnamese simply did not have the time or money that ceremonies require. This may help to explain the recent demographic changes among spirit mediums in Silicon Valley. In the past, the population of these mediums at temples was not representative of the equivalent population in Vietnam. Whereas mediums in Vietnam could be rich or poor, young or old, male or female, Silicon Valley mediums tended to be older women who had come to California to live with their adult children. One explanation for the advanced age of many California mediums is that younger people were so busy trying to subsist in their new environment, they had little time for anything else. Now with many of those basic needs met, the composition of mediums as a group is beginning to change.

Greater religious freedom in Vietnam also facilitates the revitalization of *len dong* spirit possession. Prior to *doi moi*, spirit mediums in Vietnam were sometimes arrested if caught holding possession ceremonies. Although this did not prevent mediums from persisting with their ceremonies, they held them at night, when they would be less noticeable. Today, however, spirit mediums in Vietnam say they are "freer" to sponsor possession ceremonies and are consequently less fearful, more open. Some Silicon Valley mediums were also reluctant to carry out possession ceremonies because they did not know how Americans would respond to them, and they did not want to make themselves too conspicuous. As one medium explained, "I used to think it was weird to have possession ceremonies here. This is America." But now that *len dong* are more common in both countries, mediums feel more comfortable and confident.

Spirit mediums in Vietnam and California lend legitimacy to the religion by emphasizing global interest in the *len dong* ritual. I met Ong Luong, a fourteenth-generation spirit medium, while conducting a temple survey in Hanoi. During our discussion he was quick to point out that Vietnamese practice *len dong* wherever they are. He said:

> Being Vietnamese is having *len dong*. No matter who is here, we still *len dong*. Even Vietnamese from France, America, and Italy *len dong*—they remember Vietnam.

This global interest extends to scholarly research. One of the more prominent features of a Silicon Valley temple is a photograph of a conference on *Dao Mau* held in Vietnam in 2001. The first international conference on the subject, it was organized by Ngo Duc Thinh (a contributor to this volume). When asked to explain the significance of the picture, the temple medium answered, "This shows that the religion is not superstitious ... people have gone to research about it. This convention shows that everyone in the world is researching about this religion." Photos of international conferences displayed on the walls of Silicon Valley temples contribute to revitalization by assuring younger mediums that their religious beliefs and practices are grounded in a solid and increasingly respected tradition.

The transnational exchange of ritual goods has led to increased discussions about the relationship between materialism and spirituality. The two prevailing views contradict each other. One perspective holds that *len dong* is becoming too materialistic and, as a result, is losing some of its spiritual validity. For example, one California medium expressed her opinion that since it has become easier to travel between Vietnam and the United States, "people get too caught up with … want[ing] to find a better way to sell my products or to present myself." The second perspective views lavish spending as a legitimate form of religious expression, as expressed in the phrase "wealth gives birth to ritual form" (*phu quy sinh ra le nghia*). As Malarney interprets this concept:

> The idea behind this adage is that individuals should organize their rituals according to their means. Thus, the poor man who only presents a hard-boiled egg and a bowl of rice to the spirit of his deceased parents is as virtuous as the rich man who organizes a funeral with a thousand guests. This principle itself recognizes that people can perform the same ritual differently, but derive the same moral benefit.[20]

The transnational movement of people and goods has generated an abundance of available religious items and a rise in the number of such items used in ceremonies, leading to an increased concern with materialism. One Silicon Valley medium compared the numerous outfits and accessories found in a typical ceremony today with the simpler accoutrements of earlier years: "Long ago when I became a medium [and] there were only two colors, red and blue outfits, with one fan." Others explained that since people who are able to move to California have relatively more money, *len dong* ceremonies tend to be more lavish in the States. Instead of being restricted to basic clothing, practitioners can afford to buy more elaborate wear, using finer cloth or prettier patterns.

This materialistic direction prompts some skeptics outside the religion to claim that ceremonies are only for "show-off mediums" (*dong dua*). "*Dong dua*" is a term to describe competition between mediums who seek to best one another in terms of clothing, money spent on a ceremony, or the number of gifts distributed to guests. Mediums hold mixed views of *dong dua*. Some deny its existence in Silicon Valley, while others say it exists, but that they do not participate in it. Some mediums believe that *dong dua* provides evidence that the religion is becoming more materialistic, but others feel that competitive ceremonies are a normal extension of spiritual concerns. Proponents of the first view said that "real" mediums do not *dong dua*, whereas proponents of the second view said that since people have more money now, they should spend it on the spirits. According to this point of view, the enhanced reputation of someone who is *dong dua* is thus due not to materialism, but to a high level of devotion. A medium who gives abundantly to the spirits, relative to what she has, will enjoy a better reputation among other mediums. This latter view of *dong dua* is consistent with the idea that "wealth gives birth to ritual form."

The increase in ritual goods has created new arenas of conflict between spirit mediums in Silicon Valley and Vietnam. Jenny wants to have an initiation ceremony in Vietnam, but has heard several negative things about Vietnamese temples. "Unfortunately," she said, "a lot of *len dong* nowadays is more like a business than a religion." She went on to explain that some Vietnamese temples try to solicit overseas Vietnamese mediums because they are richer and will pay more for a ceremony. "It's not about dedication, it's not about God, it's about money and opportunity." Whereas Jenny has only heard stories, Hoa was the unfortunate victim of a theft in Vietnam. Having lost her entire life savings to a deceptive Vietnamese

---

[20] Malarney, *Culture, Ritual, and Revolution in Vietnam*, p. 10.

spirit priest (*thay cung*), Hoa says she is too sad to have a possession ceremony anywhere—in Vietnam or in Silicon Valley.

Problems between Vietnamese and overseas Vietnamese commonly arise from differences in wealth. As more individuals sponsor possession ceremonies in Vietnam, one hears more stories about Vietnamese mediums taking advantage of their American counterparts. These problems are not unique to spirit mediums; they occur in all aspects of life and relate to cultural differences. Vietnamese often perceive Americans as wealthy and, in Vietnamese culture, there are many social situations in which it is acceptable to ask wealthier family members for money. However, many overseas Vietnamese have become accustomed to American norms, and they resent requests for money, donations, or assistance. These cultural conflicts were powerfully expressed in the film *Daughter from Danang.*[21] In the film, a young woman returns to Vietnam to find her mother and succeeds in discovering members of her family, but when they ask her for money, she becomes upset, feeling that her Vietnamese family is only out for material gain. Such tensions often cause great pain in relationships between Vietnamese and overseas Vietnamese.

As *len dong* grow in popularity, the increased use of ritual goods exacerbates differences between Silicon Valley temples. People evaluate temples on comparative wealth, size, the origins of the items displayed, and the number of participants involved in possession ceremonies. For example, one of the newest and wealthiest temples places a heavy emphasis on making sure that the display of the altar and the ceremonial procedure are exactly the same as they were in Vietnam. To do so, the temple medium took care to order all of the materials for her altar from Vietnam. Silicon Valley mediums are, however, divided in their views about the authenticity of ritual goods. Whereas some mediums said that items purchased in Vietnam carried more spiritual efficacy (*linh*), others said they did not. Built at a time when communication with Vietnam was very limited, many California temples contain mostly handmade altar goods or those purchased at Chinese markets. These older temples are less wealthy, and they include few, if any, ritual items from Vietnam. Temples are also distinguished by size. People regard larger temples as attractive because they can accommodate larger crowds, as well as more spirits, and the altar is bigger. Conversely, smaller temples may appeal to certain people because they can signify the presence of smaller, more tightly knit groups of mediums.

Differences between temples sometimes lead to competition and conflict that are expressed in sorcery accusations. People may claim that a temple is popular or wealthy or has a large number of initiates because someone in the temple is seeking help from spirits of the underworld. In Vietnam, tension between materialism and spirituality "is often expressed in the critical adage 'buying and selling spirits' [*buon than ban thanh*]."[22] Although it is considered normal to ask for some material benefits, there is a limit to the extent of favors an individual should request from the spirits. It is not uncommon to hear Silicon Valley mediums question each other's motives; if a medium asks the spirits for too many material goods, she may be accused of sorcery.

Although the increasingly global nature of the flow of people and material culture has led to increased competition between Silicon Valley temples and mediums, certain behaviors help to foster social harmony. Silicon Valley mediums

---

[21] Gail Dolgin and Vicente Franco, *Daughter from Danang* (Berkeley, CA: American Experience and the Independent Television Service, 2002).

[22] Malarney, *Culture, Ritual and Revolution in Vietnam*, p. 101.

downplay class differences by placing a greater value on effort over authenticity and by emphasizing the unique qualities of each temple. Although ritual goods from Vietnam carry a special status, temples containing more imported goods are not considered to be better or more authentic than other temples. Rather, the higher status of certain goods derives from the effort that one has invested in obtaining them. Virtually every spirit medium told us that it is not important where the goods come from, it is only important that the medium has put effort into getting them. Effort involves time spent shopping for the spirits, making spirit clothes or offerings, or traveling to Vietnam. As Ba Tuyet explained:

> If I want something I will get it, but I have to go searching for it. Even if it is expensive I have to buy it. For someone who is not devoted anything will do. God sees that I put in the effort to get these items.

Other mediums were equally committed to laboring for the spirits. Ba Thuong spent more than one year fashioning handmade clothes for the spirits on her altar, and the devotees of Jenny's temple are proud that some of their ceremonial items are handmade. With effort as the major criteria for the ranking of spiritual efficacy, the older, poorer temples share an equal standing with newer and wealthier temples.

Mediums also reduce conflicts and level differences in wealth by emphasizing that each temple is special and unique. While one temple is known for being the oldest in Silicon Valley, another is famous for having been constructed with materials from Vietnam, and a third is renowned for its use of handmade offerings. These local variations have the practical effect of attracting different populations. Spirit mediums who have resided in Silicon Valley the longest still continue to support the older temples, but those who are newly introduced to the religion or have recently immigrated from Vietnam often find the newer temples much more appealing. Both of the older temples serve a predominantly older generation. These contrast with smaller, relatively poorer temples patronized by a larger number of participants in the twenty- to thirty-year-old age bracket. Many of these younger mediums distinguish themselves from their elders by identifying as Vietnamese-Americans and by taking a different approach to the religion, making it "more Asian-American," for example, by including more male mediums.

CONCLUSIONS

Since the beginning of the post-war Vietnamese diaspora, the *len dong* ritual has crossed several international borders. Although it is predominantly a religion of Vietnam, as one Silicon Valley medium put it, *"len dong* is not just for Vietnamese, people in America have *len dong* too." This essay has discussed some of the history of *len dong* in Silicon Valley, focusing on the effects of *doi moi* on religious belief and practice. As we have seen, as transnational contact between mediums and the long-distance trade in ritual items have become more frequent, the number of temples and mediums has proliferated and revitalized the ritual. At the same time, an increase in the use of ritual goods has led to discussions about the relationship between materialism and spirituality. Differences in wealth and in ideas about wealth sometimes lead to competition and conflict, but they are tempered by complementary mechanisms that promote social harmony. One such mechanism is localization—Silicon Valley mediums emphasize the unique characteristics of each temple. This appreciation for the distinct, local qualities of each *len dong* temple is not a new feature; it has long defined *Dao Mau* and has contributed greatly to the persistence and spread of the religion.

GIFTS FROM THE SPIRITS: SPIRIT POSSESSION AND PERSONAL TRANSFORMATION AMONG SILICON VALLEY SPIRIT MEDIUMS

Karen Fjelstad and Lisa Maiffret

INTRODUCTION

Cross-cultural studies of spirit possession religions have found that illness is a route to initiation in many cultures. Although illness is a precipitating factor for some Silicon Valley mediums, others do not experience any pain, disease, or disorder. However, while people become mediums for a variety of different reasons, once they embark on the journey leading to mediumship, their lives and selves begin to change. Some mediums report that they recover their health, and many say that they come to view life differently. What they all share in common, regardless of how they describe their experiences, is a feeling that their lives improve as a result of mediumship. The process of becoming a medium can thus be viewed as therapeutic,[1] as mediums claim that they have become stronger, happier, and healthier people.

In her study of Puerto Rican spiritists, Joan Koss-Chioino describes healing as "a process of cognitive and emotional restructuring of self in both inner and outer worlds."[2] Using this concept of healing—one extending far beyond the cessation of pain or illness—this essay explores why people in Silicon Valley become mediums, how their views of self and others are shaped by mediumship, and what constructs the mechanisms of "healing" or personal transformation. Data for this essay were collected from California mediums, but many of their reasons for becoming a medium have also motivated individuals in Vietnam.[3] However, the particular stresses that lead to mediumship, and the ways in which people describe their

---

[1] See Nguyen Thi Hien, "The Religion of the Four Palaces: Mediumship and Therapy in Viet Culture" (PhD dissertation, Indiana University, 2002).

[2] Joan Koss-Chioino, *Women as Healers, Women as Patients: Mental Health Care And Traditional Healing in Puerto Rico* (Boulder, CO: Westview Press, 1992), p. 35.

[3] See, for example, Kirsten W. Endres, "Spirit Performance and the Ritual Construction of Personal Identity in Modern Vietnam," in this volume.

experiences of possession and transformation, vary from country to country. As we shall see, the personal histories of Silicon Valley mediums present some unique variations.

The focus of this chapter was determined, in part, by the spirit of the Young Prince (*Cau Be*). While conducting an interview on another subject, *Cau Be* spontaneously possessed a medium and told one of the authors, through the medium, that the current interview topic "sucked" and a more interesting subject would be the personal stories of mediums and how spirits enhance mediums' lives. We decided to follow the spirit's advice and began to collect data for this chapter. As it turned out, California mediums embraced this topic with fervor, and several mediums requested to be interviewed because they did not want to be "left out" of the research project.

Data for this chapter were collected through participant-observation and ethnographic interviews at several different temples, but many of these case studies involve mediums belonging to a single temple.[4] Temple affiliation is important for two reasons. First, mediums belonging to a particular temple know one another, and many have influenced each other's decision to enter mediumship. Second, the mediums from a single temple share common ritual practices and religious beliefs.[5] This particular temple (*den*)[6] is an offshoot of one of the earliest Silicon Valley temples, which was established in the 1980s. After the original master medium (*dong thay*) died in the 1990s, the *den* changed locations, and a new *dong thay* was selected. Then, during the course of this research, the temple split again. The second division occurred as the result of ritual differences. Mediums of this newer temple are especially enthusiastic, and their spiritual exuberance is expressed in the length of their *len dong*, which often last twelve hours or longer, and the frequency and intensity of possession outside the context of spirit possession ceremonies (*len dong*). Mediums of the temple are likely to be possessed by *Tu Phu* spirits while attending *len dong*, watching videos of possession ceremonies, or even driving down the road! Some mediums at the older temple were concerned about the spontaneous possession, fearing that it would someday veer out of control, and others could not bear the long ceremonies (this was especially true of seniors and those who were concerned about going to work the following day). These differences eventually led to an amicable division. The newest temple does not yet have a *dong thay*, but it is currently sponsoring spirit possession ceremonies.

THE CALL TO MEDIUMSHIP

People in California become mediums for a variety of reasons. Some people initially encountered *len dong* because they were part of a family of mediums, while others participated as a way to create or maintain friendships. While all mediums acknowledged their callings as destiny, and all felt they had been the subjects of a particularly heavy fate (*can nang*), sometimes there were precipitating events. Several

---

[4] The name of the temple has been withheld to protect the confidentiality of our consultants.

[5] See Viveca Larsson and Kirsten W. Endres, "'Children of the Spirits, Followers of a Master': Spirit Mediums in Post-Renovation Vietnam," in this volume, for a discussion of temple communities in Vietnam.

[6] California mediums use the word *"den"* for any public or private temple where *len dong* rituals are held.

individuals became mediums in response to life crises—such as the loss of a loved one, financial problems, or interpersonal conflicts. These crises caused grief, mental and physical illness, stress, and generalized anxiety. For others, the love of *Thanh* (God)[7] was the motivating factor.

Mediumship tends to recur inside families. Jenny and her mother, Co Hong, are charismatic spirit mediums who feel that mediumship runs in their family and is passed through the female line.

Aged thirty-three and sixty-four, Jenny and Co Hong came to the United States as boat people in 1983. Although Co Hong had known about *Cau Be* and made offerings to him while living in central Vietnam, she did not attend possession ceremonies or become a spirit medium until after she arrived in the United States. The trip itself was a catalyst in her transformation. When they were about to embark, the family members divided themselves into two groups. It was agreed that Co Hong would leave with some of the children and then, a few hours later, her husband would bring the others. As it happened, his group was able to reach the boat, but Co Hong had to return home. Learning that they would be permanently separated, her husband tried to persuade the captain to turn the boat around. Instead, the captain shot and killed him. Two of Co Hong's daughters were on the boat when their father was killed. One, a thirteen-year-old, had been sitting on the deck. She screamed when she witnessed her father's murder and was then shot to death herself. The remaining daughter was able to escape, but Co Hong remained in Vietnam with the rest of her family. Then, within one month, her mother died. Co Hong was overcome with grief until *Cau Be*, the spirit of a young prince, came to bring the gift of divination. Although she did not become a spirit medium for several years after that visitation, Co Hong felt that *Cau Be* brought peace and contentment and helped her to continue with her life.

Jenny was the first in the family to become a spirit medium. She began attending Silicon Valley possession ceremonies at the age of twenty, partly because her boyfriend's mother was a temple caretaker (*dong den*). Describing herself as a "happy, normal girl who loved shopping and working out," Jenny related how she soon began to have unusual experiences:

> One day out of the blue I was working and I started to feel weird and within five to ten seconds tears started coming out of my eyes, and then they stopped. I started driving home, and I felt goose bumps on my back, and I started crying again. Then I started to hear voices in my head, and they said, while I was driving on the freeway, "you should get yourself into a wreck."

Jenny continued to experience uncontrollable emotions, as a result of which she soon lost her job and entered a period of financial crisis. Then she began to see spirits. She consulted her mother, Co Hong, who in turn sought advice from a temple medium who advised her that Jenny possessed the spirit root.

Co Hong was initiated into mediumship a few years later. She had been attending her daughter's ceremonies and the ceremonies of others, but did not consider becoming a medium until *Cau Be* caused her to be ill. She had been working hard, cooking and caring for grandchildren, which might certainly have wearied her,

---

[7] Silicon Valley mediums often used the terms "god" and "spirits" interchangeably, possibly because the term "god" is more socially acceptable in the United States.

but she found herself to be constantly exhausted and concluded that she was working too much. Then she began to feel unwell and spent day after day, for months, sleeping on the sofa, too weak to rouse herself. Finally, she realized that her illness was *Cau Be's* way of forcing her to become a medium.

Co Hong lives in a low-income apartment complex with Jenny's ten-year-old son, and Jenny lives with her boyfriend and his parents. Whereas Co Hong earns an income caring for her grandchildren, Jenny is employed as a file clerk for a corporation that rents DVDs. Both women are extremely charismatic, and together they form the core of the new temple. Jenny started the temple with two friends, Susie and Hung, after a series of disagreements over ritual practices at the old temple. Co Hong is slated to become the next *dong thay*, partly because she is the oldest member of the group, and partly because of her charisma and intense religious devotion. Jenny and Co Hong each have the gift of divination—their spirits have given them power to see into the future and read the fortunes of others—and people from the temple often congregate in Co Hong's small apartment to talk with the spirits.

Friendship is a strong factor prompting many people's initial exposure to *len dong*, and many mediums become involved through social networks. Good friends since high school, Susie and Faith are unmarried, college-educated spirit mediums in their early thirties. Faith is a fun-loving, outspoken salesperson, and Susie is a strikingly beautiful business student who is about to graduate with a four-year college degree. They were introduced to *len dong* spirit possession through Jenny. Part of a group of friends who have visited Jenny and sought divination through Co Hong, Faith said she was initially skeptical:

> At first I thought it was one of those voodoo black magic type of things. I'm very skeptical. I don't like fortune-telling. I don't like anything that has to do with spirits or talking about past life or future life. That stuff gives me the chills. I don't like horror movies. I like simple stuff.

However, Faith continued to visit Co Hong, mostly because her friends were attending. After two years she decided to attend a *len dong* ceremony, and she fell in love with the music.

> I was just bouncing, you know? There are three reasons why I kept going to the ceremonies. First, they happen to be my friend's ceremonies. The second was to take photographs and do the video. The third was the music.

While attending the *len dong* rituals Faith and Susie each found a sense of peace and serenity and discovered in themselves a deep love for the spirits, especially *Cau Be*. Both women became mediums in order to serve the spirit world, and they both attend possession ceremonies frequently.

It is not uncommon to find several members of a single family who are spirit mediums. Hung, a middle-aged machinist, suspected that he had the spirit root because both his father and brother are mediums in southern Vietnam. When he came to the United States as a boat person in 1987, Hung did not attend possession ceremonies because he did not know the location of any temples. Ten years passed before he and his wife visited the temple in California. He explained that his first and second visits were "okay," but he was "caught" by a snake on his third visit.

According to Hung, he was on his knees, praying to one of the spirits, when the snake, which looked "just like an anaconda," wrapped itself around his lower legs, preventing him from moving. At that moment, Hung realized that he was called to mediumship. Hung and his wife are *dong den* (temple caretakers) of the new temple. They opened the temple with Jenny and Susie, and they share financial and spiritual responsibility for it. The tiny temple occupies the main room of the Hung family apartment and is a hub of constant activity.

Hung's life was full of difficulty before he became a spirit medium. He worked on a lunch truck from two in the morning until six in the evening every day of the week. He earned very little money, and the money he did have was quickly spent. During this time, Hung's son was imprisoned for a shooting, and his eighteen-year-old daughter tried to commit suicide. Full of stress and anxiety, Hung said he wandered the streets "like a water buffalo," roaming here and there. Physically ill for three months before he attended his first possession ceremony, Hung said he had intense stomach pain and vomited everything that he ate. Everything changed when he became a spirit medium. His physical health improved, he stopped wandering the streets, he found and kept a better job, and his daughter began feeling better. This year, Hung's wife will have an initiation ceremony; both of their daughters attend temple rituals. The younger daughter already exhibits signs of *can* and wants to be initiated when she turns sixteen.

Believers are convinced that avoiding mediumship, and thereby escaping one's preordained fate, can prove harmful to other family members. Co Nga is a sixty-three-year-old medium who emigrated to the United States ten years ago. Since then, she has worked as a private health-care aide to an invalid Vietnamese senior, whom she tends in his home. Co Nga's concern over the mental illness of her son led her to consider becoming a medium. She says that her son, John, bears a heavy fate because his father carried a very strong spirit root; one of his ancestors had been a powerful medium. According to Co Nga, because John's father had failed to answer his calling to become a spirit medium, the spirits are making John ill. One time, while Co Nga was traveling in Vietnam, John heard voices telling him to destroy all of the communications technology in the house. Piling all the televisions, VCRs, and stereo equipment in the living room, John smashed everything until a neighbor called the police. After a short period of hospitalization, John returned home to live with his mother.

John takes anti-psychotic medication and sleeping pills, and attends bi-monthly sessions with a psychiatrist. Co Nga says these medications help to relieve his symptoms, but that he will only recover if someone in the family becomes a spirit medium. She promised the spirits that she would *ra dong* (hold an initiation ceremony) if they would help her son. Since then, John's symptoms have been alleviated somewhat through a combination of medication and her promise to the spirits. John attends almost every ceremony at their temple, where he plays a small drum and helps to distribute blessed gifts (*loc*).

Some individuals turn to spirit possession in response to mental illness. Thien is a thoughtful and intelligent thirty-year-old psychology student who is currently contemplating mediumship. He was hospitalized after a psychotic episode and diagnosed with bipolar disorder at the age of twenty-three. Shortly afterwards, Thien met Jenny at a Vietnamese café, and she became his girlfriend. Since his exposure to *len dong*, Thien has begun to reevaluate his diagnosis. Although he still thinks he is ill, he now wonders if many of his experiences result from the actions of spirits.

Vietnamese in Silicon Valley follow diverse routes to mediumship, some of which are familiar to their Vietnamese counterparts. As noted above, many individuals find that mediumship runs in their family and conclude that they were destined therefore to become mediums themselves, but the final decision to pursue initiation is often made in response to a particular stressor. These stressors vary from country to country. Many Silicon Valley mediums endured severe trauma when they left Vietnam, and some promised to become mediums if the spirits protected them during the journey. Others turned to the spirits while they were grieving the loss of family members who had died along the way. Californians also become mediums in response to anxieties caused by intergenerational conflict, which is intensified among immigrants. For example, Faith said she felt a lot of pressure trying to meet her parents' demands, and Hung had several problems raising his children. Silicon Valley mediums also have a strong desire to protect traditional culture. Jenny, who describes herself as "a very traditional girl," sees *len dong* as a means of maintaining cultural integrity. Many individuals have joined the Silicon Valley temple in dyads or groups. This was true, for example, of Jenny and Co Hong, Hung and his family, Faith and Susie, and Co Nga and her son—each dyad is based on ties of blood, marriage, or friendship. This is partly explained by the belief that mediumship runs in families, but it also illustrates the importance of exposure to the religion and testifies to the social nature of *len dong* spirit possession.

California mediums share a common conviction that mediumship will change one's life for the better. Part of this personal transformation entails changes in the medium's views of her or his self. It is believed that the spirits constantly accompany the medium, helping to shape her thoughts, feelings, and actions. In this context, events take on added significance: things do not just happen—they happen for a reason.

SPIRIT POSSESSION, SELF, AND PERSONALITY

The amount of influence a spirit exerts over an individual depends upon context, as well as the nature of the particular human-spirit relationship. Spirits may influence a person during normal day-to-day life, during a possession ceremony, and through spontaneous possession. The spirit is thought to be constantly "around" the medium. Some believers claim the spirits reside inside the body of the medium, while others say they hover somewhere near the head.

Mediums experience possession during a *len dong* ceremony in a number of different ways. Susie says she feels the spirit of *Cau Be* enter her body through her head,[8] at which point she begins to feel light and "feathery." Some mediums report that they continue to be aware of their surroundings because they are possessed only "from the neck down." Others say that they can see what is happening around them, but have no control over it. Jenny compared the experience of possession to simultaneously driving and riding in a car:

> When the gods come in me, then it's like I'm put in a car in a box. I can see you, but I cannot talk to you. It's like I'm in a car driving and you're in a car in the next lane, and you can see me but I cannot communicate with you. So I'm

---

[8] Co Hong says that evil spirits come up from the ground through the medium's feet.

behind, and the god's in front of me. Actually he's in me, but my soul is put behind me.

However, according to Jenny, when a medium is completely possessed she has no control over the spirit:

> Sometimes they are not in you completely, so you are still able to control yourself and control a little bit of what god says ... but when god comes in you completely, then you have no control. If they are in you half way, then you have some control.

Some Silicon Valley mediums express possession in terms of percentages. A medium might say, for example, "I was 40 percent," meaning the spirit controlled less than half of the individual.

The degree of possession during a *len dong* varies from individual to individual and spirit to spirit. Susie said that she did not "feel it" the first time she had a ceremony. She just wanted to serve the spirits and did not think she was really possessed. However, the second time she was "completely possessed" and "could not control anything." Her experience is very different from that of Hung, who was totally possessed the third time he entered a Silicon Valley temple. The degree of possession also varies depending on the spirit involved and the temple where the ceremony takes place. Mediums often feel possession more completely in temples with which they are familiar, and they tend to be more responsive to spirits with whom they have a particular affinity.

Spirits sometimes reveal themselves unexpectedly, through spontaneous expression, but this phenomenon varies among individuals and temples. Often associated with divination, spontaneous possession is usually "complete" or "100 percent," and can be viewed by the participants as either a gift or a problem. Jenny and Co Hong read fortunes while spontaneously possessed, and this is considered a blessing, but Susie's experiences are less productive. She has been possessed by the Red Tiger, who makes her growl and foam at the mouth. Co Hong's temple is unique in Silicon Valley, partly because spontaneous possession is so common, and the members try to prevent or even conceal their unexpected responses to the spirits whenever they are in a different temple. For example, one time Hung's wife attended one of the larger Silicon Valley temples with Jenny and Susie. While the Seventh Prince (*Ong Bay*) possessed the medium affiliated with that temple, Hung's wife began to raise and shake her right hand. Seeing that she was spontaneously possessed, Jenny quickly but quietly ushered her out of the building and arranged a ride home. When asked why Hung's wife had to leave, Jenny simply stated, "Sometimes people don't understand."

The intensity and frequency of spontaneous possession sets members of this temple apart from others in Silicon Valley and distinguishes them from practitioners in Vietnam as well. Several mediums from Co Hong's temple recently traveled to Hanoi, where they attended possession and initiation ceremonies. The first night *Cau Be*, the Young Prince, reportedly possessed Jenny because he was so excited to be in Vietnam. The second night he possessed her because he was upset since the mediums had purchased outfits for other spirits, but they had forgotten to buy anything for Cau. Then Susie was possessed while waiting to have her fortune told in a Hanoi temple. She had been sitting on the floor in front of the altar, but was directly facing the tiger spirits. According to Susie, this situation "opened the path" so the tiger could just "zoom" right into her. Clenching her fists, she rocked back and forth groaning while spittle ran down her chin. Although the California mediums understood that she was possessed, the temple caretakers looked shocked. The California mediums were surprised to see that the Vietnamese did not appear to experience such intense spontaneous possession. As Susie explained:

> They looked concerned, but they didn't know the trance. They don't have the same kind of trance that we have. I don't know what kind of trance they have, I think they have trance too. Our trance is completely out. Their trance is more like dancing beautifully, that's it!

Mediums are inclined to be possessed by spirits with whom they share some affinity, creating an intimate, transformative relationship between the spirit and his or her willing servant. In her study of religious practice among Haitians in New York, McCarthy Brown learned that "individuals are not comprehensible apart from the (Vodou) spirits associated with them."[9] *Tu Phu* spirits also share personality characteristics with the individuals they possess, and they influence dispositions and manners of emotional expression. Visible physical alterations accompany many of these effects; these are considered both symbols of personal transformation and proof of the sincere intentions of the devotees.

The personality and behavior of a medium often mirrors that of her spirits. Each *Tu Phu* spirit has a personal history, palace, color, and style of dancing. Mediums learn about spirit personalities by observing them during possession ceremonies, listening to songs (*chau van*), and through the direct experience of spirit possession. Often, a devotee will experience an urge to perform an action associated with a particular spirit. For example, Co Nga carries the root of the Seventh Prince (*Ong Hoang Bay*), who was the son of a king. *Ong Hoang Bay* died in battle while fighting foreign invaders. After death, his body returned to the earth, and his spirit ascended to heaven. According to Silicon Valley mediums, the Seventh Prince was intelligent, of fine moral character, helpful to his people and his nation, and distinguished for never harming women. Often, instead of punishing his enemies, he would try to persuade them to convert to the right path. *Ong Hoang Bay* also loved drinking dark tea and smoking cigarettes, particularly if they were laced with opium. Co Nga knows that she has the root of the Seventh Prince because she likes to smoke and drink tea whenever he is incarnated in a possession ceremony. As her friend and fellow medium explained:

> Often when *Ong Hoang Bay* was unoccupied, he would start to drink tea and smoke, so that is why when he goes into someone's body, they start to drink and smoke. Normally she would not be able to smoke or drink dark tea, but when possessed by the Seventh Prince, she finds smoking to be pleasant and very dark tea is tasty.

---

[9] Karen McCarthy Brown, "Afro-Caribbean Healing: A Haitian Case Study," in *Healing Cultures: Art and Religion as Curative Practices in the Caribbean and Its Diaspora*, ed. Maria Fernandez Olmos and L. Paravisini-Gebert (New York, NY: Palgrave, 2001), pp. 43-68.

Although each *Tu Phu* spirit has a unique personality, the same spirit might express itself differently through different mediums. *Cau Be* (the Young Prince) is one of the most popular *Tu Phu* spirits in Silicon Valley, often described as active, elegant, funny, and playful, depending on the medium in whom he is incarnated. Whenever *Cau Be* enters into Jenny, he is sarcastic and playful, but when he possesses her mother, he is elegant and peaceful. Faith describes Cau as carefree, but also says, "I know that when he gets down to business, he gets his shit done. That's like me, when it comes to work, I get my shit done. My boss calls me Hurricane Faith because I just sweep through." Cau exhibits various characteristics in different mediums because he can reflect an individual's personality. As Jenny explains, "Cau will play exactly who you are"; in her opinion, he does this to teach the medium a lesson.

Spirits also relate to the expression of certain emotions. *Cau Be* often acts like a two-year-old, laughing one moment and crying the next. During possession ceremonies, people treat *Cau Be* accordingly. If he behaves like a two-year-old, devotees will try to cajole and placate him by offering him fish to play with or candy to eat. Other spirits, particularly the mandarins, are stern—they often frown when incarnated in a medium. Reading the facial expressions of mediums is one way that devotees discern which spirit has been incarnated. The female spirits *Co Be Den* and *Co Bo* often possess Jenny. One of the quiet spirits, *Co Be Den*, rarely speaks, even when asked a question. As Jenny explains, *Co Be Den* is quiet because she has a limp in one leg and is uncomfortable, perhaps even embarrassed, because of her disability. Whereas *Co Be Den* is quiet, *Co Bo* is an especially kind-hearted spirit. With such empathy and a strong desire to help others, she often suffers and ends up crying.

Len dong spirit possession offers an opportunity for the expression of emotion, but there are differences among Silicon Valley mediums and temples. Whereas some mediums carry out reserved possession ceremonies, others express a wide range of powerful emotions. In some temples, the tiger spirits growl and harmful ghosts scream, *Co Bo* cries, mandarins throw their swords, and *Cau Be* giggles with glee, all in a single afternoon. Also, interpersonal tensions commonly surface during *len dong*. During one ceremony at the old temple, just before the schism that split its membership, a great deal of tension arose between two mediums who disagreed on a certain procedure. One of the mediums retreated to the garage for a good cry, while the other continued to watch the *len dong*. Finally, the temple medium, weary of the tension, solicited one of the Co spirits and begged to be allowed to quit her position, saying that she was tired of all the interpersonal problems. The medium cried and cried, and the spirits grew angry and refused to come to the ceremony. The problem was not resolved until almost all of the mediums in the temple were on their knees, begging the spirits to return.

Tu Phu devotees interpret an individual's disposition and style of emotional expression in daily life as the work of spirits. For instance, Faith is carefree and happy-go-lucky because she contains the root of *Cau Be*, whereas Susie's anger comes to her from the Red Tiger. Jenny embodies *Quan De Nhi* who is strict with ritual procedures, so that during ceremonies she feels compelled to voice an objection if a medium is not following correct protocol. Phan is stubborn, a characteristic stemming from her *Cau Be* root, so she has to do things in her own way. Spirits also influence personality characteristics normally associated with gender. For example, if a man has effeminate characteristics, then he might bear a heavy spirit root of the female spirits (*co*). If a woman is stern and angry, then she might carry the root of a mandarin.[10]

Spirits not only influence a medium's personality, they also cause short- and long-term physical changes in the people they possess. Whenever General Tran Hung Dao possesses Co Nga, her skin burns and her face begins to turn red; when *Co Be Den* possesses Susie, she feels tremendous pain in her left leg. Tien, the thirteen-year-old daughter of Hung, often finds herself yawning during *len dong*. These phenomena signify that a spirit has descended; it is not uncommon to see several people yawning during a *len dong*. Other mediums experience long-term physical changes. For Faith, becoming a medium involved a change in hairstyle that had tremendous personal significance:

> I had gorgeous hair when I was in college and high school, and for some reason I chopped it off and kept it that way, and my friends and family and coworkers are like, "why don't you leave your hair long?" I want to do what I want to do, not just what people want me to do, and I'm like, "No, I don't want to leave it long." I'm just really stubborn. But what really made me leave my hair long was *Cau*. He wanted to do just two pigtails, and the only way to do that was to have long hair. I have this tremendous love for *Cau*. I completely adore him, I would do anything he wants me to do. So I left my hair long just so that during my ceremony I would have long hair for him to wrap around. After the ceremony, I was just like, "I love my hair." It's so nice, I get so many compliments, that was a changing attribute, a physical attribute, but it really did change my life, my hair! And I kept it that way after, and everything seemed to be just going up. I have more confidence in myself, I look better, and I had a better job offer, people like me more, and so my confidence is building.

Once individuals embark on the path to mediumship, they become increasingly aware of the spirit world, often identifying with a particular spirit, and they begin to understand their feelings, thoughts, and behaviors within the context of this spirituality. There is variation in how, when, and where the mediums are influenced by the spirits, and, as we have seen, mediums describe possession differently and distinguish between various degrees of possession during a *len dong* ritual. Also, some mediums are possessed outside the context of spirit possession ceremonies, and the mediums at this particular temple perceive themselves as "different" because they experience spontaneous possession more frequently than do individuals at other temples in Silicon Valley or Vietnam. However, regardless of these variations, all mediums share the belief that the spirits influence the mediums both emotionally and physically and in a variety of different settings.

PERSONAL TRANSFORMATIONS

Spirit mediums and initiates report tremendous personal changes resulting from mediumship. Our research has found that these changes can occur before, during, or after people become mediums. Some individuals ask the spirits for a specific favor and promise to become a medium if the request is granted. For example, Co Nga

---

[10] See Barley Norton, "'Hot-Tempered' Women and 'Effeminate' Men: The Performance of Music and Gender in Vietnamese Mediumship," in this volume.

asked the spirits to help her son receive financial support from Social Security. In this case, the initiate becomes a medium to thank the spirits for their assistance. Other Silicon Valley mediums find that the stress of initiation itself has caused a transformation in the way they view the world. Many experience changes in their social world as they spend more and more time at the temples. However, some do not experience life changes until after they have had initiation ceremonies.

It is difficult to overestimate the significance of personal transformation in *len dong* spirit possession. Our interviews with California mediums revealed that discussions of personal growth and transformation were extremely common, and they often took the form of testimony; virtually every medium told us that her life had improved in significant ways. What are these changes and how do they come about? We agree with Koss-Chioino that healing reconstitutes the self in specific ways. The self, she says, "is simply a concept of the person as human, defined by the traditions and shared understandings of a particular group."[11] In the previous section, we illustrated how the process of becoming a medium can cause changes in personality and the expression of emotion. In this section, we shall describe the alterations of inner and outer self. Whereas the "inner world" refers to personal thoughts, feelings, views, and experiences, the "outer world" refers to the self engaged in social action.

A function of the spirits is to teach the mediums certain lessons and guide them in their daily lives. One of the most important lessons taught by the spirits is how to control anger. Susie described herself as having a "hot temper," which occasionally caused her to smash her fist against a wall or a brick. The Fifth Mandarin (*Ong Quan De Ngu*) modified this behavior. Whenever Susie gets too hot tempered, the Fifth Mandarin possesses her so that her body shakes, her face turns red, and her mouth gets frozen and bloated. These uncomfortable physical symptoms occur because "he tries to tell you that if you're going to have a hot temper, then this is going to happen." When Susie became a medium, she learned to control her anger by developing a combination of self-restraint and respect for one's self and others (*tu*). During one ceremony, the Fifth Mandarin told another medium "to zip her mouth" because she had spoken disrespectfully to other people. As one medium explained: "You have to *tu* your mouth. You don't say certain things."

Spirits can endow mediums with special skills. The Third Prince (*Cau Bo*) taught Susie to develop better study habits. She had asked *Cau Bo*, whom she described as "the god of education," to help with her graduate studies. A few nights later she dreamed that he had transformed into a beast and she rode on his back as they crossed the oceans—he was taking her to a school in London. Analyzing the dream, Susie said, "I guess he's warning me to let me know he is watching over what I am doing. He's there to guide certain classes." Soon after, she began to awaken at five o'clock every morning with an itchy rash. It itched so much that she could not sleep, so she would rise from her bed and start to read. A few days later she realized that *Cau Bo* had "sprinkled something" over her, forcing her to get out of bed and study.

Just as Susie has become a more diligent student because of *Cau Bo*, Faith has become a better salesperson because of *Cau Be*. The recent recipient of an all-expense-paid trip to Florida, a prize for being one of the top salespeople in her firm, Faith says that the spirits gave her personal relations, or "PR," skills. When she first started her job, she was competent and businesslike but lacked interpersonal skills. *Cau Be*

---

[11] Koss-Chioino, *Women as Healers, Women as Patients*, p. 200.

helped her develop those skills through role modeling: Cau is outgoing and expressive, and Faith has adopted those qualities. Many of the *Tu Phu* spirits are exceptionally talented, some are culture heroes and heroines, and most are worthy of emulation. Mediums change their own lives and circumstances through the imitation of these highly valued spirit behaviors.

Several spirit mediums have received gifts of divination. Trusting that they are able to see into the future, these mediums counsel individuals with specific concerns. Cross-cultural studies of fortune-tellers and spirit mediums indicate that adoption of the role of healer and advisor can bestow many rewards.[12] Some of the rewards relate to changes in occupation and social status, while others involve inner gains, such as an enhanced sense of accomplishment and the personal satisfaction of helping fellow humans in need. (Divination can be personally rewarding for mediums, but there is also some risk because they become vulnerable to the criticisms of unhappy clients.) Although currently retired from fortune-telling, Phan used to practice this in her home. Once a month she would rise in the morning and go immediately to an altar that she had dedicated to *Cau Be*. Possessing Phan in a solitary ritual, *Cau Be* would drink warm milk, play with his toy horses, and then go downstairs to read fortunes. Phan did not accept payment for these divinations.

Several California mediums report that the process of becoming a medium helps them to establish priorities. In many cases, mediums said that they used to ask the spirits for help with all their challenges and problems, large and small, but during the process of becoming a medium they learned that some things are more important than others. As Faith explained, "I still talk to *Cau Be*, but [now] it's more like a conversation, not really an asking type of basis like before." Some mediums reported they used to be concerned with gossip or what others thought about them, but now they are not. Many learned such lessons when spirits "tested" them during the process of initiation. Faith said that spirits began to test her soon after she set the date for her initiation ceremony. She had to plan the initiation, buy the spirit clothes, arrange the flowers, and organize everything for the ceremony. As a consequence, she felt stressed, and this tension spread to include everyone around her. She said, "The entire year you're tested on your patience, your temper, on almost every aspect of your character." As a result of this intense testing, Faith feels that both her personality and her philosophy of life have changed. While she used to "stress at everything," she is now more accepting and philosophical in her responses. She says, "some things are out of your control, but some things are meant to be and you just find the positive and move on."

The spirits provide hope and meaning to mediums' lives by allowing them to believe that certain things happen for a reason. Before Faith became a medium, she felt much family pressure to get married and fit the image of "a good Vietnamese woman," as she described it. Reflecting on a particularly difficult time in her life, she said, "I just felt like I was living my parents' dream, just living for the image. There's a lot of pressure when you're Asian and growing up and you want to keep that image for yourself and around your friends and family." Becoming a medium added meaning to her life. As she explained: "I never did find myself until now. I feel like this is the peak of my life right now. I just could not be any happier."

---

[12] See Janice Boddy, "Spirit Possession Revisited: Beyond Instrumentality," *Annual Review of Anthropology* 23 (1994): 407- 34.

Many mediums say their lives have been transformed following healing by *Tu Phu* spirits. In some cases, illness was the main symptom of spirit possession, but in others the illness was just one of many different symptoms. Personal transformation also occurs because mediums change the way they think about or deal with illness, even when it is incurable. One medium, who asked to be called Nefertiti, suffers from epilepsy but has never asked the spirits for treatment because, she said, her illness is not curable. Even so, Nefertiti says that becoming a medium has made her stronger and more confident, and both characteristics help her to cope with her illness.

Many mediums distinguish between yin and yang illnesses. Yin illnesses are caused by spirits, whereas yang illnesses are considered to have "natural" or "biological" causes.[13] Although yang disorders can be treated with secular medicine, yin illnesses can only be cured in the supernatural world. When unusual experiences or behaviors result from the work of spirits, they can only be treated after one discovers who the spirit is and what it wants. If *Tu Phu* spirits are making someone ill because they want that person to serve as a medium, then medication will temporarily suppress the symptoms but the spirit will eventually find another way to express its displeasure. Many mediums feel that psychiatric medications are harmful and dangerous and will only exacerbate the problem. For example, Thien had a horrible experience with psychiatric medications while he was hospitalized. He said:

> They gave me some prescription anti-psychotics that were really heavy. I would never ever give that to anybody because it's traumatic to this day. I felt like I had two-hundred-pound sandbags tied to each foot. I couldn't even walk, it was that heavy. I was a runner you know, and I felt the lightness in my legs, and they were like, here take this drug, and I was like bam! Stuck! I couldn't walk from here to across the street without struggling. Another thing, there [were] always a lot of mental side effects. I would always get serious paranoid thoughts that would not leave ... and suicidal thoughts too while I was on these prescription drugs.

After his release from the hospital, Thien went to occupational therapy for six months and regularly visited a psychiatrist in an outpatient clinic. Although the psychiatrist eventually reduced the amount of his prescribed medication, Thien quit treatment after one year because of problems with the drugs:

> Just to be fair I took it for maybe a year but there was no progress, you know? I would measure the progress by my ability to think clearly and to figure out a math problem. Just to function daily using my mind, to do daily things, I couldn't do it on these drugs. I was also depressed and pulled down. I couldn't exercise. I tried. I tried to go and run, and I couldn't even run a mile. Paralyzed!

After quitting conventional therapy, Thien met Jenny, and she diagnosed his problem: Thien was bothered by the soul of an older brother who had died as a result of miscarriage. After this diagnosis, Thien began to make offerings to his

---

[13] See Nguyen Thi Hien, "The Religion of the Four Palaces: Mediumship and Therapy in Viet Culture."

brother's spirit. Now Thien and Jenny strongly criticize psychiatric care. She has said that she would never call the police or take him to the hospital if he was experiencing a manic episode because they only make things worse. Instead, they will try to deal with any future problems within the religion. Neither Thien nor his girlfriend, Jenny, believe that his problems are entirely over, but his life has improved. Employed in a rewarding job, he has developed close relationships with the people at the temple.

Thien's case illustrates one of the most important life-changing characteristics of *len dong* spirit possession: when people become devotees or spirit mediums, they become members of a social group. Libbey Crandon-Malamud has said that medicine can be used "as a social idiom through which cultural identity negotiation takes place,"[14] and we would argue that the same can be said for religion. Shortly after he quit taking medication, Thien decided to travel to Vietnam. Watching his Vietnamese family members interact, Thien decided that many of his problems would not have existed had he grown up in Vietnam. As he explained:

> I came back to the United States, and I kind of like went back into a depression. I thought perhaps my life could have been different had I grown up in Vietnam. I would have had more social interaction with uncles and aunts, and having just anybody to talk to would have helped me through my life. It didn't have to end up like this, I was thinking to myself. So I tried to find that atmosphere like I found in Vietnam.

Although many Silicon Valley spirit mediums experienced tremendous grief, confusion, and depression prior to becoming mediums, they did not turn to counselors or therapists. Recent reports indicate that Southeast Asian immigrants in Silicon Valley underutilize mental health-care resources.[15] Many Vietnamese are reluctant to speak of such matters with strangers because they are perceived as belonging in the family domain.[16] For example, Faith had problems sleeping and eating that she associated with stress and confusion, but she did not seek outside help. As she explains, "As an Asian, you don't come out and say that you have a problem and try to seek help. You hide it and live with it, and of course it builds up and now you're a total stress ball." The idea that personal problems are best expressed within the family may be one reason that *Tu Phu* is so attractive to some Vietnamese. Members of a temple often view themselves as a unified group, and it is not uncommon to hear mediums and devotees say they are "just like a family." Because the members of a temple form such relations and *len dong* are family occasions, temples and possession ceremonies are appropriate places for the expression of distress.

The amount of time an individual spends with a group of mediums varies from person to person. In Co Hong's temple, a core group of mediums meet with each other every weekend and several times during the week. Although all of these individuals are busy working and caring for children or elders, they spend most of

---

[14] Libbey Crandon-Malamud, *From the Fat of Our Souls: Social Change, Political Process, and Medical Pluralism in Bolivia* (Berkeley, CA: University of California Press, 1991), p. 208.

[15] Personal communication with Maria Fuentes, Ethnic Population Services Specialist, Santa Clara Valley Mental Health Administration, 2004.

[16] See Tran Minh Tung, *Indochinese Patients: Cultural Aspects of the Medical and Psychiatric Care of Indochinese Refugees* (Washington, DC: Action for Southeast Asians, Inc., 1980).

their free time with each other. Much of this time involves planning ceremonies, shopping for the spirits, and talking about *Thanh*. This social support is an important vehicle of change for many mediums. Some mediums have found a supportive "family" in this milieu, while others enjoy new and important social roles.

Many temples form closely knit social groups. Photo by Erika King.

Although the process of becoming a medium entails transformation that is usually perceived as beneficial, there are certain drawbacks. Becoming a spirit medium involves a tremendous commitment of resources, especially time and money. Spirit mediums must sponsor ceremonies, attend the ceremonies of others, and perform time-consuming and costly private rituals. We have witnessed many occasions when mediums felt they had to attend a possession ceremony, even though they had competing duties. *Len dong* rituals can also drain family finances, which can be problematic for low-income mediums. However, it is important to note that becoming a medium can contribute to the family finances as well because members of a temple often share resources and loan each other money. Finally, interpersonal problems within and between temples generate a certain amount of stress. Mediums often quarrel with one another and make accusations of sorcery, which lead to conflict, anxiety, and the division of temples.

CONCLUSIONS

Although their commitment to the *Tu Phu* religion has some drawbacks, Silicon Valley spirit mediums nonetheless report that becoming a spirit medium is a life-changing event and that the benefits far outweigh the costs. As we have seen, the process of becoming a medium entails changes in the self, which involve both the private and public aspects of one's personality. Mediums experience an altered view of the self, report changes in personality and the expression of emotion, and say they comprehend life differently. At the same time, they say they develop new ways of behaving and interacting with others.

What are the mechanisms of change? Some personal transformations come about because of alterations in the self that result from role modeling and direct spirit intervention. Mediums look to the spirits for guidance. By observing and emulating the spirits, they learn to respect their elders, empathize with others, and live virtuously. Moreover, changes in behavior arise as spirits shape conduct, bestow special skills upon mediums, and help them recover from spirit-induced illnesses. The spirits can make someone's face freeze when she gets angry or force her to rise so early in the morning that she has nothing to do but study. These transformations result from changes in thinking, as mediums develop new perspectives on themselves and others. Some mediums say they have "found" themselves, while others report a greater sense of confidence, and all have insisted that they have discovered greater purpose and meaning in their lives.

The experiences of California mediums are both similar to and different from those of other Vietnamese mediums. Although individuals in both countries turn to spirit possession for a variety of reasons, people in Silicon Valley often become mediums in response to unique stressors. Some individuals discovered they had the spirit root during the trauma of leaving Vietnam, whereas others turned to *Tu Phu* after experiencing problems adjusting to life in the United States. Silicon Valley mediums also describe their possession experiences using metaphors and language drawn from their everyday life in California. They compare spirit possession to looking out the window while driving down the freeway, a familiar and time-consuming experience for most residents of the Bay Area; they "talk to god," using a monotheistic term to describe their experiences, perhaps making spirit possession more palatable to a society that is predominantly monotheistic. Moreover, although group membership and social support are important to mediums in both countries, many Silicon Valley mediums seek ties that will build upon and maintain traditional culture. Perhaps Thien expressed this best when he said, "I tried to find that atmosphere that I found in Vietnam."

"A Bit of a Spirit Favor is Equal to a Load of Mundane Gifts": Votive Paper Offerings of *Len Dong* Rituals in Post-Renovation Vietnam

Nguyen Thi Hien[1]

Introduction

Making and burning votive paper offerings, a centuries-old tradition in Vietnam, has recently regained popularity along with the revival and development of traditional festivals and other folk religious practices. Votive offerings (*hang ma*) are generally paper representations of useful things that are promised by vow and/or dedicated to the deceased, gods, or saints. The ancient ritual of burning votive offerings originates in beliefs that propitiating supernatural beings can provide hope, security, and stability to people who live in an otherwise emotionally and materially troubled state. In post-Renovation Vietnam (*doi moi*), many people are burdened with financial concerns, yet they strongly desire access to wealth, good education, and medical care. Despite an official view dismissing votive offerings as a waste of money, the tradition of dedicating them to the higher powers has expanded substantially during the post-Renovation period.

While the increase in ritual practices may be in response to the stressful and difficult living conditions for many Vietnamese, as well as their religiosity, some people have found a way out of poverty by building lucrative businesses that capitalize on the growing demand for votive paper offerings. However, while these

[1] I would like to thank the Ford Foundation for their financial support of my field research in Vietnam in the summer of 2003, as a part of my postdoctoral program at AMNH, and Dr. Laurel Kendall (curator of Asian Ethnographic Collections at the American Museum of Natural History), Dr. Karen Fjelstad (San Jose State University), and Ann Fain (University of California in Los Angeles) for their comments on my essay. This research on votive paper offerings could not have been done without the help of Mr. Ho, one of the most resourceful persons familiar with spirit possession rituals, Mr. Thao, Mrs. Nga, and their family members, to whom I would like to express my deep gratitude.

new entrepreneurs have taken advantage of a relaxed free market for the sale of their goods, cultural administrative officials have criticized the practice, as they view the burning of such offerings as superstitious and a waste of money. Thus, the government has prohibited burning votive offerings at family rituals and in temples during festivals. The Instruction issued on November 7, 1998 by the Ministry of Culture and Information—circular number 04/1998/TT-BVHTT—states: "Votive paper offerings (manikins, houses, vehicles, dollar bills, gold and silver ingots, and so on) are prohibited from being burned at temples that are recognized as historical and cultural vestiges and during festivals."[2] These governmental restrictions also affect craftsmen who are condemned in the media for making products for practices deemed "superstitious."[3] Subsequent to the 1998 Instruction, the police have discouraged people from making and burning offerings to the dead and spirits, confiscated craftsmen's tools, and issued warnings to the mediums caught using the offerings. In some cases police have detained people for many days.

Despite the restrictions, warnings, and detentions promulgated and enforced by the Vietnamese government, people continue to use votive paper offerings for ritual and other folk practices, mainly because the practice has deep roots in Kinh (Viet) culture, especially in *len dong* spirit possession performances. My field research on *len dong* mediumship in the Red River delta in the north of Vietnam provided evidence that spirit mediums and ritual sponsors choose to defy governmental policy and continue to make votive offerings to the spirits.

The offerings—varying in quantity and size depending on sponsors' financial means and religiosity—and their use have both religious and secular meanings in contemporary Vietnam. In the ritual context, the offerings are endowed with varied religious meanings, and they figure as part of a medium's technique in the performance of the *len dong* ritual. In the social context, making offerings indicates the ritual sponsor's wealth. The reciprocal relationship between the adherents (givers) and the spirits (recipients) that develops through the offerings and the spirits' returns of "favors" contains religious as well as social meanings. Mrs. Nga, a spirit medium, said that serving spirits (*hau thanh*) or performing the *len dong* ritual expresses her devotion to the spirits. She feels unhappy if there are not enough sets of the offerings. Indeed, if rituals fail, mediums tend to blame inadequate offerings, the lack of devotion, or blasphemous behavior toward the spirits.

Data collected from observations of *len dong* spirit possession rituals in the past few years, along with recent fieldwork on the handicrafts and traditions involved in the creation and use of votive paper offerings in Bac Ninh province, highlight the importance of these offerings to the *len dong* rituals of the Mother Goddess religion, a significance that persists despite the fact that these offerings remain officially condemned as "superstition." This essay will first discuss how the offerings are used popularly in conjunction with the revitalization of the rituals and will argue that the continued use of votive offerings not only keeps the tradition alive, but expands its practice. Second, by relating stories of two households, it will illustrate how some people take advantage of the relaxed open-market economy and increased consumer

---

[2] Thin Truong, "Ton trong tin nguong va bai tru me tin di doan" [Respect Folk Beliefs and Abolish Superstitions], in *Tin Nguong-Me Tin* [Religious Beliefs-Superstition], ed. Ha Van Tang and Truong Thin (Hanoi: Nha Xuat Ban Thanh nien. 1998), p. 121.

[3] See Shaun Malarney, *Culture, Ritual, and Revolution in Vietnam* (London: RoutledgeCurzon, 2002).

demands for the votive offerings. Members of these two families produce offerings both for their own rituals and for sale to others, developing their art in the creation of these paper tokens and simultaneously building a business in the open-market economy. In one household, the handicraft tradition extends over four generations, while the other household began its paper-votive-offering business quite recently. I will examine the influence of religion on their business through the concept of "blessed gifts" (*loc*) in the Mother Goddess religion. Finally, I will demonstrate how these families have succeeded in creating profitable businesses by developing a client base built both on tradition and compatibility.

WHY VOTIVE OFFERINGS?

The tradition of making votive offerings came to Vietnam from China. Originally, Chinese people used white jade for their offerings. However, the jade was very rare and expensive, so it was eventually replaced with real money, which was discarded after its use in the ritual. Then, under the T'ang dynasty (618-907), Chinese people began using fake money instead of real gold and silver ingots, and they burned the money as a way of conveying it to the spirits. Later on, votive clothes and other objects were added to the monetary offerings.[4] According to my field notes, a villager in Chuong Xa village, Bac Ninh province, related a story explaining how the tradition passed from China into Vietnam. According to the villager, a Vietnamese emissary traveled to China on a tributary mission in the thirteenth century. Learning that Chinese people made votive offerings to the dead, he ordered his people to produce the paper offerings for the anniversary of his mother's death. From then on, the Vietnamese started to use votive offerings.

Devotion to the dead and the spirits is a hallmark of what it means, traditionally, to be an upright, moral person in Kinh (Viet) culture. The living venerate the dead and other supernatural entities by going to temples, making offerings, and praying to the spirits. Votive offerings are used in a number of these ritual settings. They are offered to the dead at funerals and death anniversary ceremonies, which are celebrated with lavish banquets and votive offerings of pans, pots, kettles, bowls, plates, cups, clothes, and so on. Votives are also part of village-wide communal house ceremonies,[5] and they are offered to the kitchen gods during the New Year. Families also maintain an altar or shrine dedicated to their deceased family members and to the spirits of earth, property, and so on, where they light incense, make frequent offerings of fruit and food, and burn the occasional votive paper offering.

People make these offerings as part of their "moral obligation" toward the deceased.[6] Also, as Catherine Bell notes, such offerings represent sacrifices to the spirits and serve important spiritual purposes:

> Whether the purpose is to avert evil, placate gods, achieve communion, reconstruct idealized kinship relations, or establish the proper reciprocity of

---

[4] See Toan Anh, *Nep Cu Tin Nguong Viet Nam* [Vietnamese Old Customs and Beliefs] (Ho Chi Minh: Nha Xua Ban Thanh pho Ho Chi Minh, 1991), p. 415.

[5] Malarney, *Culture, Ritual, and Revolution in Vietnam*, p. 84.

[6] Shaun Malarney, "State Stigma, Family Prestige, and the Development of Commerce in the Red River Delta of Vietnam," in *Market Cultures: Society and Morality in the New Asian Capitalisms*, ed. Robert Hefner (Boulder, CO: Westview Press, 1998), p. 275.

heaven and earth, the offering of something—first fruit, votive money, or human beings—has been a common ritual mechanism for securing the well-being of the community and the larger cosmos.[7]

In India, for example, offerings may be "an expression of the devotee's love and devotion; they may have the purpose of bartering or thanking for a boon or of propitiating a deity."[8]

One can view offerings as the result of human analogical and rational thought. Because people believe that the spirit world is analogous to our own, they offer to the dead and spirits what they think the spirits need in the invisible world, including food, drink, money, clothes, and more. The ancient Greeks believed that a deity was no different in character from his worshipper and would be pleased by a gift. In modern society, the Kinh offer deities the daily necessities, including votive vehicles (cars, bikes, motorbikes, or ferries) and cell phones that accord with the occupation that the person making the offerings imagines the dead to practice in the invisible world. These new types of offerings reflect the innovations transforming the culture in the open-market economy in Vietnam. For instance, one day in 2000, I had a conversation with Mrs. Lan at a séance at Ms. Phuong's, a famous soul caller (*nguoi goi hon*) in central Vietnam. Mrs. Lan was waiting for her turn to "talk," via the soul caller, with her dead father, who had been a high official at the Vietnam Ministry of Education. Mrs. Lan had been informed previously by another soul caller that her father "was very busy in the other world because he also had a very important job assisting a president." In response to this news, she had bought her father a votive cellphone as an offering, thinking it would give him more flexibility with his busy schedule in the invisible world. Thus, the belief that the spirit world shares the same qualities as our own prompts many people to see to the comfort and enjoyment of the deities and the dead by sending them useful and "necessary" votive offerings.

Finally, offerings are also made in order to gain some type of favor from a spirit or deity. For instance, a person with a particular need or desire would pray to the deity to send her what she wished for. To make her wish more acceptable, the worshipper would offer a gift, usually a votive offering. Such offerings also provide a means for worshippers to make good on a promise or vow, or to show their appreciation for the spirit having granted a wish. Sometimes the giver desires his gift to memorialize his own piety, virtue, or great achievements.[9] Thus, votive offerings are an important way of appealing to the gods to grant the devotee particular favors.

---

[7] Catherine Bell, *Ritual: Perspectives and Dimensions* (New York, NY: Oxford University Press, 1997), p. 114.

[8] Gabriella Eichinger Ferro-Luzzi, "Ritual as Language: The Case of South Indian Food Offerings," *Current Anthropology* 18,3 (1977): 508.

[9] William Henry Denham Rouse, *Greek Votive Offerings: An Essay in the History of Greek Religion* (New York, NY: Arno Press, 1975 [1902]), p. 350.

VOTIVE PAPER OFFERINGS OF *LEN DONG* RITUALS[10]

Votive offerings enable adherents of the Mother Goddess religion to show their devotion to the gods and spirits, permit the devotees to associate themselves with these same gods and spirits, and provide opportunities for the living to gain favors from the spirit world. The votive paper offerings of a *len dong* ritual can vary greatly depending on the ritual's sponsor, its locale, and purpose. As part of ritual procedure, spirit mediums or sponsors are supposed to have basic sets of the votive offerings on hand, especially for major rituals such as those to celebrate an initiation, or the inauguration of a temple of the Mother Goddess religion, or the installation of spirit statues. According to Mr. Thao, a craftsman, spirit medium, and ceremony master, basic sets of paper offerings for an initiation include five small-sized horses to be given to the spirits of five directions; hats for the spirit father, household spirit, tutelary spirit, and north and south star spirits; four manikins for each of the four palaces of the Mother Goddess religion; eight forest mandarins; forest trees; a mountain with five peaks; gold and silver treasuries; a big life-sized red horse and a yellow elephant; three sets of mother goddesses with their ladies; and gold and silver ingots.

Votive paper offerings to the spirits at *len dong* rituals have multiple purposes. They serve as ritual vehicles to send a sponsor's message of a wish for good luck and prosperity, or as a way of gaining personal blessings or auspicious good fortune via the transformation of the offerings. Spirit mediums and adherents of the Mother Goddess religion also make offerings to the spirits to communicate their care and affection. Votive offerings are thought to fill certain basic needs of the spirits because the spirits need vehicles to travel, a place to dwell, and servants to help them. Manikins in the form of maids are expected to be transformed into the spirits' assistants; horses, elephants, and ferries provide transportation to the spirit realm.

The burning of the offerings sends these gifts to the spiritual realm.[11] In the course of a *len dong* ritual, after religious masters perform petition rites to specific spirits, some votive offerings are burned and the rest are kept until the mediums perform rituals to other spirits. During the rituals, the spirits receive the offerings and witness the devotions of the ritual sponsor. At that time, some of the votives are

---

[10] Besides the votive paper objects, worshippers offer plates or trays of food and drink specific to each rank of the spirits of the Mother Goddess religion. During *len dong* rituals, offerings both from ritual sponsors and participants are conveyed to spirits, who distribute the *loc* back to *chau van* singers, mediums' assistants, and all participants. Participants bring offerings to spirits; they lay them out on plates on the altars. When mediums perform the ritual and incarnate spirits, the participants will make their offerings according to the particular spirit incarnation. When asking for a cure or expressing a desire to have a child, the participants offer some money to the Tran Hung Dao spirit, some money to the mandarins for assistance in their business, or some fruit to princes and ladies for talent or auspiciousness. When participants offer food, fruit, or money to spirits, the mediums give the offerings back to them and to all members of the audience as well. Thus, the contribution and distribution of offerings break the boundaries between the visible and invisible worlds during the ritual. The ritual transforms mundane offerings into blessed gifts with auspicious power.

[11] Offerings of food and drink are transformed and handed back to those who make them after the spirits have "received and tasted." The people making the offerings are then free to consume the food and drink. In doing so, the Kinh do not say, as they would with ordinary food, that they are eating (*an*) or having a meal. Rather, they see themselves as having been granted "blessed gifts" (*thu loc*). By eating the transformed spirit food, they are then assured of receiving the favor of the spirits regarding their good health, luck, and prosperity.

burned for "spirits' needs," while others are kept intact, as these are held to be symbolic of initiates or ritual sponsors.

Votive offerings of manikins, gold, and money are made to the spirits and burned as a means of transmitting them. Initiation ritual, August 2003. Photo by Nguyen Thi Hien.

At an initiation ritual, certain votive objects have special purposes. For instance, a small banana tree placed in a pot may symbolize a particular initiate. During the incarnation of mandarins, the mediums pour water on the tree as if they were "bathing" the initiate, so he or she will be "fresh" and lively. In addition, there could be a tray of petition sheets to spirits (*so*) on which religious masters write in Sino-Vietnamese ideographs the name, address, and requests of the initiate. Four notebooks, a writing brush, an ink slab, and a pen symbolize the knowledge with which the spirits will endow the initiate. Additionally, for this particular initiate, a plate of rice grains, a pack of cigarettes, some tea, some betel and areca nuts, handkerchiefs, combs, fans, and some money might symbolize the items needed to satisfy his or her daily needs. Finally, some eggs wrapped in colorful papers, called "dragon eggs," would represent fertility. At other *len dong* rites, such as "paying off the spirits of three and four palaces" (*tra no quan tam phu tu phu*), a medium's sponsor said to be in debt ritually "pays off" the debt by offering the spirit a horse, votive money, or gold and silver ingots.

The votive paper offerings at *len dong* are used in rituals as material for specific procedures or techniques. During each incarnation, mediums' receive and witness the offerings from the sponsor and the participants. At that time, the initiate or the ritual sponsor sits on the performing stage and holds the offerings. The spirit "enlivens" the animal and manikin offerings to imbue them with symbolic souls, while a singer from the band sings: "Enliven the eyes; The eyes of manikins; Their minds are intelligent; Their ears are excellent; Their hearts are happy; Their limbs are moving."[12] After receiving the offerings, the spirit sends its blessing messages to the sponsor via the medium. During one such ritual, the spirit said:

> Today, our Le family has chosen an auspicious day, a good date and month, to prepare their petition and make modest offerings with sincere hearts, to have the ritual performed for dismissing curses and unluckiness. I, the Mandarin, come to witness the sincere heart of the Le.[13]

In the past, before Renovation, people could barely afford to buy offerings for the spirits; they often had to perform "plain" (*chay*) rituals without any offerings. The spirits understood these financial constraints and nonetheless responded to people's requests. Today, as a result of the free market, newly prosperous adherents of the Mother Goddess religion can sponsor the rituals for good health and good business and can afford to buy the necessary full sets of paper offerings. Thus making offerings serves as an indicator of the ritual sponsor's wealth.

Not only the wealth of the sponsor is on display. Ritual offerings made for a *len dong* ritual performance are sometimes perceived now as a public indicator of how wealthy particular mediums are—or at least how devoted they appear to be to the faith. Comparatively lavish displays may earn a medium a positive reputation among the factions of her or his peers.[14] In some "luxury" temples of the Mother Goddess religion (on the shores of West Lake and in Hang Quat Street in Hanoi, for example), only wealthy mediums can sponsor a ritual. These mediums may be successful vendors at Dong Xuan and Hom markets, big commodity traders, or owners of restaurants in Hanoi or other big cities. Mrs. Tuat, a Chinese goods trader in Hanoi, said that three years after her initiation as a spirit medium, she had begun to earn a better living and saved money as a result of the compassion of the spirits. Subsequently, she was able to sponsor more costly rituals. She was very happy because she could even afford to sponsor a "decent" ritual at Phu Giay, the center for the veneration of Mother Goddesses. Thus, the votive paper offerings to the spirits not only serve as commerce and gift exchange in Viet society, but they also "foster"[15] a reciprocal flow of positive religious emotions between the spirits and their followers. The mediums must offer materials symbolizing goods to the spirits in order to receive spirit favors in return. In the act of receiving these offerings, the spirits are said to witness the sincere heart of the devotees and then bestow upon

---

[12] Nguyen Thi Hien, "The Religion of the Four Palaces: Mediumship and Therapy in Viet Culture" (PhD dissertation, Indiana University, 2002), p. 203.

[13] Ibid.

[14] Offerings gain the same social meaning when families hold lavish feasts at funerals or death anniversaries. See Dao Duy Anh, *Viet Nam Van Hoa Su Cuong* [Vietnam Cultural and Historical Outline] (Ho Chi Minh City: Thanh Thuy Publisher, 1998), pp. 225-28. Dao Duy Anh writes that many households buy very costly votive offerings, believing they represent increased piety toward one's parents. The more lavish the feasts, the higher the "praise" accorded the feast-givers within the community.

[15] Marcel Mauss, *The Gift: The Form and Reason for Exchange in Archaic Societies*, trans. W. D. Halls (New York, NY: W. W. Norton, 1990 [1950]), p. 19.

them good luck, good health, and prosperity. Recipients see this favor as a great spiritual help, for as one Vietnamese adage goes: "A bit of a spirit favor is equal to a load of mundane gifts."

THE HANDICRAFT TRADITION OF MAKING VOTIVE PAPER OFFERINGS IN POST-RENOVATION VIETNAM

In Vietnam's post-Renovation period, the production of votive offerings has become more developed and the offerings themselves have come to be used more widely. As with many other handicraft traditions, the votive-offering enterprise has benefited greatly from the open market. Consequently, the tradition has spread, as some households have started to produce the offerings and sell their products to outside villages. This expansion of the handicraft trade helps to meet the demands of the local people, as well as providing a livelihood for a number of households. During my childhood in the 1970s, I remember that my mother had to go to a market far from our village in order to purchase some simple votive paper offerings, usually for the anniversary of the death of my grandfather. Today, my mother can order any votive offerings she wants right in our home village, where there are two households who began this handicraft business in the 1990s. Thus, the "local socioeconomic dynamics"[16] allow people to have easy access to votive offerings for their ritual and daily needs.

Two households provide case studies of how families function as production units for the creation of votive offerings, and also how families pursue this handicrafts enterprise in different ways and with quite a different "human resource quality."[17] The first household, the Thao family, has developed its business based on family tradition and experience. Mr. Thao, the head of the family, knows how to use the religious elements of *len dong* to encourage his small business to flourish. In contrast, the second household, the Nga family, does not really have any experience or history of involvement in this trade,[18] but instead has developed its business by relying on Mrs. Nga's position as a master medium. Her family's products are used mainly for her clients' rituals. These stories indicate that the success of each family enterprise depends also on religious dynamics and on how those involved have used their practices to develop networks of customers to whom they can sell their votive products.

The story of Mr. Thao's family enterprise, which has been producing votive offerings for four generations, provides a glimpse into the practices of the handicraft in the past, the present, and, to some extent, the future. Today, Mr. Thao's family specializes in making votive offerings exclusively for *len dong* spirit possession rituals in Chuong Xa village. The Chuong Xa people are peasant-craftsmen who supplement their incomes from farming by producing all kinds of votive paper offerings. Mr. Thao's family is one of a few households in the village that create

---

[16] Hy Van Luong, "Wealth, Power, and Inequality: Global Market, the State, and Local Sociocultural Dynamics," in *Postwar Vietnam: Dynamics of a Transforming Society*, ed. Hy Van Luong (Singapore: Institute of Southeast Asian Studies, 2003), p. 105.

[17] Ibid., p. 104.

[18] Hy Van Luong states, "The success of some households as opposed to their neighbors appears to be due partly to a combination of drive and skills acquired through formal education as well as through previous work and family experiences." In ibid.

offerings specific to *len dong*, while other households produce all other kinds of votive offerings, such as gold and silver ingots, fake dollar bills, paper utensils, and clothes for the dead.

The Thao family has produced votive offerings for four generations. Mr. Thao's wife is shown here weaving the frame of a votive elephant. Chuong Xa village, Bac Ninh province, September 2003. Photo by Nguyen Thi Hien.

Mr. Thao's family has changed the sorts of votive products they sell over time to accommodate various markets. In the past, Mr. Thao's grandparents and uncles mainly produced the offerings presented to the dead. Although the Thao family formerly made specific votive offerings for *len dong*, their primary source of income derived from the offerings used in ancestor veneration, not from spirit possession rituals. Since the Renovation and the growth of *len dong*, they have altered their business, now producing primarily for spirit possession rituals. As Mr. Thao's uncle explained:

> Before, we mainly made offerings for the rituals for good health, for good luck, and for the dead. Offerings for *len dong* were not many, for people did not conduct many spirit possession rituals and could not afford to buy as many as today. Since the Renovation, *len dong* has been quite developed, and we eventually switched our business. Nowadays, we make only votive offerings for spirit possession rituals.[19]

The Thao family has been able to capitalize on this growing market and adjust its traditional approach to making and selling the votive offerings to include the rising demand for *len dong* products.

Also, the handicraft tradition has been disseminated widely among family members of different ages and generations, a practice motivated by the need for more laborers to accommodate the seasonal demand that typifies the post-Renovation period. When the weather cools down during the spring and fall—from the first to the fourth and then from the eighth to the twelfth lunar months, respectively—novice mediums have their initiation rituals and experienced mediums perform at least two rituals to fulfill their obligations of "serving" spirits annually. During these seasons, Mr. Thao's family is usually too busy to finish all the orders in time, and consequently, Mr. Thao has to call up his nephews and nieces to work for him after their classes. He does not pay them wages, but instead gives them some money for their course books and school supplies. As a result of the added family labor, this younger generation learns their family's handicraft tradition and techniques.

According to Mr. Thao, his family receives more orders than any of the other family enterprises in his commune producing votive offerings because Mr. Thao's family only makes offerings for special orders, not for sale in the market. In Vietnamese culture, this indicates that his products are superior. My associate, Mr. Ho,[20] told me that, "his [Mr. Thao's] offerings are elaborate, carefully constructed, and reasonably priced. Thus, he has a lot of orders and does not have time to make votive offerings for a market, where the offerings are mass-produced for buyers." Mr. Thao only takes orders from master mediums who purchase the offerings for their own rituals and rituals for their initiates and clients. Mr. Nghi, a well-known master medium in Bac Ninh town, said, "I like to order votive offerings for my clients from Mr. Thao because I know where to purchase the good and full sets of the offerings. If the offerings are deficient, I do not feel happy while performing." Thus, the family's elite clientele are a testament to the dedication, refined technique, and high-quality craftsmanship that distinguish their votive paper offerings.

The adherents of the Mother Goddess religion always say that they have a "blessed gift" (*loc thanh*) when their businesses flourish. This concept is echoed in a

---

[19] Personal communication.

[20] Mr. Ho is a cameraman who has taken pictures and shot videotapes for mediums throughout an extensive area in the Red River Delta for more than twenty years.

Vietnamese adage, "one makes a living because of the graves,"[21] suggesting that ancestors or spirits can influence a person's fortunes. Viewed from the perspective of this religion, Mr. Thao's family not only has the tradition, but it also has a "blessed gift" that maintains a prosperous business. To preserve his *loc*, Mr. Thao was initiated to be a medium—the first in his family to undergo initiation. He built his own shrine dedicated to the Mother Goddess religion, and he started to practice as a spirit priest (*thay cung*). He claimed that his mediumship, along with the establishment of his own shrine, demonstrated his devotion to the spirits and that in return he received blessings and favors from them. According to his uncle, the family also sponsored elaborate rituals at a temple to pray for their flourishing business and receive the spirits' favor. As the Mother Goddess religion has become more vital, Mr. Thao, as the head of his family, continues to adhere to the faith with the expectation of receiving more blessings from the spirits.

Unlike the Thao family's enterprise, the Nga family business of producing votive offerings is not based in the handicraft tradition or on family experience in the trade. Instead, the head of the family, Mrs. Nga, was first a master medium, who then decided to make votive offerings in order to supplement her income and increase the number of clients at her mediumship rituals. Mrs. Nga has practiced as a master medium since the early 1980s,[22] and in the post-Renovation period, she has been able to perform more rituals for her clients at a reduced cost due to her newly established enterprise of manufacturing paper votive offerings. In the Nga household, her sons and daughter-in-law are able to earn extra money by producing the offerings, in addition to cultivating and selling small plants in their nursery garden. As another benefit of this new occupation, her family can now provide offerings for their own rituals—as well as for healing and initiation rituals—without having to buy them from an outside vendor. The self-provisioning of votive offerings helps to cut down on the cost of Mrs. Nga's rituals, and thus increases the size of her clientele because she is able to offer clients these services at a lower cost.

The chief laborer in Mrs. Nga's business is her daughter-in-law, Mrs. Hoa, who did not have any experience or expertise in the making of the votive paper offerings before beginning to produce them with her mother-in-law. Mrs. Hoa used to work as a street trader in Hanoi, but now she stays at home to help her mother-in-law with the rituals, cooking the food offerings, preparing food trays, and cleaning the mother's shrine on ritual days. The rest of her time is spent making the votive offerings. The household buys the bamboo frames or skeletons, along with colorful papers and patterns for cutting the designs, in the neighboring village, where the materials for these kinds of offerings are sold. They then assemble the materials with glue handmade from sticky rice flour. Having recently learned skills from other

---

[21] Shaun Malarney, "Return to the Past? The Dynamics of Contemporary Religious and Ritual Transformation," in *Postwar Vietnam: Dynamics of a Transforming Society*, ed. Hy Van Luong (Singapore: Institute of Southeast Asian Studies, 2003), p. 243.

[22] See Nguyen Thi Hien, "The Religion of the Four Palaces: Mediumship and Therapy in Viet Culture," p. 80. Mrs. Nga is a master medium in a village not far from Hanoi, in Hung Yen province. She tells her life-story as an epic tale about the compassion Mother Goddesses have shown to her, a woman destined to be a medium. She suffered from insanity before the spirits called her to mediumship. After initiation, she was healed of her affliction. Eventually she built a shrine to the Mother Goddess religion and was endowed with abilities to open gates to spirit possession on behalf of her clients and to perform spiritual healings and divinations.

craftsmen, one of Mrs. Nga's sons is now able to weave the bamboo frames of the votive manikins, horses, elephants, boats, and ferries.

As an experienced medium, Mrs. Nga not only knows how to attract novice mediums in her village and region to come to her for either rituals or fortune-telling, but she is also skilled at managing her household business. Supported by the profits from performing rituals and producing votive offerings, her eldest son has been able to expand his nursery plant enterprise and trade in bonsais, enterprises that supplement the family income. All these earnings have allowed the family to renovate the shrine and the house, and to build a two-storey brick, flat-roofed house for the youngest son. Even with the combined efforts of the entire family running their business, Mrs. Nga always takes the time to thank the Mother Goddess and other deities for the blessings and favors that have been given to her family. As a gesture of reciprocity, she has helped to equip some of her peasant disciples who are so poor that they cannot afford the costs of ritual performances. Thus, Mrs. Nga provides them with the means to perform the rituals as a service to her community, which, according to her, they are supposed to do in order to restore the religious imbalance in their lives.

The methods by which Mr. Thao and Mrs. Nga run their votive-offering enterprises in the new market economy provide us with insights into religious revitalization in Vietnam. The spirit possession rituals have served as preconditions for the development of the votive-offerings handicraft enterprise and the related improvement of people's skills in this craft.

THE ART OF PRODUCING PAPER VOTIVE OFFERINGS AND FINDING CUSTOMERS IN THE OPEN-MARKET ECONOMY

Votive offerings of clothing, vehicles, money bills, and manikins are made of bamboo frames and wrapped with colorful papers and traditional decorated patterns. These offerings resemble real world goods, but must be crafted with vivid elaboration. The craftsmen acknowledge that some day their products will be burned into ashes in a second, but they still try to make them look as beautiful as possible. In the market economy, they produce the offerings on demand for the consumers who can afford more and more elaborate votive paper offerings to give to spirits.

The process of making the offerings requires skilled and non-skilled laborers of different ages. For example, Mr. Thao buys raw materials such as colorful papers from Dong Ho village and bamboo from the middlemen who trade in this forest product, and then he forms decorative patterns with the point of a sharp knife on colorful gold papers. His wife splits strings of bamboo and weaves bamboo frames, and his children, nephews, and nieces perform the simplest tasks of gluing the paper pieces onto the bamboo frames.

Mr. Thao recognizes that in order to compete in the open market he must constantly obtain new customers. Discussing innovations to his family tradition, he told me that he must constantly improve his handicraft techniques in order to meet the demands of the "mediums' artful tastes." He listens to the comments from his customers to learn about which offerings they view as "beautiful," so that he can make them accordingly. He also learns "the good and the beautiful" (*cai hay cai dep*) from craftsmen who come from the other provinces and work for him during the peak business season of the year, when Mr. Thao's family can barely finish all the orders in time. By hiring people with certain skills from Nam Ha province, he can learn some techniques that further enhance his business.

Mr. Thao and his fellow entrepreneurs in the open-market economy must also take into account the very different incomes of their clients when making decisions about which items to make and sell. The craftsmen produce the votive offerings in different sizes to accommodate their customers' financial situations. Whereas wealthy individuals are able to afford larger, elaborate, and more expensive offerings, people in the low-income bracket can usually only afford small, plain and relatively inexpensive offerings. Thus, the marketplace requires that these items be made available in a variety of sizes, styles, and prices. Subsequently, craftsmen of votive offerings categorize their products into three sizes: extra-large (*dai*), medium (*trung*), and small (*tieu*). Mr. Thao has learned that the medium-sized offerings seem to be consumed more than the other two types, for they are large enough to satisfy many people and are the most reasonably priced. Wealthy mediums or initiates buy the extra-large offerings for use at big rituals.

The adherents of the Mother Goddess religion are both urbanites and rural peasants, most of whom are not wealthy traders, though some scholars have characterized them in this way.[23] Thus, the offerings of different sizes and prices in the open market also serve the religious demands of customers who interpret offerings more luxurious in quality and quantity as representing their stronger devotion to the spirits, devotion which they trust will win them further blessings from the spirit. Those who can only afford small and simple votive offerings for their rituals have faith that blessings will come from their devotion to the spirits.

This busy, open-market trade in large and small votive offerings fuels competition between the entrepreneurs who produce and sell them. Thousands of people in Vietnam, such as Mrs. Hoa, Mrs. Nga's daughter-in-law, still earn some thousands of *dong* a day (less than US$1) by selling petty goods in the market. Their income is barely enough for their family to live on, as they can buy only rice and vegetables for their daily food supply. Often, they have no money left over for other basic needs. Consequently, there is tremendous incentive for people like Mrs. Hoa to begin producing and selling votive offerings in the market place. The good that comes from this, of course, is that these people are able to improve their living conditions and financial situations dramatically; the downside is that their success creates more competition, thus making it more difficult for these struggling entrepreneurs to sell and receive a fair price for their wares. As a result, compatibility between buyers and sellers becomes a crucial issue, determining who will sell more offerings and who will not.

From a cultural perspective, the interaction between the craftsmen and their consumers demonstrates the importance of personal compatibility (*co duyen, hop nhau*). Mrs. Them, a master spirit medium in Ha Dong town, on the outskirts of Hanoi, said that she bought beautiful and good offerings according to her tastes and from sellers or craftsmen with whom she is compatible (*co duyen*). This expression denotes people who are fated to have excellent relationships with one another, and

---

[23] See Kirsten W. Endres, "Spirit Mediumship and the Symbolic Construction of Self and Society in Modern Vietnam" (paper presented at the Association for Asian Studies Annual Meeting, New York, NY, March, 2003); Hong Ly Le, "Tin nguong Len dong tu cai nhin cua nguoi trong cuoc" [*Len Dong* Ritual from an Insider's Perspective] (paper presented at the International Conference, "Tin nguong tho Mau va Le hoi Phu Giay" [Mother Goddess Veneration and the Phu Giay Festival], organized by the Folklore Institute, Hanoi, 2001.

in the trade sphere, to partners who have good business relationships. Thus, the selling and buying of offerings reflect not only a relationship around goods, but also one depending on harmonious cultural behaviors.

Mr. Thao's flourishing business not only demonstrates that he enjoys compatible relationships with a number of buyers, but also that he has strong connections with other master mediums. The fact that he is a medium as well as a spirit priest (*thay cung*) reveals his dynamism and enhances his ability to associate with many mediums. Traditionally, a ceremony master must know the ancient writing system of Sino-Vietnamese manuscripts, which allows him to write petitions sheets to spirits and to perform the chants in this archaic language. However, a number of masters like Mr. Thao break this convention by using *quoc ngu*, the romanized modern Vietnamese language, instead. As a ceremony master, Mr. Thao conducts the ceremonies for his clients. In addition, he has other mediums come to his shrine to perform *len dong* rituals, and he has associated closely with other master mediums in the region. Thus, the network of mediums and clients that Mr. Thao has established contributes greatly to his increasing clientele.

A highly competitive arena forces Mr. Thao to adjust his traditional production to meet the demands of his customers. To keep up with business, he has to update his techniques continuously, widen his business partnerships, and add new decorated patterns in accordance with the mediums' tastes and requirements. Although Mr. Thao adapts to market demand in these decisive ways and appreciates the fact that becoming a spirit medium has led to the growth of his business, he does not view his success in such pragmatic terms. From his perspective, one that is shared with many spirit mediums, his success is the result of *loc.*

Further, the family handicraft tradition and history play a very important part in Mr. Thao's enterprise. For instance, Mr. Ho explained to me that the Thao family probably knows the meanings of all the offerings, why they are made, and their specific purposes, whereas new producers like Mrs. Nga's daughter-in-law and her sons might produce the offerings, but they lack knowledge of the tradition and its meanings. This knowledge can be an advantage to some craftsmen because customers may think that their family history and longer experience in the trade make their votive offerings comparatively more appropriate and pleasing to the gods. Moreover, the more experienced and skilled craftsmen are able to meet the demands of customers who want specific offerings created for them that are not part of the traditional sets. For instance, Mr. Thao has a number of customers who order "an elephant with nine tusks and a cock with nine spurs,"[24] which are seen as the most precious gifts according to a Vietnamese myth. In the myth, these gifts were offered to the Hung king, but in the current context, the sponsor wanted to offer these to the spirit of mountains and waters.

Mr. Ho added that a family familiar with the tradition could design the decorative patterns of the offerings in line with the Vietnamese style. One day we

---

[24] See Huu Ngoc, *Sketches for a Portrait of Vietnamese Culture* (Hanoi: The Gioi Publishers, 1995), p. 315. According to the legend, "The Genie of the Mountains and the Genie of the Waters" (*Son Tinh Thuy Tinh*), King Hung Vuong the Eighteenth had a remarkably beautiful daughter, My Nuong. The Genies of the Mountains and Waters both fell madly in love with the princess. The king told the two suitors that he would give his daughter to the first one who would bring to him a hundred plates of sticky rice, two hundred rice cakes, an elephant with nine tusks, a cock with nine spurs, and a horse with nice red hair. The Genie of the Mountains arrived first to the palace with the required presents, and he won the princess.

went to see an initiation ritual at Mrs. Nga's shrine, and one of my colleagues, an American scholar, pointed out that the decorative patterns of the offerings were mixed with Cambodian styles. Thus, the inexperienced producer may add what he or she sees as "beautiful" and "colorful" without paying attention to the decorative combinations of the traditional patterns. The alien patterns can pose some risk to this producer because customers may not see the offerings as appropriate for them to offer to the spirits. So, for example, Mr. Thao's traditional family offerings would have an advantage over Mrs. Nga's offerings in attracting some customers. Ultimately, however, regardless of tradition or experience, both these small entrepreneurs have learned how to capitalize on market demand generated by the adherents of Mother Goddess religion, even though they run the risk of violating the government's prohibition of spirit possession rituals.

Finally, because their enterprises have made them both more wealthy than the average Vietnamese, Mr. Thao and Mrs. Nga perform their rituals and run their businesses without worrying about the government's prohibition of the spirit possession rituals and the restrictions on burning and making votive offerings. However, Mr. Thao's uncle still remembers that the local authorities would show up to confiscate the tools and materials for making the offerings until the 1980s. The producers had to hide their wares and materials, he said, until after the local officials left, at which time the craftsmen would take out their tools again and recommence work.[25] Mrs. Nga was scared to death when her village policeman came to her ritual in August of 2003 and subsequently ordered her to stop her "superstitious" practice, including performing the ritual, doing divination, and making votive offerings. She contacted me while I was in Hanoi, seeking my help in getting her "official permission" to legitimize her practice. I advised her to establish good relationships with local authorities who might be able to help in order to avoid disturbing her practice and handicraft production. A week later, ignoring the warning of the local official, she resumed her practice and business, performing the initiation ceremony for her own daughter.

CONCLUSION

The votive-offering handicraft industry has developed substantially in post-Renovation Vietnam, integrating into the open-market economy. This development has been caused by the revitalization of *len dong* spirit possession rituals because votive offerings are so important in the context of the Mother Goddess religion. The recent evolution of the handicraft tradition itself has been shaped, in part, by the impact of the free-market economy, and the traditional handicraft product has been changed to meet the demands of consumers. Meanwhile, the famous handicraft skills involved in the creation of the Dong Ho prints, which are produced in the same region, are at risk of disappearing, even though this craft tradition has been praised in folk verses and government officials have advocated its revitalization. Despite such support, today there are a few craftsmen in Dong Ho village who produce these prints because the number of their customers has declined. At the local markets before Vietnamese lunar New Year (Tet), people no longer sell and buy the prints decorated with traditional themes. Instead, they buy more votive offerings, such as clothing, hats, and shoes, to offer to kitchen gods for the ritual in their honor on the

---

[25] See Malarney, *Culture, Ritual, and Revolution in Vietnam,* pp. 84-85.

twenty-third day of the twelfth month. They send the offerings off to heaven to report the passing year to the heaven king and, in return, to bring a new message from the king to the households. Or the people will buy statues of Di Lac, a happy, smiling manifestation of the Buddha, to insure that the coming year will be prosperous and lucky.[26] In contrast to the state's legitimatization of the Dong Ho prints, the use of the votive paper offerings has been discouraged by government restrictions. Despite such opposition, the rituals have become more widespread today, thanks to the revitalization of the so-called "superstitious" practices of *len dong*. The development of the votive-offerings handicraft industry in the open-market economy in response to both the high demand of consumers for the *len dong* rituals and self-motivated producers and practitioners exemplify the revitalization of folk practices in post-Renovation Vietnam.

---

[26] Nguyen Van Huy, "Tet Holidays: Ancestral Visits and Spring Journeys," in *Vietnam: Journeys of Body, Mind, and Spirit*, ed. Nguyen Van Huy and Laurel Kendall (Berkeley, CA: University of California Press, 2003), p. 70.

"CHILDREN OF THE SPIRITS, FOLLOWERS OF A MASTER": SPIRIT MEDIUMS IN POST-RENOVATION VIETNAM

Viveca Larsson and Kirsten W. Endres

INTRODUCTION

On a bright morning in the first lunar month of the year 2000, the old temple hidden in an alley of Hanoi's old quarter is buzzing with activity. An elderly spirit priest (*thay cung*) is reading prayers from a book written in Sino-Vietnamese characters while one of the male *chau van* musicians is beating a drum to add emphasis. Mrs. Tu, a thirty-seven-year-old owner of a small business and a medium for fourteen years, is sitting cross-legged in the middle of a low platform in front of the altar, her head bowed in prayer. In preparation for her *len dong* (spirit possession) ritual, the *thay cung* invites the spirits to "witness the offerings" (*chung le*) that have been decoratively arranged on large aluminum trays and placed on the altar. The ritual assistants (*hau dang*) are busy with preparing the spirits' robes and accessories according to the order in which the spirits are going to descend during the ritual. Mrs. Tu has invited a number of guests who are now arriving: her sister, her daughter, as well as some friends and fellow mediums. Some of them bring additional offerings that are carefully arranged on trays. They are warmly welcomed by the female temple master who helps with the offerings while talking to each and everyone. Everybody seems to be in a cheerful mood and eagerly anticipating the *len dong* ritual, which is soon to start. For the duration of approximately five hours, the gathered ritual community will concentrate their attention on the spirits embodied by Ms. Tu and will share a sense of divine presence while clapping their hands to the music, exchanging stories, smoking cigarettes, and receiving "blessed gifts" (*loc*) as a token of the spirits' benevolence.

In *len dong* mediumship, the concept of a ritual community features most prominently during a ritual performance. Mediums, regular devotees of the Four Palace religion, *chau van* musicians, and ritual assistants gather in a public temple (*den*) or in the private shrine (*dien*) of a temple master in order to arrange, perform, or

The spirit, the medium, and the audience all enjoy the ceremony. Photo by Viveca Larsson.

witness the ritual embodiment of the spirits associated with the four palaces (*Tu Phu*). With possibly very few exceptions, they strongly believe in the spirits' efficacy in bestowing health and material well-being, and many of them share a medium's fate (*can dong*) of having been summoned into the spirits' service (*hau thanh*). Victor Turner's concept of the *communitas* that evolves out of such liminal "moments in and out of time" comes to mind here.[1] But the notion of sharing a "heavy fate" (*nang so*) that can be eased only by becoming a medium also reaches beyond the boundaries of the ritual setting and creates a sense of belonging to a wider community of faithful adherents to the Four Palaces religion. This, however, does not mean that *len dong* mediums represent a cohesive group that subscribes to standardized religious doctrines and ritual knowledge. As a nonformalized religion, *len dong* mediumship strongly relies on individual temple masters who shape their followers' conceptualizations by their own personal motives, experiences, and levels of knowledge. In this essay, we shall focus on the community of *len dong* spirit mediums and the different social roles that are constructed within and around this community. In particular, we shall discuss how relationships among spirit mediums in general and between master mediums and their followers in particular are knit and nourished. Furthermore, we shall explore the role of *doi moi* (Renovation) in forming an idealized, nostalgic view of the past and will analyze the significance of *len dong* mediums' narratives in sifting and evaluating the dynamic changes that *len dong* mediumship has been experiencing in post-renovation Vietnam.

"CHILDREN OF THE SPIRITS..."

In contrast to the situation of ordinary believers, who visit the temples associated with the Four Palace religion in order to present small sets of offerings and pray for

---

[1] Victor Turner, *The Ritual Process: Structure and Anti-Structure* (Chicago, IL: Aldine Publishing, 1969), pp. 94-113.

their own and their families' well-being, a medium's fate (*can dong*) centers on the notion of a destined relationship with one or several spirits of the *Tu Phu* pantheon.[2] When a destined medium's sufferings have reached a critical stage, he or she usually seeks the help of a reputed fortune-teller (*thay boi*) or a fortune-telling medium (*dong boi*) who—depending on what the reading holds—decides whether or not it would be advisable, or even imperative, for this person to enter into the spirits' service. If the destined person for some reason does not or does not yet wish to be initiated as a medium, then he or she is given the option of having a special ritual organized in order to ask for a delay. Often, the decision to enter mediumship (*ra dong*) is accompanied by much anguish. Mrs. Vuong relates her story:

> I have been destined [to become a medium] for a long time, but I kept it secret because of my financial situation. I was very afraid because each ritual is so expensive, so I was pondering how I could manage to follow [the call of the spirits]—I would commit a deadly sin if I didn't follow, but then again where should the money come from?[3]

In contemporary Hanoi, *len dong* rituals have become increasingly sumptuous and expensive. A modest initiation ritual may cost over three hundred US dollars, and each *len dong* ritual costs at least two hundred US dollars. Considering that these amounts are roughly half of the annual income of an average Hanoian, entering into mediumship can place a heavy burden on the family budget.[4] However, mediums see this expenditure as an investment that earns this-worldly interest, since they believe the problems in their lives will significantly ease after the initiation. Mrs. Vuong felt that her personal situation would not improve unless she entered mediumship: "I saw that my life was too miserable. I felt that ever since I got married with my husband, everything I did was doomed—my emotional life [*tinh cam*], my domestic life [*doi noi*], and my communal life [*doi ngoai*]—everything was just miserable."

However, since her husband strongly opposes *len dong* mediumship, Mrs. Vuong has to hide the fact that she is now a practicing medium. She therefore keeps her ritual robes at her master's temple and is very anxious lest her husband become suspicious. On the other hand, relatives may also be an important source of support for a medium. As an example, Mr. Duc wanted his young daughter to become a medium because he believed that it would give her high morals. He explains that the Four Palace religion teaches people how to be good, and he believes the blessings bestowed by the spirits upon their worldly children will also benefit their families. As a little girl, Mr. Duc's daughter always followed him on his visits to different temples, and although the entire family believes in the spirits, it is only she who has entered mediumship.

A destined person becomes a medium with the help of a master (*dong thay*). Master mediums either operate in their own private shrines (*dien*) or in public

---

[2] See Kirsten W. Endres, "Spirit Performance and the Ritual Construction of Personal Identity in Modern Vietnam," and Karen Fjelstad and Lisa Maiffret, "Gifts from the Spirits: Spirit Possession and Personal Transformation among Silicon Valley Spirit Mediums," this volume.

[3] Interview with Mrs. Vuong, August 2002, Hanoi.

[4] General Statistical Office, *Result of the Survey on Households Living Standards 2002* (Hanoi: Statistical Publishing House, 2004), p. 86.

temples (*den*) in their custody. For a medium, it is important to choose the right master. Usually, a medium would base her choice on recommendations by friends or relatives, age compatibility, and the master's personality. It is important to select a kind master, but equally important is his or her knowledge of the spirits and proper ritual conduct. Last but not least, the question of money may also influence a medium's choice because initiation rituals may differ considerably in price depending on the master's requests. Whether or not a master medium accepts a person as a follower may also depend on a variety of reasons. For Master Canh, the most important condition is that teacher and student have a predestined affinity (*nhan duyen*):

> When I feel comfortable with a person, I readily accept [him or her as a follower]. But there are also cases when it becomes obvious that I don't like a person, even though he or she may have a lot of money, and this proves we do not have that affinity [*khong co duyen*].[5]

Some people are destined to become mediums. Photo by Viveca Larsson.

The master-follower relationship is sealed with a ritual called *doi bat nhang*, which literally means "carrying an incense holder on one's head." It involves a petition or "decree" (*lenh*) written in Sino-Vietnamese characters with the name and age of the initiate, votive money, areca nuts, fruits, and cigarettes as offerings, and an

---

[5] Interview with Master Canh, March 2005, Hanoi.

incense holder. The new follower sits down in front of the altar and covers his or her head with a red veil (*khan phu dien*), the most important ritual insignia of a medium. The master then invokes the spirits to accept the new follower. A sign of divine approval is sought by throwing two ancient coins (*xin dai*). Then the votive money is burnt, and the decree is placed upon the temple altar—it symbolizes the new "incense child" (*con nhang*) of the temple and is kept there for life. In earlier times, temples kept an incense holder for each follower, and when these followers came to worship at the temple on the first and fifteenth of the lunar month, they lit a joss stick. Temples in rural areas may still maintain this tradition, but as the number of mediums in the capital kept growing, urban masters abolished the practice of keeping numerous incense holders, for lack of space, and now keep only their followers' decrees.

After the *doi bat nhang* ritual, the new disciple is invited to participate in various temple activities, for example, ritual performances of the master or of one of his or her followers, and to join pilgrimages to temples in other provinces. The new medium thus gradually becomes acquainted with the group network of the master's followers and, as part of the preparations for the initiation ritual, with the master's teachings and style of ritual performance. The initiation ritual is called "the opening of the palaces" (*mo phu*), and the initiate can choose at which temple he or she would like the initiation to take place—usually this is the master's temple, but the master can also "borrow" a temple that is in another master's custody.

During the initiation ritual, the four palaces (symbolized by four large bowls covered with votive paper in the colors of the palaces) are opened by the mandarin spirits embodied in the master. Then the Second Lady is summoned to "hand over the role of the medium" to the initiate. While the master withdraws from the platform in front of the altar, the new medium starts to perform his or her first *len dong* ritual. Stage fright is not uncommon. Master Canh comments that new mediums often remind him of fish out of water since they are "new to the surroundings," but he adds that mediums with a "sincere heart" (*that tam*) and true religious devotion can rely on the spirits' guidance during their ritual performance.

Mediums usually feel that their lives ease noticeably after entering into mediumship.[6] At the same time, mediums shoulder a great responsibility since they are now obliged to serve the spirits for the rest of their lives by performing at least two *len dong* rituals each year. As mentioned above, this obligation can have serious economic implications, although mediums stress that it is the "sincere heart" that counts rather than presenting the spirits with lots of expensive offerings. Besides fulfilling their ritual duties, mediums have to lead a virtuous life (*song dao duc*); if they failed to do so, they would incur the spirits' punishment in the form of illness, bad luck, or loss that would affect the whole family. But the spirits do not necessarily transmit their rules (*phep thanh*) through divine revelations. The adage "children of the spirits, but followers of a master" (*con nha thanh nhung co canh nha dong*) in fact suggests that the master plays a crucial role in providing his or her followers with spiritual guidance and instructions for proper ritual and moral conduct. The following section will provide deeper insights into the teacher-student relationship

---

[6] See Endres, "Spirit Performance and the Ritual Construction of Personal Identity," Fjelstad and Maiffret, "Gifts from the Spirits," and Barley Norton, "'Hot-Tempered' Women and 'Effeminate' Men: The Performance of Music and Gender in Vietnamese Mediumship," this volume.

between masters and their followers and explore what it means to become a "good medium."

"...BUT FOLLOWERS OF A MASTER"

Both male and female mediums can become masters. However, prestigious master mediums presiding over prosperous temples seem predominantly to be male, at least in an urban space like Hanoi.[7] As one male master puts it, "'one male medium equals one thousand female mediums' [*mot dong nam bang ngan dong nu*], both in terms of numbers and significance because men are not only able to perform rituals, but they can also teach, and they are more skillful in praying and preparing the offerings." The idea that male intellectual abilities are superior to those of females derives from Confucian conceptions that associated knowledge with masculinity and reserved societal leadership roles for men of learning.[8] This bias also extended into the spiritual realm since men were traditionally given a strong preference in handling important ritual affairs from which women were usually excluded. Sources dating back to the French colonial period indicate that male mediums engaged in the socially esteemed worship of Saint Tran, whereas mediums of the Four Palace religion were exclusively female and were disdained by those in "good society."[9] Interestingly, the resurgence of mediumship in the *doi moi* era has facilitated an overlapping of these formerly separate and gendered ritual realms: just as the worship of Saint Tran is no longer confined to male mediums,[10] the Four Palace religion is no longer an exclusive realm for female practitioners.[11] Though some mediums (male and female) still claim male superiority, this view is most certainly not shared by all. One female master maintains, for example, that females even have a deeper understanding of the holy mothers because they themselves are (most often) caring mothers. In contrast, Thanh, a young assistant to a female temple master, sees no gendered difference between male and female masters' competencies. For him, a master's skillfulness is not determined by his or her gender, but instead is based on personal and individual talent. However, he adds that in reality, "people may still think more highly about male mediums than female mediums," which may be a reason for the apparent dominance of male master mediums in contemporary Hanoi.

---

[7] Barley Norton, "Music and Possession in Vietnam" (PhD dissertation, SOAS, University of London, 2000), p. 67.

[8] Luong Van Hy, *Revolution in the Village: Tradition and Transformation in North Vietnam, 1925-1988* (Honolulu, HI: University of Hawai'i Press, 1992), p. 70; Alexander Soucy, "The Buddha's Blessing: Gender and Buddhist Practice in Hanoi" (PhD dissertation, Australian National University, Canberra, 1999), p. 228.

[9] See Thien Do, *Vietnamese Supernaturalism: Views from the Southern Region* (London and New York, NY: RoutledgeCurzon, 2003), pp. 97-105; Phan Ke Binh, *Viet Nam Phong Tuc* [Vietnamese Customs] (Ho Chi Minh City: Nha Xuat Ban Thanh Pho Ho Chi Minh, 1995 [1915]), pp. 239-40; Pham Quynh Phuong, "Hero and Deity: Empowerment and Contestation in the Veneration of Tran Hung Dao in Contemporary Vietnam" (PhD dissertation, La Trobe University, Australia, 2005), p. 165; as well as "Tran Hung Dao and the Mother Goddess Religion," this volume.

[10] See Pham Quynh Phuong, "Tran Hung Dao and the Mother Goddess Religion."

[11] See Norton, "'Hot-Tempered' Women and 'Effeminate' Men."

Whether or not a medium can become a master is first of all a matter of his or her fate, which is regarded as "heavier" than the fate of an ordinary medium. But equally important are his or her knowledge and social abilities. A *chau van* musician relates his definition of a proficient master as follows:

> A proficient master medium ... has to be well grounded [*phai co goc*] and has to have thorough knowledge of the Mother [Goddess] religion, [he or she] has to know all the legends and holy days of the Four Palace religion. Moreover, a master has to guide [the followers'] hearts and get a good reputation in order to be called proficient.

A good reputation is often established by a medium's ability to cure illnesses, in particular if these illnesses have been caused by "yin" disorders, for example, insanity.[12] Master Canh relates that one of the first mediums he initiated was a madman whose family insisted that Canh should "open the palaces" for him. This was a very risky decision for a new master since it would have ruined his reputation forever if the man did not show any signs of recovery after the initiation. But luckily he did, and after three years as a medium, his madness vanished completely. Other masters may become reputed to be expert fortune-tellers, an ability that is said to have been bestowed upon them by the spirits (*an loc boi*). Master Phuong, for example, was a famous fortune-telling medium (*dong boi*) who transmitted messages of the Seventh Prince to those who came to seek her advice on different matters at her private temple near the Pomelo Market (Cho Buoi) in Hanoi. After thirteen years of practicing mediumship, Phuong, who is now in her mid-thirties, decided to operate as a master and started to organize initiation rituals.

Once mediums have established themselves as masters, they have to make sure their reputations do not get damaged. For this reason, novice mediums are required to perform exclusively at the temple of their initiation during the first three years. During this time, the master teaches his novice followers the proper rules of ritual performance and monitors their progress during their *len dong* rituals. Most masters take their followers on pilgrimages to famous temples throughout the northern region. These temples are usually dedicated to a certain spirit of the *Tu Phu* pantheon, and masters "present" their novice mediums to these spirits by conducting a short introduction ritual called *trinh giau*. After three years, mediums are considered to have had sufficient training and may perform at any temple of their choice. Master Canh comments:

> [The three-year period is necessary] because if [new mediums] perform inadequately, how can you let them go to the provinces? ... Sometimes, a medium doesn't even know in which order [he or she] is supposed to serve the spirits; it is terrible! If I am with [the medium], I can correct [him or her] right away, but if I'm not there ... that would leave me in a very bad light. People would say: 'Certainly, the master of this medium isn't worth a thing; this is why this medium also performs [the ritual] so badly!'

---

[12] The yin world is associated with the dead, ancestors, and with spirits; see Nguyen Thi Hien, "The Religion of the Four Palaces: Mediumship and Therapy in Viet Culture" (PhD dissertation, Indiana University, 2002), pp. 103-8.

Besides the basic rules of proper ritual conduct, master mediums may also develop their personal styles of spirit embodiment.[13] This involves not only variations in their bodily movements or the use of certain accessories for certain spirits,[14] but also variations in the selection of spirits embodied during a ritual: masters with the spirit root (*can*) of a less commonly embodied spirit of the *Tu Phu* pantheon, for example, may pass this inclination on to their followers and thus notably shape a temple community's performative focus and style.

A proficient master has to set an example for his followers, not only in terms of ritual conduct, but also in displaying polite manners and high morals. Masters require their followers to conform to the rules of the group, citing the adage "whichever group you go with, you have to follow their rules" (*di co nao canh nao phai theo canh day*), but it is the master's responsibility to teach these rules:

> If a master knows how to teach his followers really well, then the students will also be proficient. A master who is ridiculous will bring forth ridiculous students; if a master likes telling dirty jokes, his students will do so as well. This is why a master always has to be careful about such things, and this is quite difficult.[15]

Temple communities may significantly differ in size depending on the number of followers a master has gathered, and bonds between followers are naturally stronger within smaller temple communities. Long-established and well-reputed masters may have several hundreds of followers for whom they feel responsibility— Master Duong compares his task as a master with that of a train guard who can cause immeasurable disaster if he performs his job carelessly. Masters often perceive their work as hard, but at the same time rewarding, in particular if they witness improvements in the lives of their followers. Many mediums assert that they feel that they are raised inside the religious community as if in a family, and they refer to their master not only as a teacher (*thay*) but also as a parent. Moreover, they feel respect and gratitude to their master, who they believe saved their lives by initiating them. When a master conducts his or her own rituals, the temple is usually crowded with followers, which mediums believe will render the ritual more efficacious. Besides attending ritual events, mediums often pay a visit to the temple on the first and the fifteenth of the lunar month and pay respect to their master on the occasion of the lunar New Year (*Tet Nguyen Dan*).

As mentioned above, masters also organize pilgrimages to remote temples. These trips usually start at night or very early in the morning and may take up to several days. For a master's group of mediums, as well as noninitiated followers, these trips provide a joyous opportunity to get to know each other more closely, as well as to experience a temporary release from their daily chores.[16]

---

[13] See Claire Chauvet, "Du commerce avec les esprits des Quatre Palais: Étude d'un culte de possession à Ha Noi (Viet Nam)" (PhD dissertation, Université de Paris-X, 2004), p. 227.

[14] For example, the Tenth Prince (*Ong Hoang Muoi*) most often dances with a flag since he is said to have been skillful in martial arts. However, master mediums who like to stress the prince's alleged love for poetry prefer to perform a dance holding a fan (as a writing sheet) and a joss stick (symbolizing a pen).

[15] Interview with Master Canh, March 2005, Hanoi.

[16] See Philip Taylor, *Goddess on the Rise: Pilgrimage and Popular Religion in Vietnam* (Honolulu, HI: University of Hawai'i Press, 2004) for a detailed account of pilgrimages in southern

SPIRITUAL SOLIDARITY AND MUNDANE JEALOUSY

Mediums claim they feel a good sense of community among the "children of the spirits," in general and between followers of the same master, in particular. Their shared fate eases communication between them and often fosters strong friendships and mutual help. Mrs. Hong, for example, offered an unemployed fellow medium a job in her flower shop, and Mrs. Mai offered to store the ritual robes of her fellow mediums who had to hide their ritual practice from their families. Mediums also invite each other to participate in their rituals, to which the invitees usually contribute some money and additional offerings. The redistribution of offerings (*phat loc*) as blessed gifts during the ritual performance also acts as an important mechanism for consolidating relationships between a medium and his or her invitees, as well as between masters and their followers. Although Hanoi's hectic pace may not allow for many leisurely social gatherings, the mediums of a small village in the outskirts of Hanoi enjoy meeting in the temple or at their homes every morning to exchange stories about life and mediumship.

However, just as in a large extended family, mediums sometimes vie with each other for their master's attention and appreciation or engage in petty quarrels. Mrs. Nguyet, a relatively wealthy, novice medium of Master Canh's group, fell out with most of his followers because she made a huge fuss over the fact that one of them, Mr. Duc, did not attend her ritual and did not send any contribution for it, although she (Mrs. Nguyet) previously had contributed 200,000 Vietnamese dong (approximately twelve US dollars, which is a rather large amount) to his ritual. It turned out that Mr. Duc was feeling sick that day, and, moreover, as a factory worker, he did not have enough money to make such a big contribution. Master Canh then had to act as a mediator between the two of them, but this episode and the fact that Mrs. Nguyet displays her wealth too conspicuously created animosity among his followers, and she no longer invites them to attend her rituals. Feelings of envy and jealousy are not uncommon; for example, they often arise when another medium can afford to buy more expensive ritual robes and offerings or if his or her performance is praised as particularly skillful.[17] Jealousy may occur when a medium thinks his or her master pays more attention to other followers. In fact it often happens that a master does pay more attention to the novice mediums. But Master Canh explains that he has to "pamper" the newly initiated more than his more experienced followers when he distributes divine gifts during his performances because, just as in a family, as the elder siblings grow up, they receive fewer special treats since these are reserved for their young siblings. Generally, a master should not show favoritism toward certain followers, but Master Canh says this is very difficult because he does not feel the same closeness or destined affinity (*nhan duyen*) with each of his followers.

Masters of different temples often know each other or have heard about each other by word of mouth. *Chau van* musicians who typically play at many different temples are an important source of information and gossip about what is going on in

---

Vietnam; also see Alexander Soucy, "Pilgrims and Pleasure-seekers," in *Consuming Urban Culture in Contemporary Vietnam*, ed. Lisa B. W. Drumond and Mandy Thomas (London and New York, NY: Routledge, 2003), pp. 125-37.

[17] See Endres, "Spirit Performance and the Ritual Construction of Personal Identity."

other groups. With perhaps a few exceptions, master mediums are usually not in close contact with each other.[18] Since gathering a large clientele of devoted followers enhances a master's status and prestige, relationships between masters of different temples can be rather competitive. Furthermore, there are few occasions for masters to meet each other because there is no such thing as a council of masters in *len dong* mediumship.

NOSTALGIA FOR THE PAST

The openness and ease with which master mediums practice *len dong* mediumship as a profession and build their temple communities is a rather recent phenomenon in Vietnam. After 1954, the Communist Party staged a zealous secularization campaign aimed at stamping out so-called unsound customs (*hu tuc*) and wasteful superstitions (*me tin di doan*). Ritual practices that engaged supernatural forces in dealing with human agonies and anxieties were strictly banned, and spirit practitioners were portrayed as unscrupulous and mercenary frauds who took advantage of people's credulity and had concerns for nothing but their own personal gain.[19] *Len dong* rituals were branded as a superstitious squandering of labor and resources that lacked any "scientific basis" (*co so khoa hoc*) and were harmful to the people's economy and ideology (*tu tuong*). In a 1975 educational primer on "establishing new customs," two cartoons depict *len dong* settings with the following captions: "How utterly nonsensical a medium is! They abandon their work and spend their money for ridiculous rituals!" "Inviting each other to a *doi bat nhang* ritual—it is lavish and expensive, and brings forth nothing but more worries!"[20] Spirit temples were destroyed, turned into warehouses, or simply abandoned; ritual paraphernalia were confiscated or thrown into village ponds; and many diviners, spirit priests, and other ritual experts had to undergo a period of reeducation (*cai tao*).

These severe restrictions notwithstanding, *len dong* rituals were henceforth conducted in secret, usually in small private shrines, but mediums who could afford it also went by train to remote temples in the mountainous region, even though the authorities there were said to be even stricter than in the Red River delta. The following narration is an edited summary of octogenarian Master Thuyet's account of the "hard times" she went through as a medium initiated in the mid 1960s:

> In the past, it was so difficult [*kho khan lam*] to perform a ritual. Robes were not readily available—I only had one single robe for all the spirits! The fabric could be found in shops on Hang Ngang or Hang Dao Street, but I had to be careful since trading was illegal. I would whisper to the shopkeeper what I wanted, and the bargain took place out of sight under the staircase. Later, I was able to buy another robe, so I had one for the lady spirits and one for the mandarin spirits. When I went to a temple to perform a ritual, I placed the robes on the bottom of a basket and pretended to be a vegetable seller by putting veggies on top. Spirit

---

[18] See also Nguyen Thi Hien, "The Religion of the Four Palaces," p. 96.

[19] Shaun Malarney, *Culture, Ritual, and Revolution in Vietnam* (New York, NY, and London: RoutledgeCurzon, 2002), p. 83.

[20] *Xay dung nhung phong tuc tap quan moi* [Building New Customs] (Hanoi: So Van Hoa Thong Tin, 1975), p. 43.

insignia like swords or sabres could be improvised, but flags were not available, so for the Tenth Prince, mediums would wave their red veil [*khan phu dien*] instead. Votive money [*vang*] and paper objects were not available either. During the period of state subsidy [*thoi gian bao cap*] I had to sell twenty kilos of dried noodles in order to have enough money to serve the spirits! As for offerings, we only had some fruit, like five tangerines for a poor medium and ten for a rich one, some areca nuts, and maybe a few pieces of candy. During a ritual, only five to ten people were present, and all of them were mediums. We would talk very silently for fear of being discovered and arrested by the police. We had to perform the rituals without music [*hau vo*], and nobody dared clap their hands during the dances of the female spirits. At that time, it was very difficult for the *chau van* musicians to make a living. Mediums also used the red veil to mark the descent and ascent of the different spirits, but they did not change robes since they only had a single one or two. The movements were the same as nowadays, but the ritual would not take longer than an hour since there was no music, and we could not change robes and distribute a lot of offerings as blessed gifts. When Nguyen Van Linh became general secretary in 1986, things got better and I started to buy lots of scarves and robes for *len dong*![21]

Master Thuyet's narration highlights the tremendous effort that master mediums and their followers had to make in order to keep the community of spirit mediums alive during the period of state subsidy. Before *doi moi*, not all of the destined mediums dared to be initiated. Mrs. Huong says that at that time being a medium would have significantly decreased her chances of finding a husband because very few people dared to be associated with "superstitious practices." Although she had severe problems due to her *can*, she gave in to her desire to get married and have a family and decided to pray instead of being initiated. It was only after 1986 that she finally felt it was safe to enter mediumship. Many elderly mediums relate stories of being caught by the authorities and having their identity cards and robes confiscated. Sometimes they allegedly received a warning by the spirits in their dreams and avoided the arrest. But they were not always so lucky. Master Ngoc narrates:

One day we were going to a temple close to Hanoi. We stayed there from the morning until the evening and prayed and performed and at nine o'clock in the evening, the police came. All the authorities, policemen, and villagers came to arrest people, and they took away all our identity cards. They asked: "Who is the leader, the organizer of this superstition?" Everybody was so afraid and moved aside, but I said: "I am. I am the organizer for this." They wanted me to sign [a confession], but I refused. I said: "OK, I have led people here to pray and worship, but you have also made a mistake. If it was forbidden, you should have put up a sign telling that it was forbidden! We have been here praying all day, and nobody told us anything. We didn't come here to make trouble, to break the law, or murder; we pray because it is a sacred temple and the landscape here is beautiful. We come here with gifts, with good things, and we do not harm the local people![22]

---

[21] Interview with Master Thuyet, January 2004, Hanoi.

[22] Interview with Master Ngoc, May 2000, Hanoi.

However, the police refused to return the identity cards and robes, however hard Master Ngoc tried to convince them to return them. For several days, she continued to discuss the issue with the local authorities and boldly stood up to them, trying to appeal to their respect for the late president:

> I quoted Ho Chi Minh's words, saying "First-time thieves may be released!" I told them, "I am sure that when you were in the battlefield, your mothers came here to pray so that you are now back and have power. Of course, it was wrong of me that I didn't report that we were going to worship here, but you were wrong not to tell us outsiders that it was wrong. It is our first time, and you should think of that and forgive us. If we made a mistake, you can make us pay a fine; this is more reasonable. Please give us our robes and identity cards back, otherwise [my followers] will say it is my fault that I got them into trouble, and their husbands will kill me." I said if they didn't give back our things, I would jump into a well and that would make the problem worse. After that, they returned the things and even arranged for my transport back to Hanoi, which also saved my dignity, and I returned to Hanoi to give the robes back to my followers.[23]

Mediums claim that the Four Palace religion survived because there was a strong faith in every medium. Mr. Tam, a medium and organizer of pilgrimages, notes that during those difficult years, there used to be a really nice and cheerful community of mediums. Sometimes they met in the temple, where they would stay for the whole day to pray, chat, and to share a meal. According to his opinion, a meal brings people together regardless of their wealth or backgrounds. These were hard times, he adds, but he remembers them as "happy days" because there was a strong feeling of solidarity. In contrast, he feels that nowadays many people just come and go and do not seem to have time to reflect and pray; they just come to the temple for blessed gifts from the spirits.

This nostalgia for the past is consistent with Mila Rosenthal's findings among retired female factory workers in Hanoi, who fondly remember the period of state subsidy as a time when there were no rich and poor, and "[e]veryone was equal."[24] The shared hardships during those times of severe food shortages had fostered neighborly solidarity and sentimental relations (*tinh cam*) that have been gradually replaced by a rush for economic success and material gain, corresponding with the rising materialism of the post-Renovation era. At the same time, the slackening of Party-state restrictions on ritual practices and the intensification of market relations have facilitated a resurgence of religious activities, as well as a considerable increase in ritual expenditures.[25] The impact of this development on *len dong* mediumship will be the focus of the next section.

---

[23] Ibid.

[24] Mila Rosenthal, "'Everyone was Equal': Nostalgia and Anxiety among Women Workers in a State-Owned Textile Factory," in *Doi Moi in Wirtschaft und Gesellschaft: Soziale und ökonomische Transformation in Vietnam*, ed. Rainer Klump and Gerd Mutz (Marburg: Metropolis-Verlag, 2002), p. 208.

[25] See, for example, John Kleinen, *Facing the Future, Reviving the Past: A Study of Social Change in a Northern Vietnamese Village* (Singapore: Institute of Southeast Asian Studies, 1999).

EMBODYING MARKET RELATIONS

Vietnamese official and scholarly discourse distinguishes between religion (*ton giao*) and belief (*tin nguong*).[26] Whereas *ton giao* designates institutionalized religions such as Buddhism, Christianity, and Islam, *tin nguong* refers to popular religious beliefs and practices, such as ancestor and spirit worship. In this essay, we have chosen to speak of the Four Palace religion as a *religion* rather than a popular religious practice because mediums subscribe to a belief in a system of symbolic representations and practices that provides them with a framework for addressing their human concerns. Since the beginning of *doi moi*, the conception of *tin nguong* has gradually widened and now seems to include a broader range of beliefs and practices than before.[27] However, whereas many of the temples dedicated to the spirit pantheon of the Four Palace religion have received official recognition as historical sites (*di tich lich su*), spirit mediumship is still lingering on the edge of illegality and so far has not been acknowledged by state authorities as a reputable religious practice.[28] Yet since the early 1990s, interventions by local authorities have gradually subsided and given way to tolerance. Nowadays, the police no longer bother to interfere with mediums' ritual practices: Master Canh's private temple is located on the top floor of his house, located in an alley of a densely populated neighborhood. When a neighbor reported him to the police because he felt disturbed by the amplified *chau van* music that reverberated for hours throughout the vicinity, the police just kindly asked Master Canh to please turn down the volume. As for the *len dong* rituals, they explained to his outraged neighbor that they had no legal justification to interfere since there was freedom of belief (*tu do tin nguong*).

The onset of *doi moi* triggered feverish endeavors throughout the country to rebuild, renovate, and refurbish religious structures, such as ancestral halls, Buddhist pagodas, village communal houses, and temples dedicated to the worship of spirits and deified heroes. Master mediums were able to resume their duties associated with their roles as custodians and owners of temples; some of them had managed to rescue and hide ancient statues from burnt-down temples and now sought the permission of the old temple masters to place them on the altars of their newly built private temples. In rural areas, as well as in the capital, public temples were rebuilt with the help of donations from the population and the approval of the authorities. Mediums now have more options in choosing the master and temple of their initiation, and they are free to be initiated at a temple that is considered to be particularly sacred (*thieng*).

In contemporary Hanoi, it seems that the number of initiated mediums has been growing rapidly. At the same time, the religious revitalization has also widened the existing avenues for generating an income from spirit mediumship. Shops in Hang Quat and Hang Ma openly display their range of supplies for *len dong* mediums, whole family enterprises earn their livelihood by manufacturing votive paper

---

[26] See Pham Quynh Phuong, "Tran Hung Dao and the Mother Goddess Religion."

[27] Nguyen Thi Hien, "The Religion of the Four Palaces," p. 77; and Shaun K. Malarney, "Return to the Past? The Dynamics of Contemporary Religious and Ritual Transformation," in *Postwar Vietnam: Dynamics of a Transforming Society*, ed. Hy Van Luong (Singapore: ISEAS, 2003).

[28] For a discussion of the changing official attitude, see Karen Fjelstad and Nguyen Thi Hien, "Introduction," this volume.

offerings,[29] and *chau van* musicians, ritual assistants, and spirit priests (*thay cung*) . who specialize in prayers that precede a *len dong* ritual enjoy a busy schedule of engagements that often requires them to perform at several rituals per day. With an increasing number of followers, master mediums can also become quite wealthy. Although ritual fees and donations from followers are mostly used to maintain and enlarge the temple, this income usually also has to sustain the master and his or her family. Master mediums therefore tend to stress their moral integrity by expressing their own contempt for mercenary materialism[30] and by emphasizing their efforts to help poor destined mediums to cover their costs. Mediums generally acknowledge that no master can carry out his or her duties free of charge, as charity (*lam phuc*), but masters who are felt to overcharge their followers may be accused of "trading in spirits" (*buon than ban thanh*), and this may damage their reputations quite significantly.

Mediums who were initiated during the period of state subsidy view the substantial growth of their community with mixed feelings. On the positive side, they feel that spirit mediumship is emerging from the margins of society, where it had been disdained as involving obsolete superstitions practiced by backward (*lac hau*) and uneducated simpletons—and is now more widely accepted as a respectable religious practice. On the negative side, however, elderly mediums criticize the new generation of mediums for not properly observing the spirits' rules and for entering into mediumship in order to tap the spirits' assumed efficacy for the sole purpose of improving their material well-being and economic success.[31]

The intensification of market relations has not only enhanced popular belief in the spirits' efficacy in fostering economic success but also contributed to "new" spirits associated with trade being adopted into the pantheon.[32] An example is the Second Lady Cam Duong (*Co Doi Cam Duong*). Since she is a recent addition to the spirits embodied during *len dong* rituals, the Second Lady Cam Duong's rank in the sequence of spirit embodiment is a contentious issue among master mediums. To illustrate this point, Master Canh once related a lengthy discussion about the issue of whether the Second Lady Cam Duong should be "served" (*hau*) before the Third Lady or after the Little Lady. In contrast, octogenarian Master Thuyet advocates that the Second Lady Cam Duong should not be included in the *len dong* mediums' spirit pantheon:

> I'm telling you, the Second Lady Cam Duong is not part of the spirits' pantheon. This pantheon comprises [twelve holy princesses], but not the Second Lady Cam Duong. So this is why I follow [the teachings of] my old master and serve [the spirits] correctly. But nowadays, the newcomers [*thanh nien*] have changed many things. ... Mainly mediums who trade in cloth serve [the Second Lady Cam

---

[29] See Nguyen Thi Hien, "'A Bit of a Spirit Favor Is Equal to a Load of Mundane Gifts': Votive Paper Offerings of *Len Dong* Rituals in Post-Renovation Vietnam," in this volume.

[30] See Pham Quynh Phuong, "Hero and Deity," pp. 224-25.

[31] Increased materialism is also an issue among overseas Vietnamese mediums living in the United States; see Karen Fjelstad, "'We Have *Len Dong* Too': Transnational Aspects of Spirit Possession," in this volume.

[32] The assembly of spirits embodied during a *len dong* ritual is essentially open to accommodate new additions; another example is the addition of Tran Hung Dao to the pantheon (see Pham Quynh Phuong, "Tran Hung Dao and the Mother Goddess Religion," in this volume).

Duong], because she used to trade in silk. She died during a sacred hour [*gio thieng*] and thus became a genie [*hien thanh*], but she does not belong to the spirits' pantheon![33]

Furthermore, and this is particularly true for urban mediumship, the growing prosperity has set new standards in ritual requirements concerning such details as the amount and quality of offerings for redistribution, and the use of votive paper offerings, spirit robes, and costume jewelry. For destined mediums from the poorer levels of society, an initiation has thus become almost unaffordable. Last but not least, many mediums are said to engage in status competition by lavishly displaying their wealth during their *len dong* rituals, and some even go into debt in order to impress their invitees. Master Duong, who is in his late forties, expresses his disapproval as follows:

Nowadays, many mediums borrow money in order to *len dong*, what for? To compete, to vie with each other; they see their friend give one piece, so they have to give ten pieces! But this is so dangerous; it can hurl the whole family economy into crisis ... After coming home from a ritual, they start fighting with their husbands and children and run away helter-skelter, then they start embezzling money little by little in order to have money to perform and again run away helter-skelter ... Many people think that nowadays they just have to *len dong* and they will have a lot of money, right? Money is [the fruit of] my labor, so how can it be a religious thing now, this cannot be right![34]

Master Canh is approximately the same age as Master Duong, and many of his followers live on very modest incomes. He generally thinks that a medium's heart (*tam*) is more important than the amount of money he or she spends on *len dong*, but at the same time he upholds the view that the amount spent on *len dong* rituals naturally adjusts to the current overall economic situation:

[The amount spent on rituals] adapts to economic circumstances. If the country prospers, mediums spend a lot on rituals, but if the social economy drops, then ritual expenditure also drops. [Spending a lot on rituals] does not necessarily mean that a medium competes [*dua*]. It all depends on the heart [*tam*] of the medium. I never assess a ritual according to the amount spent. But just like [when I buy clothes] for my parents, I have to buy beautiful clothes for the holy ladies and the holy mandarins because who would buy ugly clothes for their parents? Or talking about offerings, would you present your parents with rotten meat or a burnt chicken? [Buying beautiful robes and offerings] means I respect the spirits like my parents, and it is the heart of the person that counts, not the money.[35]

Although Master Canh supports his less affluent followers to a certain degree, he also thinks that, under the present circumstances, entering into mediumship is only possible for those who have sufficient financial means to conduct their rituals

---

[33] Interview with Master Thuyet, January 2004, Hanoi.

[34] Interview with Master Duong, March 2005, Hanoi.

[35] Interview with Master Canh, March 2005, Hanoi.

properly. Serving the spirits with only one robe, he says, would nowadays be improper:

> The old ladies say that in former times they made one robe and went to serve the spirits. That was in former times ... but today you can't just have one red robe and then go and serve all of the spirits, with the excuse of a heavy fate [*can mang*], this is not right! Talking about mediumship, the fate goes together with the financial means. [Before the revolution], mediumship only prevailed within the bourgeoisie. The workers or the poor could not do it [*khong lam duoc*], even if they knew they had a heavy fate.[36]

This is a claim that certainly deserves further research, but for the moment it at least opens up a few interesting points for consideration. If we assume it is true that prerevolutionary mediumship was practiced only by the bourgeoisie,[37] at least in urban Hanoi, then we could conclude that "the hard times" during the period of state subsidy provided poor fated mediums an equal opportunity to enter mediumship since neither offerings nor robes were available in sufficient quantity, no matter how rich a person was. In post-Renovation Vietnam, the economic upsurge has improved the general living standards in both rural and urban areas and thus also made it possible for destined low-income workers and petty traders to become initiated. At the same time, the widening gap between rich and poor slowly creates significant differences in the amounts they can spend on rituals, and may in the future again exclude those who cannot afford to keep up with the new ritual aesthetics determined by the demands of the new consumer culture in modern late-socialist Hanoi.

It is not surprising, then, that elderly spirit mediums idealize and fondly remember the difficulties of the past, when everybody was equally poor and sentiments of community and solidarity were strong. Even if they feel grateful that the open-door policy of the *doi moi* era has made their religion prosper, many of them regret the loss of a strong sense of community. Whereas mediums in the pre-Renovation era focused on maintaining the community and fostering strong sentimental relationships (*tinh cam*), the newer mediums of today are said to focus predominantly on material success in the new market-oriented economy. The narratives of these older mediums also seem to lend the elderly mediums legitimacy because the hardships they experienced fulfilling their religious duties during times of legal persecution and severe food scarcity mark them as "genuine mediums" (*that dong*) and set them most clearly apart from those mediums whom they classify as belonging to the new category of "show-off mediums" (*dong dua*). The generation gap between spirit mediums is also reflected in elderly mediums' occasional critical comments about young initiates who claim they have experienced economic benefits as a result of the religion. Yet transactions with the spirit world for material comfort (besides other this-worldly benefits) have always been a central element of Vietnamese popular religious practice, and the wealth of adages and proverbs that

---

[36] Ibid.

[37] This observation was also made by several authors of the French colonial period, for example, Maurice Durand, *Technique et panthéon des médiums viêtnamiens (Dông)* (Paris: École Française d'Extrême-Orient, 1959). However, scholarly opinions on this issue differ; see, for example, Nguyen Thi Hien, "The Religion of the Four Palaces," which treats the Four Palace religion as a folk belief that has long prevailed in all layers of Viet society.

scorn material interests in religious matters indicates that the relationship between spirituality and materialism has long been perceived as antagonistic.[38] We agree with Pham Quynh Phuong's findings that the boundaries between spirituality and materialism have become more blurred in the post-Renovation era, and even though spirit mediums may be critical of the increasing emphasis on conjuring wealth in *len dong* mediumship, they believe strongly in the efficacy of the spirits in bestowing blessed gifts (*loc*), not only in terms of easing their burdens of fate, but also in terms of economic gains.

CONCLUSIONS

In contemporary urban Vietnam, spirit mediums of the Four Palace religion constitute a community that shares feelings of being closely connected with the spirit world, as well as belonging to a specific group network of a temple master's followers. Between masters and their followers, there is a strong interdependency: masters provide their followers with spiritual guidance and moral support in their personal affairs, and they initiate destined mediums into the ritual practice of serving the spirits, while mediums contribute to the maintenance of, and improvements to, the temple, and they sustain their masters' livelihood by paying donations and fees for ritual services and other temple activities, as well as by introducing prospective new followers to the temple community. Mediums' participation in rituals and pilgrimages nourishes the bonds between fellow mediums and may foster sentimental relationships (*tinh cam*) that result in mutual help and strong friendships. However, as we have shown in this essay, social inequalities between followers, as well as a master's alleged favoritism toward certain disciples, may trigger feelings of envy and jealousy, and mediums sometimes bicker with each other over ritual or personal matters and may reject antisocial group members. Besides profound religious and ritual knowledge, a master therefore has to possess strong social competencies and communicative skills in order to settle disputes and foster feelings of mutual respect and solidarity among his or her followers.

Elderly mediums, many of whom are retired and thus not necessarily forced to eke out a living in the new economy, tend to idealize the past by fondly remembering the solidarity among spirit mediums during the period of state subsidy. Their narratives also lend them legitimacy as "genuine mediums" and earn them respect based on their past and present efforts to preserve the religion and the community. Adherents of the Four Palace religion draw upon this collective memory of a strong faith and a mutually supportive community in order to assess critically the creative potential that allows *len dong* mediumship to hybridize by incorporating dynamic transformations in post-Renovation Vietnam. At the same time, this memory may entail a "vision for the future for which the past acts as prologue."[39] Master Duong bemoans the fact that masters have no legal power to guide their followers, and therefore he strongly advocates establishing an organization that will teach the religion and issue certificates in order to provide master mediums "with

---

[38] See Taylor, *Goddess on the Rise*, p. 84; Pham Quynh Phuong, "Hero and Deity," p. 202.

[39] Hue-Tam Ho Tai, "Introduction: Situating Memory," in *The Country of Memory: Remaking the Past in Late Socialist Vietnam*, ed. Hue-Tam Ho Tai (Berkeley, CA: University of California Press, 2001), p. 2.

legal authority and spiritual principles to guide everyone toward doing it right." Otherwise, he thinks the religion will become "exceedingly chaotic" (*hon loan vo cung*). But even though state authorities no longer persecute the practitioners of *len dong* mediumship, the Four Palace religion is still a long way from being officially recognized as a "national religion" (*quoc dao*). Yet the fact that in the past the religion survived "from village to village, and from town to town" convinces mediums to trust that *len dong* spirit mediumship will continue into the future and help to create—in line with Party aspirations—a strong country and a prosperous society.

DO THE FOUR PALACES INHABIT
AN EAST ASIAN LANDSCAPE?

Laurel Kendall

Let me confess at the outset that this task runs against my instincts as a writer of ethnography even as the idea has intrigued me since my first visit to Vietnam in 1991. Comparisons of popular religious phenomena are a tricky business, and when using secondary literature to make them, it is all too easy to mistake apples for oranges, regional or even local variations for national essentialisms. I am among the guilty. In my first book, I compared "Korean shamans"—but really only shamans in the Seoul style (*Hanyang kut*)—with "Chinese shamans"—but really only shamans from Taiwan, Fujian, and the Hong Kong New Territories. My discussion was consistent with ethnographic understandings of these local traditions but not for "Korean" and "Chinese" shamans in general.[1] Comparisons seemed much easier a few decades ago when the structuralist paradigm gave us an unrealistically tidy sense of "kinship systems," "inheritance practices," "men," "women," and "ancestors," uncomplicated by cognizance of variations across time and space— which is to say "history," "region," and "class"—the "constructed" nature of our categories, and the "contingency" of any commonsense label. Even anthropologists of my generation have learned to talk this way, and if we don't let lingo swamp substance, our anthropology is the better for these critical lenses.

Consider, for example, how several of the studies in this volume, those by Karen Fjelstad and Lisa Maiffret,[2] Kirsten Endres,[3] Pham Quynh Phuong,[4] and especially Barley Norton,[5] complicate the simple constructs of another generation, the old expectation that possession rituals (*len dong*) enable disempowered women to become, for a time, powerful male gods, and enable men to explore their feminine

---

[1] Laurel Kendall, *Shamans, Housewives, and Other Restless Spirits: Women in Korean Ritual Life* (Honolulu, HI: University of Hawai'i Press, 1985).

[2] Karen Fjelstad and Lisa Maiffret, "Gifts from the Spirits: Spirit Possession and Personal Transformation among Silicon Valley Spirit Mediums," this volume.

[3] Kirsten W. Endres, "Spirit Performance and the Ritual Construction of Personal Identity in Modern Vietnam," this volume.

[4] Pham Quynh Phuong, "Tran Hung Dao and the Mother Goddess Religion," this volume.

[5] Barley Norton, "'Hot-Tempered' Women and 'Effeminate' Men: The Performance of Music and Gender in Vietnamese Mediumship," this volume.

dispositions in cross-dress, make-up, and elaborate flowery coiffures. This happens, but to leave it at that would be a gross reduction of the complex *len dong* ritual, where a single medium crosses and recrosses gender boundaries in alternating categories of deities, dressing and undressing the particular colorations of status, age, and ethnicity. As a further complication, different mediums embody the variety of these spirits in distinctive individual styles, and many have special relationships with particular deities and goddesses, whom they carry into their daily lives and sometimes into their personalities. "Effeminate men" and "hot-tempered" women find their counterparts in the spirit world, but not all of these human/divine relationships cross genders; some are less about transgendering than salesmanship or being a good student, and some mediums seem to be cultivating their inner child in their affinity for childlike gods. Possession rituals like the Vietnamese *len dong*, Korean *kut*, and Burmese *nat pwe* suggest fun-house mirrors on multiple ways of being; something we are better able to appreciate in light of a more sophisticated gender theory that has sensitized researchers to diverse and sometimes contradictory ways of doing, being, and performing "masculine" and "feminine."

Speaking across cultures is further complicated when the discussion turns on such elusive concepts as "shamans," "spirit possession," and "trance," all of which have been giddily applied to a wide variety of phenomena.[6] Broadly researched and brilliantly generalized work, like Mircea Eliade's *Shamanism: Archaic Techniques of Ecstasy*[7] or I. M. Lewis's *Ecstatic Religion*,[8] tickle the imagination and have prompted a great deal of writing in these areas, but they have also been faulted for simplifying or eliding complexities and contradictions implicit even in the ethnographies they cite.[9] Meticulous comparisons, on the other hand, engender sterile typologies, and pigeonholing makes for earthbound pigeons. Introducing "Asian shamanism" on the basis of a quarter century of observation, religious scholar Peter Knecht had cause to throw up his hands: "the amount of significant variations of what is called 'shamanism' that have been brought to light by recent research makes a clear definition that goes beyond very general terms impossible."[10]

[6] See, for example, Alice Kehoe's call for a highly restricted use of the word "shaman" in Alice Beck Kehoe, *Shamans and Religion: An Anthropological Exploration in Critical Thinking* (Prospect Heights, IL: Waveland Press, 2000) and Mari Womack's critique of Kehoe's position in "Emics, Etics, 'Ethics,' and Shamans," *Anthropology Newsletter* 42,3 (2001): 7; Roberte Hamayon's discussion of ethnographers' overreification of "trance" in R. N. Hamayon, "Are 'Trance,' 'Ecstasy,' and Similar Concepts Appropriate in the Study of Shamanism?" in *Shamanism in Performing Arts*, ed. M. Hoppal and P. Paricsy (Budapest: Akademiai Kiado, 1995), pp. 17-34; and Erika Bourguignon's attempt to bring order to the chaos of possession terminology. See Erika Bourguignon, "'Possession' and 'Trance' in Cross-Cultural Studies of Mental Health," in *Culture-bound Syndromes, Ethnopsychiatry, and Alternate Therapies*, Mental Health Research in Asia and the Pacific 4, ed. W. P. Lebra (Honolulu, HI: University of Hawai'i Press, 1976), pp. 47-55.

[7] Mircea Eliade, *Shamanism: Archaic Techniques of Ecstasy* (New York, NY: Pantheon, 1964).

[8] I. M. Lewis, *Ecstatic Religion* (Harmondsworth: Penguin, 1969).

[9] Jane Monig Atkinson, "Shamanisms Today," *Annual Review of Anthropology* 21 (1992): 307-30; Janice Boddy, *Wombs and Alien Spirits: Women, Men, and the Zar Cult in Northern Sudan* (Madison, WI: University of Wisconsin Press, 1989) and "Spirit Possession Revisited: Beyond Instrumentality," *Annual Review of Anthropology* 23 (1994): 407-34; Kehoe, *Shamans and Religion*; Kendall, *Shamans, Housewives, and Other Restless Spirits*.

[10] Peter Knecht, "Introduction," in *Shamans in Asia*, ed. C. Childon and P. Knecht (London and New York, NY: RoutledgeCurzon, 2003), pp. 1-30.

But if comparison—in the rigorous, controlled sense of an older social science—is ultimately disappointing—either too broad to be verifiable or too precise to fire the imagination—is there no space for a meaningful ethnographic conversation? This essay is premised on the existence of such a space. Its aim is to suggest not rules or defining principles so much as resonances from a broader East Asian world that might enrich a discussion of the Mother Goddess religion in Vietnam and, through this encounter, let the mother goddesses and Saint Tran raise some questions for the study of popular religious practices in other places. Cross-referencing is already implicit in the study of Vietnamese popular religion; for example, two recent works, Shaun Malarney's *Culture, Ritual, and Revolution in Vietnam*[11] and Phillip Taylor's *Goddess on the Rise*,[12] combine their citations of a rich tradition of Vietnamese scholarship with ethnographies of China, Korea, and Japan to frame discussions and draw points of comparison. In a similar manner, twenty years ago, publications on Korean popular religion brought a wealth of Korean folklore and ethnographic research into dialogue with Chinese and Japanese ethnographies.[13]

As is already amply evident, my discussion is cast within the frame of two broad and imperfect constructs, "popular religion" and "East Asia." The term "popular religion" is used to emphasize "practice" over "theology" and to obscure arbitrary distinctions between "elite" and "folk" practice. At the same time, its presumption of holism should not obscure the complexities of class, gender, locality, or other interests that are the substance of any dynamic popular culture.[14] "East Asia" confounds the feudatories of academe insofar as Vietnam is commonly subsumed under the intellectual projects of "Southeast Asian Studies" and the contemporary realities of this region and its recent past undeniably have an impact upon popular religion. From another corner of Southeast Asia, Jean DeBernardi's work among overseas Chinese, long resident on the Malay Peninsula, highlights the dilemma. Should her *Rites of Belonging* be considered a work of "East Asian" ethnography, owing to the ritual and symbolic referents her subjects deploy, or a study of a "Southeast Asian" community, influenced by the cultural politics of the Malaysian state?[15] DeBernardi's ethnography is necessarily and effectively both.

"Crypto-Confucian societies" highlight the most obvious common legacy of China, Vietnam, Korea, and Japan to a lesser degree, but even permitting the problematic commonsense understanding of "Confucianism," which has come to

---

[11] Shaun K. Malarney, *Culture, Ritual, and Revolution in Vietnam* (New York, NY: RoutledgeCurzon, 2002).

[12] Philip Taylor, *Goddess on the Rise: Pilgrimage and Popular Religion in Vietnam* (Honolulu, HI: University of Hawai'i Press, 2004).

[13] See, for example, Roger L. Janelli and Dawnhee Yim Janelli, *Ancestor Worship and Korean Society* (Stanford, CA: Stanford University Press, 1982); Kendall, *Shamans, Housewives, and Other Restless Spirits*; Kwang-Kyu Lee, "Ancestor Worship and Kinship Structure in Korea," in *Religion and Ritual in Korean Society*, Korea Research Monograph 12, ed. L. Kendall and G. M. Dix (Berkeley, CA: Institute of East Asian Studies and Center for Korean Studies, University of California, 1987); Arthur P. Wolf and Robert J. Smith, "China, Korea, and Japan," in *Religion and Ritual in Korean Society*, ed. L. Kendall and G. Dix (Berkeley, CA: Center for Korean Studies and Institute of East Asian Studies, University of California, 1987), pp. 185-99.

[14] Catherine Bell, "Religion and Chinese Culture: Toward an Assessment of 'Popular Religion,'" *History of Religions* 29,1 (1989): 35-57.

[15] Jean DeBernardi, *Rites of Belonging: Memory, Modernity, and Identity in a Malaysian Chinese Community* (Stanford, CA: Stanford University Press, 2004).

mean many things to many different scholars, the term elides a common legacy of Mahayana Buddhism and a cosmology underpinning more-or-less mutually intelligible systems of medicine, geomancy, divination, and traditional models of statecraft, all of which saturate popular religion in Vietnam.

The Mother Goddess religion is a juncture for several threads that seem to run through the ornate and complex tapestry that, for want of better language, I am calling "East Asian popular religion." The analogy of "thread" and "tapestry" is carefully chosen; a tapestry requires multiple threads to make a complex design through diverse points of intersection; not all threads intersect, and the resulting design is not necessarily a precisely replicable pattern. Metaphoric "threads" are neither "rules," nor "principles," nor "types," and as "generalizations," they are very modest ones. That there are striking visual similarities between the performance of *len dong* in Hanoi and *kut* in Seoul should not obscure the fact that there are other kinds of spirit mediums in Vietnam—notably those who are the exclusive devotees of Saint Tran and those who speak for the dead—and not all shamans in Korea dress in costumes, dance, and mime like the *mansin* who perform *kut* in and around Seoul and, traditionally, in northern Korea. Although these rituals are not "Korean" and "Vietnamese" archetypes, the comparison of *len dong* in Hanoi with *kut* in Seoul is resonant, interesting, and potentially useful.[16] The point is not to define an "East Asian shamanism" or "mediumship" or "possession ritual," but rather to follow some Vietnamese threads as they configure with others in interesting patterns. The analogy of moving threads also allows for historical contingency, a recognition that popular religious practices are highly fluid, which is well evidenced in the different presentations in this volume, from Ngo Duc Thinh's discussion of the long gestation of the Mother Goddess religion[17] to Pham Quynh Phuong's contemporary portrait of how the Mother Goddesses' *ong dong* and *ba dong* are appropriating Saint Tran, and how Saint Tran's adherents are affiliating themselves with Mother Goddess temples.[18] Threads can also weave themselves through and beyond an arbitrary "East Asia" (that includes Silicon Valley) and intersect with other threads from, say, Burma or Cambodia.

WHO ARE THE GODS AND GODDESSES?

The Mother Goddess religion includes a particular style of ritual practice. Whether one calls the *ong dong* and *ba dong* "mediums" or "shamans," what they do is at once distinct from the journeying shamanisms of several of Vietnam's ethnic minorities (who are more nearly "classical" shamans in Eliade's terms) and of a piece with those rituals performed throughout the (Han) Chinese world, Korea, the Ryukyus, (at least ancient) Japan, and by lowland majorities in Burma, Cambodia, Thailand, and Laos. In these traditions, the deities are brought into the here and now, "manifested" (my word) or "incarnated" (Nguyen Thi Hien's word) as an active presence realized in and through some manner of performance, where music, dance,

---

[16] L. Kendall and Nguyen Thi Hien, "Entertaining Power, Transcending Eliade: Perspectives from Korea and Vietnam" (paper, Seventh International Conference of the International Society for Shamanic Research, Changchun, Jilin, China, August 21-15, 2004).

[17] Ngo Duc Thinh, "The Mother Goddess Religion," this volume.

[18] Pham Quynh Phuong, "Tran Hung Dao and the Mother Goddess Religion," this volume.

song, costumes, props, and theatrical business play a part.[19] Each god's presence is evidenced through the practitioner's own body in situations of greater ritual complexity and instrumental intention than would be associated with, say, table-rapping mediums in western Spiritualism. The word "séance," sometimes used to gloss the *len dong* of Vietnam, leaches these events of an aesthetic and ritual complexity that should rather be emphasized. The possibility of deities entering into ritual transactions with humans makes a weave with other themes common to popular religion in East Asia, where deities and ancestors, although distinguished from one another, ride upon some common premises. Most obviously, it is assumed that both deities and ancestors were once living people, albeit where reincarnation is a possibility, a mortal life is not necessarily the first chapter in a deity's existence. The possibility of continued social engagement between the living and those who once lived is assumed and enacted in ritual through idioms of asymmetrical reciprocity: offerings and petitions (from the living), bestowals of favor (from gods and ancestors), and return expressions of gratitude or indebtedness (from the living). But whereas ancestors evoke "family" and the intimacies of personal memory, deities are powerful and more distant beings—figures of legendary proportion. Idioms of asymmetrical relationships between mere mortals and powerful beings appear in Nguyen Thi Hien's discussion of votive offerings,[20] Ngo Duc Thinh's discussion of the dynamics of *len dong* ritual,[21] and in the several essays that discuss paths of initiation, most poignantly in Fjelstad's stories of refugees who are miraculously rescued by the deities they subsequently serve.[22] Offerings are made to the spirits as a way of securing their benevolent regard (sometimes expressed in Vietnam as "compassion" or "pity," *thuong*), and in both Korea and Vietnam, the idiom of gifting has similar grounding in more mundane cultural practices. Discussing the significance of offerings at a ceremony, Nguyen Thi Hien describes how Vietnamese give gifts to a powerful benefactor, or to a potential benefactor on such occasions as, for example, when seeking help in finding a job for one's child. If the appeal brings a good result, further gifts of gratitude are in order.[23]

Deities come garbed in the imagery of antique courts and armies.[24] Mandarins, courtly dames, princes, pages, and generals like Tran Hung Dao populate the ritual imaginaries of Asian states in a very different form from the animal spirits of North

---

[19] Ngo Duc Thinh, "Hau Bong as Viewed from the Angle of the Performing Arts," *Vietnamese Studies* 12,192 (1999): 56-60 and "*Len Dong*: Spirits' Journeys," in *Vietnam: Journeys of Body, Mind, and Spirit*, ed. Nguyen V. H. and L. Kendall (Berkeley and Los Angeles, CA: University of California Press, 2003), pp. 253-72.

[20] Nguyen Thi Hien, "'A Bit of a Spirit Favor Is Equal to a Load of Mundane Gifts': Votive Paper Offerings of *Len Dong* Rituals in Post-Renovation Vietnam," this volume.

[21] Ngo Duc Thinh, "The Mother Goddess Religion."

[22] Karen Fjelstad, "'We Have *Len Dong* Too'": Transnational Aspects of Spirit Possession," this volume.

[23] Nguyen Thi Hien, "The Religion of the Four Palaces: Mediumship and Therapy in Viet Culture" (PhD dissertation, Indiana University, 2002), p. 122.

[24] Gods appearing in Korean shamans' *kut* partially confound this generalization. Some—historical generals—are legendary figures. Most are known only by title ("Official," "Buddhist Sage," and so forth) and have a relationship with a client household, where particularly potent deity slots are inhabited by ancestors—known or distant—a child who died of smallpox, a grandmother who prayed on mountains, a shaman, an ancestor who was some sort of official. The Korean household of shamanic practice can be seen as a microcosm of a kingdom that recognized exemplary figures as tutelary gods.

Asian shamanisms, where power emerges from a harsh natural landscape.[25] In East Asian popular religion, power is expressed in its most familiar form through evocations of the state, albeit in premodern fancy dress. Some of Pham Quynh Phuong's informants have a highly articulate sense of this when they describe the coexistence of the Mother Goddess and Saint Tran as the civil and military components, the yin and yang, of the dynastic bureaucracy, both tasks "essential for a country."[26] According to Jean DeBernardi, Chinese spirit mediums in Penang make a similar distinction, "drawing on a classical model of authority in which the normative powers of civil leaders found their complement in the coercive powers of military leaders—a dualism that also informs the popular religious images of the gods," with the military gods, here too, performing "self-mortifying acts of endurance."[27]

GODS AND NATIONAL HEROES

The quasi-historical imaginary of the Four Palace religion and the cult of Saint Tran reconciles history and religious devotion within the frame of the twenty-first-century Vietnamese nation-state insofar as the deities of the Mother Goddess religion are commonly regarded—by folklorists and practitioners alike—as historical figures honored as national heroes, some more explicitly than others, and Tran Hung Dao perhaps most explicitly of all. Ngo Duc Thinh's essay is full of examples.[28] Such figures tie recent and distant pasts together in a national story, as when a devotee describes Saint Tran as "a great hero...like general Vo Nguyen Giap" (and note how easily informants cite contemporary phenomena to explain antique images). Arguably, such claims and the possibility of rehabilitating popular religion as national culture are particularly possible in a part of the world where premodern states ritualized history by commemorating heroes, exemplary men and women, and mythic figures. Ngo Duc Thinh relates that in dynastic times, heroic figures, including heroic or regal women, "have been deified by kings," who bestowed rank designations. Premodern Chinese and Korean states similarly "appointed" or

---

[25] Piers Vitebsky, "From Cosmology to Environmentalism: Shamanism as Local Knowledge in a Global Setting," in *Counterworks: Managing the Diversity of Knowledge*, ed. R. Fardon (London: Routledge, 1995) pp. 182-203, and *The Shaman: Voyages of the Soul, Trance, Ecstasy, and Healing from Siberia to the Amazon* (London: Macmillan Reference Books, 1995). But note how the imagery of the state appears in the landscape of shamanic journeys when a Manchu shaman in a (possibly) seventeenth-century text is forced to navigate a Sinicized underworld and is disciplined by one of its magistrates, a fitting literary metaphor for a colonized imagination, or when the spirit army of the Tay shaman in northern Vietnam must ask permission of various spirit mandarins in order to navigate their domains. See, for example, Stephen Durrant, "The Neisan Shaman Caught in Cultural Contradiction," *Signs* 5,2 (1979): 338-47; Caroline Humphrey and Urgunge Onon, *Shamans and Elders: Experience, Knowledge, and Power Among the Daur Mongols* (Oxford: Clarendon Press, 1996); Margaret Nowak and Stephen Durrant, *The Tale of the Nisan Shamaness: A Manchu Folk Epic* (Seattle, WA: University of Washington Press, 1977); La Cong Y, "The Perilous Journey of the Then Spirit Army: A Shamanic Ritual of the Tay People," in Nguyen and Kendall, *Vietnam: Journeys of Body, Mind, and Spirit*, pp. 239-51.

[26] Pham Quynh Phuong, "Tran Hung Dao and the Mother Goddess Religion."

[27] DeBernardi, *Rites of Belonging*, p. 90.

[28] Ngo Duc Thinh, "The Mother Goddess Religion."

bestowed official titles upon particular spirits and established or recognized temples to venerate them as gods.[29]

This woodblock print portrays the well-defined hierarchy of the Mother Goddess religion. Although located beneath the Buddha and the four kings of the four realms, the mother goddesses (*Thanh Mau*) reign supreme in the world of *len dong*, governing the four realms of the cosmos. Below them, in descending order, are the ranks of spirits who appear in a *len dong* ritual: mandarins, dames, princes, damsels, and pages. Most mediums today use more expensive wooden sculptures rather than prints. A contemporary artisan made this print after a black and white illustration. American Museum of Natural History 70.3/5815.

---

[29] See also, for Vietnam, Nguyen Van Huyen, *Contribution a l'étude d'un génie tutélaire annamite Li-Phuc-Man* (Hanoi: BEFEO, 1938); and *Le Culte des Immortels en Annam* (Hanoi: Imprimerie d'Extrême Orient, 1944), pp. 20, 86, 150. For China, see Valerie Hansen, *Changing Gods in Medieval China, 1126-1276* (Princeton, NJ: Princeton University Press, 1990); C. K. Yang, *Religion in Chinese Society* (Berkeley, CA: University of California Press, 1961); James L. Watson, "Standardizing the Gods: The Promotion of T'ien Hou ("Empress of Heaven") along the South China Coast, 960-1960," in *Popular Culture in Late Imperial China*, ed. D. Johnson, A. J. Nathan, and E. S. Rawski (Berkeley, CA: University of California Press, 1985), pp. 292-324. For Korea, see Yi Nung-hwa, *Chosŏn musok ko* [Reflections on Korean Shamanism], trans. Yi Chae-gon (Seoul: Peangnuk, 1976 [1926]); Pak Hŭng-ju, *Seoulŭi Maŭlgut* [Seoul's Village Rituals] (Seoul: Sŏmundang, 2001); Yi Chae-gon *Seoulŭi min'gan sinang* [Folk Beliefs of Seoul] (Seoul: Paeksan Ch'ulp'ansa, 1996). The ancient Chinese Book of Rites included provisions for making sacrifices to kings, generals, and martyrs as part of an official cult; Valerie Hansen's research suggests that in twelfth-century China, the titles were more broadly bestowed upon local deities as a means of maintaining a finger on the pulse of local society. See Hansen, *Changing Gods in Medieval China*, pp. 3, 37-38, and chap. 4.

The well-developed field of Chinese popular religion suggests an uneasy relationship between a premodern state desirous of appropriating popular religion into its own moral order via a spirit world that runs parallel to, and is approached as if it were, the imperial administration,[30] and a fertile, creative field of popular religious practice, capable of generating or reappropriating local cults for its own needs.[31] In Vietnam, several local cults seem to have merged, at different historical moments, into cults that venerated such figures as Goddess Lieu Hanh,[32] the Granary Queen,[33] and the Lady of the Realm,[34] accommodating the mutating needs and desires of a community of worshippers. Pham Quynh Phuong observes that not only have historical figures been deified, some deities have very likely been historicized.[35] To search for the "real" origins of such figures is misguided; it fails to appreciate the messiness, openness, and geographical and ontological fluidity that is the very stuff of an adaptable, dynamic, and vital popular religion.

In contemporary Vietnam, where popular religion still bears the onus of "superstition," deities who can be identified as national, historical heroes carry an aura of respectability. According to Pham Quynh Phuong, in some sites the veneration accorded to the politically more acceptable Tran Hung Dao eclipses the veneration shown to King Bat Hai. Her description of the spread of Tran Hung Dao's veneration to settings and ritual contexts where he was not honored in the past is an excellent example of this phenomenon, as is her claim that some communities have recently refashioned legends in order to position their deities as state-approved national heroes, although this move may have been made in the past as well. If the Chinese Imperial view assumed either a colonization from the top[36] or a push-pull

---

[30] Emily Martin Ahern, *Chinese Ritual and Politics* (Cambridge: Cambridge University Press, 1981); Arthur P. Wolf, "Gods, Ghosts, and Ancestors," in *Religion and Ritual in Chinese Society*, ed. A. P. Wolf (Stanford, CA: Stanford University Press, 1974), pp. 131-82; Yang, *Religion in Chinese Society*.

[31] See Stephan Feuchtwang, *Popular Religion in China: The Imperial Metaphor* (Richmond: Curzon Press, 2001); Meir Shahar and Robert P. Weller, *Unruly Gods: Divinity and Society in China* (Honolulu, HI: University of Hawai'i Press, 1996); Watson, "Standardizing the Gods." Kenneth Dean's work in southeast China suggests that one means of appropriation was to bring local deities into the fold of ecclesiastical Taoist practice. See Kenneth Dean, *Taoist Ritual and Popular Cults of Southeast China* (Princeton, NJ: Princeton University Press, 1993), p. 18. Ngo Duc Thinh suggests that Chinese Taoism has had a strong influence on the ultimate form of the Mother Goddess pantheon, but what exists today seems far less colonized by Taoist cosmology than the practices that Dean describes; the Mother Goddess religion is not under the authority of an organized Taoist clergy. Taoist influence is also evident where figures like the Jade Emperor and the Seven Stars appear in the Korean shaman pantheon, but the names seem almost coincidental. Organized Taoism was not unknown in Korea, but seems to have had a more circumscribed role in Korean religious life in dynastic times. We need to know a great deal more about how "Taoism" was historically present in Korean and Vietnamese popular religion.

[32] Pham Quynh Phuong, "Following the Footsteps of the Goddess of Vancat Village" (paper, International Conference on Mother Goddess Worship and the Phu Giay Festival, Hanoi, March 31-April 1, 2001).

[33] Ngo Duc Thinh, "The Belief in the Granary Queen and the Transformation of Vietnamese Society" (paper, American Anthropological Association, Annual Meeting, Chicago, IL, March 27-30, 2003).

[34] Taylor, *Goddess on the Rise.*

[35] Pham Quynh Phuong, "Tran Hung Dao and the Mother Goddess Religion."

[36] Dean, *Taoist Ritual and Popular Cults of Southeast China.*

process between state and locality,[37] Pham Quynh Phuong's study of the Tran Hung Dao cult—from a time when the state no longer confers rank status on deities but does authorize history—suggests a bottom-up struggle to make the local a part of the approved and permitted national story.[38]

The fifth mandarin is dancing with a sword, reenacting his old battles. Initiation ritual in Phu Giay, Nam Dinh province, August 2003. Photo by Nguyen Thi Hien.

ENTERTAINMENT FOR WHOM?

Heritage claims for the Mother Goddess religion are tied, not only to the identification of its gods and goddesses as national heroes, but also to the artistic content of its rituals. Frank Proschan's assertion that not only the deities of *len dong* but their costumes, accoutrements, and music constitute a "living history museum" of Vietnam[39] struck a resonant chord with Vietnamese scholars attending a historic first international conference on the Mother Goddess religion in Hanoi in 2001. Professor Ngo Duc Thinh has drawn attention to the performance elements of *len dong* rituals, to gesture, dance, music, and particularly the poetic *chau van* songs that are sung to invoke and entertain the spirits.[40] This music has wide popularity in

---

[37] Hansen, *Changing Gods in Medieval China*; Watson, "Standardizing the Gods."

[38] Pham Quynh Phuong, "Tran Hung Dao and the Mother Goddess Religion."

[39] Frank Proschan, "Len Dong (Hau Bong): A Living Museum of Vietnamese Cultural Heritage" (paper, conference on Mother Goddess Veneration and the Phu Giay Festival, Hanoi, March 31-April 1, 2001).

[40] Ngo Duc Thinh, "Hau Bong as Viewed from the Angle of the Performing Arts."

secular contexts, where it can be heard on CD recordings.[41] Barley Norton suggests that music not only invokes gods, it creates and genders them.[42] This link between possession rituals and performing arts is familiar to me from Korea, where the entertainment value of *kut* and its links to other genres of Korean folk performance have long been recognized.[43] That several Korean shaman rituals are now officially designated as Intangible Cultural Properties (*muhyŏngmunhwaje*) is of interest to Vietnamese folklorists concerned with the preservation of the Mother Goddess religion. As in Korea, the case for the artistic merit of this body of practice is undeniable, but why is this so?

The several essays in this volume suggest that mediums worship the spirits by performing them—that the idea of entertainment and the creation of an atmosphere of pleasure and beauty are central to the work of *len dong* as envisaged by its adherents. *Len dong* mediums describe what they do as "fun" (*vui*) for both deities and humans;[44] incarnated in the medium, the deity listens with pleasure to the musicians and is inspired to shower them with money, another bestowal of blessed gifts (*loc*), which is a central idiom of the ritual. Mediums speak of how deities who are pleased with beautiful costumes, music, and offerings make a beautiful (*dep*) performance. Similarly, in Korea, the ability to entertain is a core attribute of the shaman;[45] dancing and feasting gods "play" (*nolda*), and their satisfaction gives the ritual an auspicious outcome. The pleasures of performance, in both *len dong* and *kut*, can be understood as a meta-offering, something that pleases the deities and thereby generates auspiciousness (*loc*, Korean *pok*, Chinese *fu*), which participants come to

---

[41] Nguyen Thi Hien, "The Religion of the Four Palaces"; Barley Norton, "'The Moon Remembers Uncle Ho': The Politics of Music and Mediumship in Northern Vietnam," *British Journal of Ethnomusicology* 11,1 (2002): 71-100; Dong Hai To, Phan Dang Nhat, Ngo Duc Thinh, and Pham Van Ty, "Hymns of the Cult of Holy Mothers," in "The Cult of Holy Mothers in Vietnam," special issue, *Vietnamese Studies* 12,192 (1999): 61-72.

[42] See Norton, "'Hot-Tempered' Women and 'Effeminate' Men," this volume.

[43] See Daniel A. Kister, *Korean Shamanist Ritual: Symbols and Dramas of Transformation* (Budapest: Akademiai Kiado, 1997); Du-hyun Lee (Yi Tuhyŏn), *Han'guk kamyŏn'guk* [Korean Masked-Dance Drama] (Seoul: Munhwa Kongbobu, Munhwaje Kwalliguk, 1969) and "Role Playing through Trance Possession" (paper, Wenner-Gren Foundation Symposium 89 on Theater and Ritual, New York, NY, August 23-September 1, 1982) and *Kyŏnggido todang kutŭi kongyŏnjŏk ch'ukmyŏn* [Performance Aspects of Kyŏnggi Province *todang kut*] in *Han'guk musokkwa kongyŏn* (Seoul: Seoul National University Press, 1995), pp. 248-55; Yim Seuk Jai, "Han'guk musok yŏn'gu sŏsŏl" [Introduction to Korean "Mu-ism"], *Journal of Asian Women* (Seoul) 9 (1970): pp. 73-90. This link is particularly strong for hereditary shamans of southern Korea (*tan'gol mudang*) who are trained from childhood in singing and dancing to please the spirits. According to Ch'oe Kil-sŏng, particularly beautiful daughters born into *mudang* families sometimes received training as artistically accomplished courtesans (*kisaeng*), assuming the *mudang* role on retirement, and boys were trained as musicians and mountebanks. See Ch'oe Kil-sŏng, *Han'guk musok ŭi yŏn'gu* [Research on Korean "Mu" Practices] (Seoul: Asia Munhwasa, 1978). But even among the charismatic shamans (*mansin*) of Seoul and northern Korea, there are sometimes close autobiographical connections between performing arts and a divine calling. See Laurel Kendall, "Of Gods and Men: Performance, Possession, and Flirtation in Korean Shaman Ritual," *Cahiers d'Extrême-Asie* 6 (1991/1992): pp. 45-63.

[44] Karen Fjelstad, "Tu Phu Cong Dong: Vietnamese Women and Spirit Possession in the San Francisco Bay Area" (PhD dissertation, University of Hawai'i, 1995).

[45] See Yim, "Han'guk musok yŏn'gu sŏsŏl." In fact, this artistic capacity was one means by which Yim distinguished the *mudang* of Korea from the north Asian shamans of Eliade's study.

"feel" through the pleasure of participation. Entertainment in the form of music, dance, and displaying beautiful costumes is also deployed as a means of winning the auspicious regard of regal spirits. Could this also be why these rituals emphasize the feminine? Barley Norton's discussion of the complex gendering of mediums and the deities they incarnate leaves the impression that, hot-tempered women aside, it is more likely and appropriate for the male medium to assume "feminine" attributes in daily life than the reverse.[46] Inevitably, I think of Korea where—deep-voiced female shamans aside—male shamans are commonly expected to put on traditional feminine dress—in effect to become women—before donning the gods' costumes, or Burma, where "effeminate" men are gaining prominence in a formerly female form.[47] Is the courtly entertainment of a dancing woman part of the idiom of an offering in all of these forms? What is the preferred gender of a court dancer?

Once the pattern becomes legible, it is possible to see it in other places. According to Arthur Waley, in ancient China intermediaries with the spirits were called *wu* (Korean *mu*). "Some *wu* danced, and they are sometimes defined as people who danced in order to bring down the spirits."[48] In Japan, the shrine priestesses (*miko*) who dance for the resident deities (*kami*) in Shinto shrines perform a highly formalized and conventionalized ritual, but there is some suggestion, or at least speculation, that they were more shamanic in the past.[49] If this is so, perhaps they were less like the lively (sometimes described as "ecstatic") *mansin* of northern Korea and more like the decorous and graceful *ba dong* and *ong dong* of Vietnam and the *tan'gol mudang* of southern Korea, calling the spirits into the here and now of a ritual space and securing an auspicious outcome by their ability to please them with appropriate entertainment. Outside the frame of "East Asia," rituals honoring Burmese *nat* (*naq*) (spirits, demi-gods) similarly evoke legendary histories of kings, local rulers, and particularly princes who met untimely deaths.[50] Their male and female "wives" are described as "dancing" in order to please them, but these entertainments, as revealed in Lindsey Merrison's documentary, *Friends in High Places*, are also elaborate theatricals. Royal god play is also evident in possession rituals in Laos[51] and Cambodia.[52]

Pham Quynh Phuong describes an historic contrast—now blurring—between the *len dong* (or *hau bong*) style of ritual performance and the exorcistic cult of Tran Hung

---

[46] Norton, "'Hot-Tempered' Women and 'Effeminate' Men."

[47] Naoko Kumada, "Spirit Cult and Gender: Spirit Mediums in Post-socialist Burma, New and Old Religious Forms" (paper, annual meeting of the Society for the Anthropology of Religion and the American Ethnological Society, Providence, RI, April 24-26, 2003).

[48] Arthur Waley, *The Nine Songs* (San Francisco, CA: City Lights Books, 1973), p. 9.

[49] Carmen Blacker, *The Catalpa Bow* (London: George Allen and Unwin, 1975); William P. Fairchild, "Shamanism in Japan," *Asian Folklore Studies* (Tokyo) 21 (1962): 1-122.

[50] Benedicte Brac de la Perrière, "Être épousée par un naq: Les implications du mariage avec l'esprit dans le culte de possession birman (Mayanmar)," *Anthropologie et Société* 22,2 (1998): pp. 169-82; Melford E. Spiro, *Burmese Supernaturalism* (Englewood Cliffs, NJ: Prentice Hall, 1967).

[51] Monique Selim, "Les génies thérapeutes du politique au service du marche," in *Essai D'Anthropologie Politique sur le Laos Contemporain: Marché, Socialisae, at Génies*, ed. B. Hours and M. Selim (Paris: L'Haramattan, 1997), pp. 299-352.

[52] Didier Bertrand, "Spécificité d'une pratique médiumnique de possession dans le Cambodge contemporain" (paper, Fourth Conference of the International Society for Shamanic Research, "Le chamanisme: perspectives religieuses at politiques," Chantilly, France, 1997).

Dao, whose mediums perform feats at once frightening and thrilling.[53] Their ability to cut their own tongues, pierce their cheeks, or strangle their own necks witnesses potent exorcistic powers in a manner that recalls the slashing and piercing displays of the *tang-ki* (spirit mediums) of Southwest China and Taiwan.[54] Exorcistic powers, demonstrated through feats, are also a part of Korean *kut*, where shamans become knife-riding generals or spirit warriors who wield their blades to attack the inauspicious forces surrounding afflicted persons. The strikingly similar re-creations of antique weaponry deployed in some of these displays evokes a common imagery of military might such as one might see on a Chinese opera stage. Martial power, packaged in the imagery of kingdom and empire, is mustered to intimidate and exorcise ghosts and other malevolent spirits. Tran Hung Dao "still has his own army just as he did when he was alive," a devotee explains to Pham Quynh Phuong.

When the artistic or entertainment value of possession rituals becomes a rationale for their rehabilitation, it is tempting to read "performance" with a secular gloss, but at the risk of losing its significance as a means of transacting with spirits.[55] The foregoing suggests that the music, dance, drama, and feats of divine power associated with possession-centered rituals, not just in Vietnam, but throughout the region, are the engine on which these rituals run, one source of their efficacy. This is not to deny the national heritage value of *len dong* or to forget that these claims are probably necessary for its survival. Indeed, Professor Ngo Duc Thinh and his students and colleagues have played an important role in garnering official respect for this tradition by inducting the mother goddesses into the domain of folklore studies and studies of national culture in Vietnam.[56]

UNDER THE CLOUD OF SUPERSTITION

No aspect of East Asian popular religion—and not just East Asian popular religion—is more problematic to a modernist gaze and more likely to provoke the ire of a zealous reformer than the cost of rituals. Not only in the high socialisms of China and Vietnam, but in Meiji Japan, under Republican China's New Life Movement, and as a tenet of the New Village Movement of Park Chung Hee's Korea, material manifestations of religious practice were attacked as exploitative and as being based on backward superstitions.[57] Several authors in this volume witness some obvious

---

[53] See Pham Quynh Phuong, "Tran Hung Dao and the Mother Goddess Religion," this volume.

[54] Alan J. A. Elliott, *Chinese Spirit-Medium Cults in Singapore* (London: Department of Anthropology, The London School of Economics and Political Science, 1955); J. J. M. de Groot, *The Religious System of China* (reprint: Taipei: Ch'eng-wen, 1967 [1892-1910]); David K. Jordan, *Gods, Ghosts, and Ancestors: Folk Religion in a Taiwanese Village* (Berkeley and Los Angeles, CA: University of California Press, 1972); Donald S. Sutton, *Steps to Perfection: Exorcistic Performers and Chinese Religion in Twentieth Century Taiwan* (Cambridge, MA: Harvard University Press, 2003).

[55] For Korea, see, for example, Keith Howard, "Preserving the Spirits? Rituals, State Sponsorship, and Performance," in *Korean Shamanism: Revivals, Survivals, and Change*, ed. K. Howard (Seoul: Royal Asiatic Society, Korea Branch, 1998), pp. 187-207.

[56] "The Cult of Holy Mothers in Vietnam," special issue, *Vietnamese Studies* 131 (1999).

[57] See, for example, Kirsten W. Endres, "Beautiful Customs, Worthy Traditions: Changing State Discourse on the Role of Vietnamese Culture," *Internationales Asienforum* 33,3-4 (2002): 303-22, and "Local Dynamics of Renegotiating Ritual Space in Northern Vietnam: The Case of the Dinh," *Sojourn: Journal of Social Issues in Southeast Asia* 16,1, (2001): 70-101; John Kleinen, *Facing the Future, Reviving the Past: A Study of Social Change in a Northern Vietnamese Village*

points of sensitivity: practitioners (master mediums) who provide ritual services on behalf of invisible spirits receive material compensation, mediums spend large sums hosting *len dong* rituals, master mediums are paid for their services on behalf of clients and apprentices. Efficacy is an act of faith, charlatanry and exploitation a possibility. These issues, resonant throughout the region, could be bundled together under a common rubric of "religious materialism," that is, the use of material goods, entertainments, and gifts of cash to achieve health, prosperity, and good fortune. While such practices are commonly associated with popular religion, they are often outside the experiences and conceptual apparatuses of those who study it. S. J. Tambiah has effectively critiqued the founding fathers of the anthropology of religion who, following the iconoclasm of the Protestant Reformation and the rationalism of the Enlightenment, distinguished "religion," as a matter of faith and doctrine, from "magic," the performance of instrumentally intended acts that aimed to bring about tangible results by appealing to spiritual agents through or with things, by venerating images, using talismans, or giving offerings to gods.[58] The intellectual genealogy that Tambiah charts is not merely academic; it has affected the

---

(Singapore: Institute for Asian Studies, 1999); Hy Van Luong, "Economic Reform and the Intensification of Rituals in Two Northern Vietnamese Villages, 1980-90," in *The Challenge of Reform in Indochina*, ed. B. Ljunggren (Cambridge, MA: Harvard Institute for International Development, 1993), pp. 259-92; Malarney, *Culture, Ritual, and Revolution in Vietnam*; David G. Marr, *Vietnamese Tradition on Trial: 1920-1945* (Berkeley and Los Angeles, CA: University of California Press, 1981); Taylor, *Goddess on the Rise*; and the essays in this volume. For China, see Ann S. Anagnost, "Politics and Magic in Contemporary China," *Modern China* 13,1, (1987): 40-61, and "The Politics of Ritual Displacement," in *Asian Visions of Authority: Religion and the Modern States of East and Southeast Asia*, ed. C. F. Keyes, L. Kendall, and H. Hardacre (Honolulu, HI: University of Hawai'i Press, 1994), pp. 221-54, and *Natural Past-Times: Narrative, Representation, and Power in Modern China* (Durham, NC: Duke University Press, 1997); Prasenjit Duara, "Knowledge and Power in the Discourse of Modernity: The Campaign against Popular Religion in Early Twentieth-Century China," *Journal of Asian Studies* 50,1, (1991): 67-83; Stephan Feuchtwang and Ming-ming Wang, "The Politics of Culture or a Context of Histories: Representations of Chinese Popular Religion," *Dialectical Anthropology* 16 (1991): 251-72; Zufeng Luo, *Religion under Socialism in China*, ed. D. E. MacInnis and Z. Xi'an (Armonk, NY: M. E. Sharpe, 1991); Mayfair Mei-hui Yang, "State Secularization and the Numinous Foundations of Indigenous Civil Societies" (paper, American Anthropological Association 102nd Annual Meeting, Chicago, 2003), p. 481. For Japan, see Helen Hardacre, *Shinto and the State, 1868-1988* (Princeton, NJ: Princeton University Press, 1989). For Korea, see Ch'oe Kil-sŏng, "Misin t'ap'ae taehan ilgoch'al" [A Study of the Destruction of Superstition], *Han'guk Minsokhak* [Korean Folklore] 7 (1974): 39-54; Laurel Kendall, "The Cultural Politics of 'Superstition' in the Korean Shaman World: Modernity Constructs its Other," in *Healing Powers and Modernity: Traditional Medicine, Shamanism, and Science in Asian Societies*, ed. L. Connor and G. Samuel (Westport, CT: Greenwood Press, 2001); Boudewijn Walraven, "Our Shamanistic Past: The Korean Government, Shamans, and Shamanism," *Copenhagen Papers in East and Southeast Asian Studies* 8 (1993): 5-25, and "Shamans and Popular Religion around 1900," in *Religions in Traditional Korea, Proceedings of the 1992 AKSE/SBS Symposium*, ed. H. H. Sorensen, SBS Monographs Number 3 (Copenhagen: The Seminar for Buddhist Studies, Center for East and Southeast Asian Studies, University of Copenhagen, 1995), pp. 107-29, and "Interpretations and Reinterpretations of Popular Religion in the Last Decades of the Choson Dynasty," in *Korean Shamanism: Revivals, Survivals, and Change*, ed. K. Howard, pp. 55-72. These are not meant to be exhaustive lists so much as indications of a widespread modernist response to popular religion in many political guises.

[58] Stanley Jeyaraja Tambiah, *Magic, Science, Religion, and the Scope of Rationality* (Cambridge: Cambridge University Press, 1990).

religious policies of nonwestern states, as is well documented for China[59] and Japan.[60] As students of popular religion, we deal, on one level, with the limitations of our own conceptual apparatus—a problematically Western notion of "religion"[61]— and on another, with tensions on the ground where we do our work—between policy and practice, between contradictory world views sometimes embodied in the same person, between informant self-justifications, nostalgia, hearsay, and observations. That the cult of Saint Tran is categorized as a "folk belief" relative to "religion," or a "folk religion" or "traditional religion" rather than a "high" or "world" religion is not an ontological truth, but an historically and politically contingent fact of the social field in which spirit mediums, devotees, policy makers, and scholars all function. In the People's Republic of China, distinctions between "religious superstition" and "feudal superstition" separated what was grudgingly permitted from what was emphatically suppressed.[62] In 1970s South Korea, the label "superstition" permitted the destruction of sacred sites and the banning of rituals, subsequently revalued as "national culture."[63]

By the measure of both modernist utilitarian ideology and socialist morality, veneration of the Mother Goddess was, and to some degree remains, a highly problematic domain of social practice, with some spirit mediums still subject to harassment and many others carrying vivid memories of a time when they had to hold their rituals in secret or not at all. Epithets of "superstitious" or "primitive" that predate socialism have followed the mother goddesses and their devotees to Silicon Valley. The life history material collected in Hanoi by Viveca Larsson and Kirsten Endres[64] speaks of how, in the not-so-distant past, carved images, costumes, and musical instruments, numinous in their own setting, could be confiscated and destroyed as the paraphernalia of superstition, and threats of confiscation have not disappeared. At the same time, mediums reveal that suppression was never absolute; popular religion persisted in secret, although costumes were simpler, music was sometimes omitted, and only simple votive paper objects were produced and purchased.[65]

---

[59] Myron L. Cohen, "Being Chinese: The Peripheralization of Traditional Identity," *Daedalus* 120,2 (1991): 113-33; Feuchtwang and Ming-ming Wang, "The Politics of Culture or a Context of Histories"; Mayfair Mei-hui Yang, "Putting Global Capitalism in Its Place: Economic Hybridity, Bataille, and Ritual Expenditure," *Current Anthropology* 41,4 (2000): 477-509, and "State Secularization and the Numinous Foundations of Indigenous Civil Societies."

[60] Hardacre, *Shinto and the State*.

[61] Talal Asad, *Genealogies of Religion: Discipline and Reasons of Power in Christianity and Islam* (Baltimore, MD: Johns Hopkins University Press, 1993); Wilfred Cantwell Smith, *The Meaning and End of Religion* (San Francisco, CA: Harper and Row, 1978); Tambiah, *Magic, Science, Religion*.

[62] Anagnost, "The Politics of Ritual Displacement."

[63] Ch'oe, "Misin t'ap'ae taehan ilgoch'al"; Laurel Kendall, "Who Speaks for the Shaman When Shamans Speak of the Nation?" in *Making Majorities: Constituting the Nation in Japan, Korea, China, Malaysia, Fiji, Turkey, and the United States*, ed. D. Gladney (Stanford, CA: Stanford University Press, 1998), pp. 55-72.

[64] See Viveca Larsson and Kirsten W. Endres, "'Children of the Spirits, Followers of a Master': Spirit Mediums in Post-Renovation Vietnam," this volume.

[65] See also Nguyen Thi Hien, "The Religion of the Four Palaces"; Norton, "'The Moon Remembers Uncle Ho.'"

One consequence of the value judgments implicit in discussions of popular religion in Vietnam is the climate of self-justification and ambivalence, which many of these essays describe.[66] Devotees of Tran Hung Dao express contempt for mediums of the Four Palaces; old mediums are critical of new mediums; rural mediums see Hanoi mediums as frivolous and superficial; mediums accuse master mediums of being too mercenary; and temple keepers criticize other temples for ostentatious display. At the same time, everyone seems to be looking over their shoulders at the local authorities, whose critical posturing may be only one layer in their own complex interaction with popular religion. In Larsson and Endres's essay, a policeman is persuaded to return confiscated costumes and ID cards when the medium appeals to private sentiment: "I am sure that when you were in the battlefield your mother came here to pray, so that you are now back and have power."[67] One of Nguyen Thi Hien's informants, Mrs. Nga, is harassed with dire threats from the local police (because a foreigner was seen attending one of her rituals), but still manages to hold a large and elaborate initiation for her daughter a week later. Rumors abound of party members and civil servants who dance for the Mother Goddess in secret; Endres describes Cuong, a cadre of the communist youth organization in his village who doubles as a medium,[68] while Mrs. Thu, in Pham Quynh Phuong's account,[69] finds it more advantageous to trade employment as a court secretary for life as a master medium, enjoying the patronage of her former colleagues. Ambiguity is at the literal heart of the tradition, captured in Endres's gloss of a negatively valued "idealism," which contains in its ideograph the positive connotation of a true (or sincere or loyal?) heart.[70]

The tension of ambivalence between official antisuperstition policies and adherence to popular religion, between claims to virtuous practice and accusations of exploitation and fraud, between skepticism and faith is by no means unique to Vietnam. Although the notion of "superstition" is a modern and Western-identified concept implying erroneous science;[71] it would be difficult to imagine a society that recognizes the agency of spirits acting through human beings but does not have skeptics and does not admit the possibility of fraud. Endres gives a fine example of how notions of efficacy can turn on questions of situation-specific legitimacy that are outside a rationalist/materialist frame: a destined medium may be possessed by deities, but she could also be possessed by ghosts, and the authenticating judgment of a master medium may be subject to dispute.[72]

---

[66] Norton, "'The Moon Remembers Uncle Ho,'" p. 75.

[67] Larsson and Endres, "'Children of the Spirits, Followers of a Master,'" this volume.

[68] Endres, "Spirit Performance and the Ritual Construction of Personal Identity in Modern Vietnam," this volume.

[69] Pham Quynh Phuong, "Tran Hung Dao and the Mother Goddess Religion," this volume.

[70] Endres, "Spirit Performance and the Ritual Construction of Personal Identity in Modern Vietnam."

[71] Mary R. O'Neil, "Superstition," in *The Encyclopedia of Religion*, vol. 4., ed. M. Eliade (New York, NY: Macmillan, 1987).

[72] Endres, "Spirit Performance and the Ritual Construction of Personal Identity in Modern Vietnam."

WEALTH, MORALITY, AND RITUAL

All of the essays in this volume describe a popular religious tradition that is flourishing in tandem with the opening of the market and the subsequent expansion of consumption, a phenomenon witnessed by other accounts of religious revival in both Vietnam[73] and China.[74] A great deal of writing on Vietnamese popular religion is particularly concerned with the question of "moralizing money."[75] Studies of the Mother Goddess religion bear witness to the moral anxieties induced by the speed of transition from an impoverished, cautious, and necessarily restrained time to the current flowering of ritual commodities and the rising cost of participating in lavish rituals. The Mother Goddess religion seems to be particularly rich in material accoutrements: Temples are renovated with carved votive images, altars, and decorations. Music and multiple costumes—"more beautiful than in the past," the tailors insist—have returned. Rituals are decorated with colorful piles of offering food, incense, and paper votive goods, ranging from simple to elaborate, some of which now find their way to temples in Silicon Valley. The essays by Karen Fjelstad[76] and by Nguyen Thi Hien both suggest the value of addressing popular religion through material objects. It would be difficult to imagine an activity more at odds with a utilitarian and Marxist perspective than the still illegal but highly popular use of votive offerings that Nguyen Thi Hien describes—objects manufactured and bought in order to be burnt as offerings.[77] Her essay offers a vivid example of the ambiguities that surround lingering legal strictures against "superstition." The production of paper votive goods is flourishing today as a Red River Delta cottage industry. China experienced a similar revival in the demand for paper votive goods,[78] and as Nguyen Thi Hien and I learned in 2003, some Chinese dealers do a brisk trade in paper houses, cars, and household equipment made with cheaper Vietnamese labor. In Vietnam itself, the production of votive goods for *len dong* is a growing industry. Some families have given over their votive-paper-offering business completely to this line, and households with no prior experience manufacturing votive paper offerings produce successfully for the spirit medium market. With the aid of Nguyen Thi Hien's descriptions of votive paper production, it is possible to understand how the mediums quoted in several other of the essays in

---

[73] See, for example, Endres, "Beautiful Customs, Worthy Traditions," and "Local Dynamics of Renegotiating Ritual Space"; Kleinen, *Facing the Future, Reviving the Past*; Hy Van Luong, "Economic Reform and the Intensification of Rituals"; Malarney, *Culture, Ritual, and Revolution in Vietnam*; Nguyen Thi Hien, "The Religion of the Four Palaces"; Nguyen and Kendall, *Vietnam: Journeys of Body, Mind, and Spirit*; Taylor, *Goddess on the Rise*.

[74] See, for example, Dean, *Taoist Ritual and Popular Cults of Southeast China*; Hill Gates, *China's Motor: A Thousand Years of Petty Capitalism* (Ithaca, NY: Cornell University Press, 1996); Helen F. Siu, "Recycling Rituals: Politics and Popular Culture in Contemporary Rural China," in *Unofficial China: Popular Culture and Thought in the People's Republic*, ed. P. Link, R. Madsen, and P. G. Pickowicz (Boulder, CO: Westview Press, 1989); Mayfair Mei-hui Yang, "Putting Global Capitalism in Its Place."

[75] Compare with Robert W. Hefner, "Introduction: Society and Morality in the New Asian Capitalisms," in *Market Cultures: Society and Morality in the New Asian Capitalisms*, ed. R. W. Hefner (Boulder, CO: Westview Press, 1998).

[76] Fjelstad,"'We Have *Len Dong* Too,'" this volume.

[77] Nguyen Thi Hien, "'A Bit of a Spirit Favor Is Equal to a Load of Mundane Gifts,'" this volume.

[78] Siu, "Recycling Rituals"; Yang, "Putting Global Capitalism in Its Place."

this volume experience their world as a place of rising material expectations and costs, but, as Nguyen Thi Hien also notes, this is a complex market, adjusted to different tastes and pocketbooks. In her account, votive paper offerings for *len dong* are saturated with religious meaning on at least two levels: the objects themselves are regarded as ritually instrumental, and beautiful offerings are particularly efficacious.[79] The reverse is also true; Endres describes a failed initiation attributed to a paper horse of the wrong size whose leg broke when it was burnt.[80]

At another level, religious adherents believe that successful artists and entrepreneurs—like musicians who play at *len dong* and tailors who fashion the spirit mediums' costumes—enjoy special blessings from the goddesses. Nguyen Thi Hien relates the story of a son in one family of votive paper makers who became a medium in order to properly honor the goddesses who give the family its livelihood; many musicians, votive statue carvers, and some tailors are mediums too. The manufacture of votive goods, as a form of market production, is thoroughly integrated into the moral economy of gifts and favors enacted in devotions to the Mother Goddess. And to the degree that *len dong* evokes the imagery of premodern East Asian states, it is also worth remembering that one product of the state—money—is a necessary ritual prop and symbol of auspiciousness throughout East Asia. Indeed, the oldest known examples of votive paper coins were found in China's Xinjiang province in a Tang dynasty tomb dated to 667 CE.[81]

Karen Fjelstad's essay provides a global dimension to the booming market in ritual goods by describing the flow of temple fittings, costumes, and music from Vietnam to the overseas Vietnamese community in Silicon Valley as local temples and mediums are revitalized by contact with the source.[82] Reminiscent of Louisa Schein's work with originally Laotian Hmong who travel from the United States to China in search of an "authentic" connection with their ethnic roots,[83] Fjelstad's essay documents the stories of some of the Silicon Valley mediums who visit Vietnam to connect with more efficacious temples, as do the immigrant mediums in Marseilles studied by Martine Wadbled.[84] These mediums all move within a logic of religious practice in Vietnam where mediums and other devotees make pilgrimages to important and efficacious sites.[85] Once installed in Silicon Valley, new shrine

---

[79] Nguyen Thi Hien, "'A Bit of a Spirit Favor Is Equal to a Load of Mundane Gifts.'"

[80] Endres, "Spirit Performance and the Ritual Construction of Personal Identity in Modern Vietnam."

[81] See Roderick Cave, *Chinese Paper Offerings* (Oxford: Oxford University Press, 1998). Votive paper clothing was also found in a fifth-century grave in Xinjiang, and its use is documented from eighth-century China. Production flourished in twelfth-century China when votive paper was sold in specialized shops in the northern Sung capital of K'aifeng. See Ellen Johnston Laing and Helen Hui-ling Liu, *Up in Flames: The Ephemeral Art of Pasted-Paper Sculpture in Taiwan* (Stanford, CA: Stanford University Press, 2004), pp. 11, 181 n. 2. "Burning money" remains significant in revived Chinese practice. See Yang, "Putting Global Capitalism in Its Place."

[82] Fjelstad, "'We Have *Len Dong* Too.'"

[83] Louisa Schein, "Forged Transnationality and Oppositional Cosmopolitanism," in *Transnationalism from Below*, ed. M. P. Smith and L. E. Guarnizo, Comparative Urban and Community Research (New Brunswick and London: Transaction Publishers, 1998).

[84] Martina Wadbled, "Les thánh dans la migration: Même les esprits s'acculturent" (paper, Fourth Conference of the International Society for Shamanic Research, Chantilly, France, 1997).

[85] Nguyen Thi Hien, "The Religion of the Four Palaces"; Taylor, *Goddess on the Rise.*

accoutrements that have been acquired in Vietnam become the focus of moral claims for more or less appropriate temple practices: for example, some mediums complain that *other* mediums engage in status displays through the material contents of their shrines, and some mediums express strong, but by no means uniform, sentiments about the virtue of buying expensive goods, fabricating them oneself, or acquiring them with great difficulty. Fjelstad summarizes: "One perspective holds that *len dong* is becoming too materialistic and, as a result, is losing some of its spiritual validity ... The second perspective views lavish spending as a legitimate form of religious expression."[86] Some of the ambiguities of popular religious practice in the homeland are also evident in the diaspora. Nostalgia contemporizes a tension between sincere rituals and conspicuous display that must be very old in the Confucian/crypto-Confucian world, a tension between the virtue of performing rituals with a sincere heart and the necessity of evidencing one's virtue through elaborate ritual performances.[87]

But whatever the antiquity of this strain, it is heightened in contemporary Vietnam by utilitarian notions associated with modernity, as well as by a socialist morality and vastly expanded possibilities for material consumption. Predictably, Cuong, the young cadre turned spirit medium in Endres's account, emphasizes the virtue of a pure heart over luxurious offerings.

Nguyen Thi Hien points out that studies of the Mother Goddess religion, beginning with Maurice Durand's,[88] have largely confined their ethnography to (relatively) wealthy entrepreneurs in Hanoi for whom rituals are a means to more wealth. In her dissertation, she describes the complexity of the *len dong* world, arguing that it is not exclusively urban, that adherents are not exclusively petty traders, and that rituals address a variety of concerns, from ill children to marriage prospects to insanity. At the same time, and almost in spite of herself, she provides ample evidence to suggest that the anxieties of petty traders find expression in popular religion.[89] Tran Hung Dao's mediums, who take pains to distinguish themselves from performers of *len dong*, imply that the mother goddesses' promises of prosperity are lesser stuff than the health and security Saint Tran provides, but at the same time, they incorporate her altars into the Saint's temples in the belief that "if a pagoda has no Mother Goddess altar, it has no money." In a similar vein, Phillip Taylor suggests that the sense of moral disapprobation hovering over urban petty traders in Ho Chi Minh City engenders the common perception that their devotion to the Goddess of the Realm is motivated by mercenary desires.[90] Taylor turns the question of motivation around, suggesting that the risks and anxieties inherent in market transactions cause petty entrepreneurs to seek comfort through their religious devotions. This position is also explicit in Endres's essay in this volume[91]

---

[86] Fjelstad, "'We Have *Len Dong* Too,'" pp. 106-07.

[87] Laurel Kendall, *Getting Married in Korea: Of Gender, Morality, and Modernity* (Berkeley, CA: University of California Press, 1996), chap. 3; Malarney, *Culture, Ritual, and Revolution in Vietnam*, p. 10.

[88] Maurice Durand, *Technique et panthéon des médiums viêtnamiens (Dông)* (Paris: École Française d'Extrême-Orient, 1959).

[89] Nguyen Thi Hien, "The Religion of the Four Palaces."

[90] Taylor, *Goddess on the Rise*, pp. 87-88.

[91] Endres, "Spirit Performance and the Ritual Construction of Personal Identity in Modern Vietnam."

and in Le Huong Ly's writing (cited by Endres in this volume) and is a tack I have also taken in describing contemporary Korean shaman rituals, which now overwhelmingly address business concerns.[92] The link between religious activities and boom/bust entrepreneurship is one of the most striking features of popular religion in East Asia today. Studies from China and Vietnam, where market culture has resumed, and South Korea, where economic growth took place at a remarkable rate, have a great deal to tell us regarding the interface between religion and economics in relentlessly contemporary settings. Indeed, one may ask whether popular religion can exist in a late capitalist setting without material display, self-justifications, and moral contradictions. But recent and dramatic developments should not blind us to a link between economics and a popular religion that has been present in the region for a very long time. Valerie Hansen traces the flowering and regional diffusion of popular religious cults in China to the growth of commerce in the twelfth century.[93] Although Korean popular religion is most commonly associated with rural life, Pak Hŭng-ju's study of the numerous shrines along Seoul's Han River suggests that most of them owe their origins and patronage to robust commercial activities on the southern periphery of the capital.[94] The Red River Delta's long integration into the economic life of Hanoi must certainly have fostered the rich religious traditions of petty traders and producers.

Even so, spirit mediums who remember the period before Renovation experienced *doi moi* as a radical transformation. The essay by Endres[95] and the essay coauthored by Larsson and Endres[96] both suggest that many mediums view the present with surprising ambivalence, sentiments that also reverberate in Fjelstad's descriptions of Silicon Valley mediums.[97] These essays speak of tensions and rivalries that the mediums describe as a new phenomenon and attribute to the materialism of the post-*doi-moi* moment. Larsson and Endres's essay[98] takes us back, via informants' memories, to pre-*doi-moi* times, when spirit mediums carried on in secret, if at all, risking fines and imprisonment, hiding each other's costumes, and helping each other out. As Larsson and Endres record them, spirit mediums recollect (and dare I say romanticize?) a time of hardship, when everyone hung together for protection in performing their dangerous and necessarily covert work. Larsson and Endres and Fjelstad and Maiffret[99] all speak of the importance of fellowship among spirit mediums as a buffer, not only against out-and-out suppression, but also against the social disdain that is sometimes manifest in their own families. Larsson and Endres suggest that gilded memories of shared hardships in the past foster solidarity among small communities of adherents. Affinity seems to be an important element, not only in the smooth ritual interplay between a medium and her attendants, but in generating the sense of "fun" that Fjelstad's informants see as central to their

---

[92] Laurel Kendall, "Korean Shamans and the Spirits of Capitalism," *American Anthropologist* 98,3 (1996): 512-27.

[93] Hansen, *Changing Gods in Medieval China*, pp. 75, 78, 139, 165.

[94] Pak Hŭng-ju, *Seoulŭi Maŭlgut*.

[95] Endres, "Spirit Performance and the Ritual Construction of Personal Identity in Modern Vietnam."

[96] Larsson and Endres, "'Children of the Spirits, Followers of a Master.'"

[97] Fjelstad, "'We Have *Len Dong* Too.'"

[98] Larsson and Endres, "'Children of the Spirits, Followers of a Master.'"

[99] Fjelstad and Maiffret, "Gifts from the Spirits."

rituals.[100] These memories are juxtaposed against complaints that mediums have now become more mercenary, that they "join for economic reasons," that only wealthy people can afford to participate, that devotees only come to *len dong* for the gifts they receive and not out of devotion, that initiation rituals have become so expensive that those who really need them cannot afford them, that busy people have less time to socialize with each other after temple ceremonies, but at the same time, and with a now obvious sense of contradiction, they speak of the affection shared among a circle of spirit mediums. Endres describes competitive displays, jealousies between mediums, and complaints that master mediums overcharge for the use of their shrines. The Silicon Valley mediums feel that as overseas Vietnamese, they are particular targets for exploitation when they hold their rituals in temples in Vietnam. Echoing many of these complaints, one of Fjelstad's Silicon Valley mediums observes, "it's (now) more like a business than a religion."

I have heard a similar nostalgia expressed in South Korea, where shamans chastise other shamans—city shamans, younger shamans, famous shamans—for exploiting clients, initiates, and colleagues, and everyone reminisces about the good quality of human relationships in times of past privation.[101] The old people in Helen Siu's study of religious revival in a Chinese market town are similarly concerned with what they see as the superficial materialism of a younger generation that indulges in elaborate ritual expenditures for the sake of status rather than sentiment.[102] What do such filtered reminiscences tell us? They are not necessarily untrue. They do seem to witness—in South Korea, south China, and Vietnam—a commonly held feeling that economic competition affects the tone of human relationships in the circles of practitioners of popular religion no less than anywhere else. In Silicon Valley, competition between temples is manifest in behavior long familiar to anthropologists: accusations of sorcery leveled against particularly popular temples. But it is also possible to see in complaints about the mercenary character of *other* mediums or shamans an anxiety that may be endogenous to this kind of religious practice, which is always to some degree or in some respect a "business," however awkwardly the notions of "religion" and "business" cohabit the same professional space. In Korea, rivalries between shamans can become extremely bitter because shamanship is an overtly paid profession and shamans compete for clients, apprentices, and popular colleagues who will invite them into their busy schedule.[103] In Vietnam, does "medium-talk" reveal real, if subtle changes? Is popular religion becoming more of a commodity, as evidenced in the prominence of highly paid "masters" who receive paying clients and have shrines to rent? The micro-politics of the spirit medium world are a potentially rich field of inquiry.

Beyond any attempt to sort truth from self-justification from nostalgia, it is interesting to observe how the inevitable tensions between religious practice and its critiques play out in a contemporary language of historical rupture and vanishing authenticity. This is the undertow that is pulling mediums (like the Korean shamans with whom I am more familiar)[104] into a folkloric vision where they might reposition themselves as curators of endangered cultural traditions, drawing on a new

---

[100] Fjelstad, "Tu Phu Cong Dong."

[101] Kendall, "Korean Shamans and the Spirits of Capitalism."

[102] Siu, "Recycling Rituals."

[103] See Kendall, "Shamans, Housewives, and Other Restless Spirits."

[104] Kendall, "Who Speaks for the Shaman when Shamans Speak of the Nation?"

language of "legitimacy" and "authenticity" that is not yet their own. All of the participants in the UCLA workshop on the Mother Goddess religion—scholars who have sought out the *ong dong* and *ba dong* and shown an unabashed interest in their work—have been a part of this dynamic.

SUMMARY AND CONCLUSION

I have tried to make an argument for some common themes in the study of popular religion in East Asia, with some sideways glances at Southeast Asia. In casting this particular net, some things have slipped out, most particularly the central theme of both the essay coauthored by Karen Fjelstad and Lisa Maiffret[105] and the contributions to this volume by Kirsten Endres[106] and Barley Norton:[107] when people become mediums, what does it mean? What is the relationship between personal biography and selection by the deities, or between personality, gender affinity, and the roles performed in and out of possession? Do the deities abet transformations that would not take place if the gods were not present, or do they exaggerate traits already present? Is possession therapeutic? Do people feel better? On what basis do they make this claim? These are questions that have intrigued scholars of spirit possession worldwide, with seminal work done in Africa and among Afro-Caribbeans. Although notions of "destiny" may evoke a common East Asian horoscope scheme, this is only a small part of the story. "Why?" and "How?" may be the broadest questions one can ask of the *ong dong* and *ba dong*, questions that can draw in an enormous literature that is global in its scope, but the search for possible answers is microspecific and best addressed through individual case histories, such as the essays in this volume provide. This discussion is inevitably on the agenda for Vietnamese popular religion.

Some of the threads that have run through the contributions to this collection and into this essay might not be so obvious. Scholars of Vietnam have witnessed the play between history and popular religion, national heroes, and gods. I have tried to suggest that the historical imaginary of the premodern state is a particularly strong common thread that has not been sufficiently traced through in discussions of "shamans" and "mediums" in East (and possibly also Southeast) Asia. Such imaginaries are not only conducive to the rehabilitation of possession rituals as national culture, they are critical to understanding their logic of efficacy, why the deities are empowered, and how people appeal to their power. The imaginary of an antique state informs local understandings of the power claimed by deities who appear either as noble beings who are entertained and offered tribute to secure their good will or as warriors who exorcise through military feats. Divine entertainments have a high aesthetic content; this is part of their appeal as cultural heritage in the present tense. The logic of these rituals, that powerful beings return favors for being provided with entertainment and offerings, makes sense in terms of the expectations people would form on the basis of their collective experience of asymmetrical human interactions, for example, interactions between commoners and the agents of state authority, throughout the region. It also assumes "ritual materialism," doing things

---

[105] Fjelstad and Maiffret, "Gifts from the Spirits."

[106] Endres, "Spirit Performance and the Ritual Construction of Personal Identity in Modern Vietnam."

[107] Norton, "'Hot-Tempered' Women and 'Effeminate' Men."

with things, the *bête noir* of a rational, utilitarian worldview manifest in the "antisuperstition" policies of various governments throughout the region over the course of the twentieth century. Ritual materialism also evokes an older tension implicit in Confucian attitudes toward ritual: a sincere heart is better than an ostentatious ritual, but by what means does one evidence a sincere heart?

The authors in this volume suggest an ambivalent play between faith and skepticism, official posturing and private devotion, nostalgia for a simpler time and exuberant consumption, legal strictures and unabashed defiance. These arguments may be worth listening to, not for the truth or falsity of any claim they make, since they generally cannot be proved or falsified, but for the arguments' sake. What do they tell us about the experience of contemporary life through the practice of popular religion? Attitudes toward business seem to be particularly freighted with ambivalence, partly as a socialist legacy but also consistent with a crypto-Confucian disdain for the market that is, at the same time, so necessary and celebrated. One makes bargains with the gods, money is transmitted to the other world, and coins and cash are symbols of good fortune. One aspect of the dynamism of popular religion is the contradictions at its core, contradictions that keep pace with an uncomfortable and contradictory world.

GLOSSARY

Compiled by Kirsten W. Endres

ái nam ái nữ	transsexual (also: hermaphrodite)
âm dương	Yin and Yang
bản mệnh	destiny; one's fate
bắt đồng	to be "seized" by the spirits
bệnh âm	spiritually ill
buôn thần bán thánh	buying and selling spirits; trading in spirits
các Cô	lit. all ladies; here: referring to all Holy Lady spirits
căn đồng	a medium's fate, root of a spirit
căn số	destined aptitude (here: for mediumship)
chầu văn	liturgical music played during *lên đồng* rituals
chư vị	Assembly of Spirits
chứng lễ	to witness the offerings
Cô	here: Holy Princess spirits
cô hồn	wandering souls
con nhang	lit. incense child; disciple, follower of a master; also: *con nhang đe tử*
cộng đồng đức ông	Assembly of male spirits
cộng đồng Tứ Phủ	Assembly of spirits of the Four Palaces
cung văn	musician specializing in *chau văn* music
đàn nguyệt	moon-shaped lute
đàn nhị	two-stringed fiddle
đàn tranh	sixteen-stringed zither
đạo	faith, religion
Đạo Mẫu	Mother Goddess religion
Đạo Tứ Phủ	Four Palace religion
đền	(public) temple; also called *miếu*
Địa phủ	Earth palace
điên	mad
điện thờ	(private) temple or shrine
đình	village communal house

đội bát nhang	to carry an incense holder (on one's head)
đồng bóng	spirit possession
đồng cô	effeminate (male) medium
đồng cốt	(female) medium; nowadays the phrase implies a derogatory meaning
đồng đền	temple medium, temple caretaker; also: *thủ nhang đồng đền*
đồng đua	competitive mediumship, a "show-off medium"
đồng mê	an "uncontrolled" or "obsessed" medium
duy tâm	spiritual matters, idealism, idealistic
duy vật	material matters materialism, materialistic
ghế	chair (here: a medium acting as a "seat" for the spirits)
gia	incarnation of a certain spirit in a medium
giáng	descend (referring to a spirit's descent)
hầu bóng	service to the spirits (lit. serving the shadows)
hầu dâng	ritual assistants who participate during a *lên đồng* ritual
hầu đồng	a service performed by a medium
hầu đúng phép thánh	to perform according to the spirit's rules
hầu làm cảnh	to serve spirits for **their** beauty
hầu làm việc	working ritual
hầu thánh	lit. to serve the spirits
hầu vo	serving (the spirits) without music
hầu vui	convivial spirit possession
hồn, tâm hồn	soul, heart-soul
khăn phủ diện	red veil used to mark the spirits' descent and ascent during a *lên đồng* ritual
kiếp trước	previous incarnation
làm phúc	to practice charity
làm tôi đôi nước	servants to both realms
linh	(spiritually) efficacious
lộc; lộc thánh	a blessed gift bestowed by a spirit; *phát lộc*: to distribute offerings transformed into "blessed gifts"
mã	paper votive object; *vàng mã*: votive paper money
Mẫu	Mother Goddess, Holy Mother (also: Thánh Mẫu)
Mẫu Thượng Thiên	Mother Goddess of Heaven
Mẫu Thượng Ngàn	Mother Goddess of Mounts and Forests
Mẫu Thoải	Mother Goddess of Water
mê tín dị đoan	superstition
mõ	wooden slit drum
mở phủ	palace-opening ritual; initiation as a medium
múa võ	martial dance (of Mandarin spirits)

nạng số	a "heavy" (difficult) fate
ngài	honorific for addressing high-ranking personalities and deities
Ngọc Hoàng	Jade Emperor, Ruler of Heaven
ngũ hành	five basic elements: metal, wood, water, fire, earth
người có đồng	a person who is fated for mediumship
người gọi hồn	soul caller
người hầu	medium (lit. a servant of the spirits)
Nhà Trần	family of Trần Hưng Đạo
Nhạc Phủ	Forests and Mountains Palace
nhân duyên	destined affinity (usually between husband and wife)
nhập	to incarnate
nóng tính	hot-tempered
ông đồng/bà đồng	male/female medium
ốp vào	to be embodied (here: spirit embodiment)
phách	bamboo clappers
phép thánh	the spirits' rules
phủ	lit. "palace," but also used to refer to temples dedicated to the spirits of the Four Palaces (e.g., Phủ Tây Hồ)
ra đồng	enter mediumship
sáo, tiêu	bamboo flutes
sớ	petition sheet for spirits
sống đạo đức	to lead a virtuous life
tâm	heart
tâm lý	psychology, psychological
tam sinh	(offering consisting of) a whole boiled duck, a chicken, and a pig head
thanh đồng	novice medium (formerly: a medium of Trần Hưng Đạo)
thanh la	small gong
Thánh tổ Hải Quân	Ancestor of Navel Forces
thật đồng	genuine, true medium
thật tâm	true-hearted, sincere
thầy bói	fortune-teller
thầy bùa thầy phù thủy	those who specialize in worshipping the nether world's souls
thầy cúng	spirit priest, ritual specialist, ceremony master
Thiên phủ	Heavenly Palace
thiêng	sacred, spiritually efficacious
Thoải phủ	Water palace
thu lộc	to have been granted spirit favors, receiving *lộc*, sharing *lộc*; this expression is used for sharing the meal after a *lên đồng* ritual
thương	pity, compassion
tịn ngưỡng	belief

tình cảm	emotion, sentiment
tôn giáo	(institutionalized) religion
trả nợ	to repay one's debt
trình giầu	ritual of introducing a new medium to the spirits by presenting areca nuts
trống	small-headed drum
Tứ Phủ	Four Palaces
tỳ bà	pear-shaped lute
Vua Cha Bát Hải	Father King of Eight Oceans
xem bói	to read someone's fortune
xiên lình	to pierce the cheeks with a pin
xin đài	to seek a sign of the spirits' approval by throwing two coins (if they fall head and tails, it means the spirits approve)

SOUTHEAST ASIA PROGRAM PUBLICATIONS
Cornell University

Studies on Southeast Asia

Number 39 *The Indonesian Supreme Court: A Study of Institutional Collapse,* Sebastiaan Pompe. 2005. 494 pp. ISBN 0-877277-38-9 (pb).

Number 38 *Spirited Politics: Religion and Public Life in Contemporary Southeast Asia,* ed. Andrew C. Willford and Kenneth M. George. 2005. 210 pp. ISBN 0-87727-737-0.

Number 37 *Sumatran Sultanate and Colonial State: Jambi and the Rise of Dutch Imperialism, 1830-1907,* Elsbeth Locher-Scholten, trans. Beverley Jackson. 2004. 332 pp. ISBN 0-87727-736-2.

Number 36 *Southeast Asia over Three Generations: Essays Presented to Benedict R. O'G. Anderson,* ed. James T. Siegel and Audrey R. Kahin. 2003. 398 pp. ISBN 0-87727-735-4.

Number 35 *Nationalism and Revolution in Indonesia,* George McTurnan Kahin, intro. Benedict R. O'G. Anderson (reprinted from 1952 edition, Cornell University Press, with permission). 2003. 530 pp. ISBN 0-87727-734-6.

Number 34 *Golddiggers, Farmers, and Traders in the "Chinese Districts" of West Kalimantan, Indonesia,* Mary Somers Heidhues. 2003. 316 pp. ISBN 0-87727-733-8.

Number 33 *Opusculum de Sectis apud Sinenses et Tunkinenses (A Small Treatise on the Sects among the Chinese and Tonkinese): A Study of Religion in China and North Vietnam in the Eighteenth Century,* Father Adriano de St. Thecla, trans. Olga Dror, with Mariya Berezovska. 2002. 363 pp. ISBN 0-87727-732-X.

Number 32 *Fear and Sanctuary: Burmese Refugees in Thailand,* Hazel J. Lang. 2002. 204 pp. ISBN 0-87727-731-1.

Number 31 *Modern Dreams: An Inquiry into Power, Cultural Production, and the Cityscape in Contemporary Urban Penang, Malaysia,* Beng-Lan Goh. 2002. 225 pp. ISBN 0-87727-730-3.

Number 30 *Violence and the State in Suharto's Indonesia,* ed. Benedict R. O'G. Anderson. 2001. Second printing, 2002. 247 pp. ISBN 0-87727-729-X.

Number 29 *Studies in Southeast Asian Art: Essays in Honor of Stanley J. O'Connor,* ed. Nora A. Taylor. 2000. 243 pp. Illustrations. ISBN 0-87727-728-1.

Number 28 *The Hadrami Awakening: Community and Identity in the Netherlands East Indies, 1900-1942,* Natalie Mobini-Kesheh. 1999. 174 pp. ISBN 0-87727-727-3.

Number 27 *Tales from Djakarta: Caricatures of Circumstances and their Human Beings,* Pramoedya Ananta Toer. 1999. 145 pp. ISBN 0-87727-726-5.

Number 26 *History, Culture, and Region in Southeast Asian Perspectives,* rev. ed., O. W. Wolters. 1999. Second printing, 2004. 275 pp. ISBN 0-87727-725-7.

Number 25 *Figures of Criminality in Indonesia, the Philippines, and Colonial Vietnam,* ed. Vicente L. Rafael. 1999. 259 pp. ISBN 0-87727-724-9.

Number 24 *Paths to Conflagration: Fifty Years of Diplomacy and Warfare in Laos, Thailand, and Vietnam, 1778-1828,* Mayoury Ngaosyvathn and Pheuiphanh Ngaosyvathn. 1998. 268 pp. ISBN 0-87727-723-0.

Number 23   *Nguyễn Cochinchina: Southern Vietnam in the Seventeenth and Eighteenth Centuries*, Li Tana. 1998. Second printing, 2002. 194 pp. ISBN 0-87727-722-2.

Number 22   *Young Heroes: The Indonesian Family in Politics*, Saya S. Shiraishi. 1997. 183 pp. ISBN 0-87727-721-4.

Number 21   *Interpreting Development: Capitalism, Democracy, and the Middle Class in Thailand*, John Girling. 1996. 95 pp. ISBN 0-87727-720-6.

Number 20   *Making Indonesia*, ed. Daniel S. Lev, Ruth McVey. 1996. 201 pp. ISBN 0-87727-719-2.

Number 19   *Essays into Vietnamese Pasts*, ed. K. W. Taylor, John K. Whitmore. 1995. 288 pp. ISBN 0-87727-718-4.

Number 18   *In the Land of Lady White Blood: Southern Thailand and the Meaning of History*, Lorraine M. Gesick. 1995. 106 pp. ISBN 0-87727-717-6.

Number 17   *The Vernacular Press and the Emergence of Modern Indonesian Consciousness*, Ahmat Adam. 1995. 220 pp. ISBN 0-87727-716-8.

Number 16   *The Nan Chronicle*, trans., ed. David K. Wyatt. 1994. 158 pp. ISBN 0-87727-715-X.

Number 15   *Selective Judicial Competence: The Cirebon-Priangan Legal Administration, 1680–1792*, Mason C. Hoadley. 1994. 185 pp. ISBN 0-87727-714-1.

Number 14   *Sjahrir: Politics and Exile in Indonesia*, Rudolf Mrázek. 1994. 536 pp. ISBN 0-87727-713-3.

Number 13   *Fair Land Sarawak: Some Recollections of an Expatriate Officer*, Alastair Morrison. 1993. 196 pp. ISBN 0-87727-712-5.

Number 12   *Fields from the Sea: Chinese Junk Trade with Siam during the Late Eighteenth and Early Nineteenth Centuries*, Jennifer Cushman. 1993. 206 pp. ISBN 0-87727-711-7.

Number 11   *Money, Markets, and Trade in Early Southeast Asia: The Development of Indigenous Monetary Systems to AD 1400*, Robert S. Wicks. 1992. 2nd printing 1996. 354 pp., 78 tables, illus., maps. ISBN 0-87727-710-9.

Number 10   *Tai Ahoms and the Stars: Three Ritual Texts to Ward Off Danger*, trans., ed. B. J. Terwiel, Ranoo Wichasin. 1992. 170 pp. ISBN 0-87727-709-5.

Number 9   *Southeast Asian Capitalists*, ed. Ruth McVey. 1992. 2nd printing 1993. 220 pp. ISBN 0-87727-708-7.

Number 8   *The Politics of Colonial Exploitation: Java, the Dutch, and the Cultivation System*, Cornelis Fasseur, ed. R. E. Elson, trans. R. E. Elson, Ary Kraal. 1992. 2nd printing 1994. 266 pp. ISBN 0-87727-707-9.

Number 7   *A Malay Frontier: Unity and Duality in a Sumatran Kingdom*, Jane Drakard. 1990. 2nd printing 2003. 215 pp. ISBN 0-87727-706-0.

Number 6   *Trends in Khmer Art*, Jean Boisselier, ed. Natasha Eilenberg, trans. Natasha Eilenberg, Melvin Elliott. 1989. 124 pp., 24 plates. ISBN 0-87727-705-2.

Number 5   *Southeast Asian Ephemeris: Solar and Planetary Positions, A.D. 638–2000*, J. C. Eade. 1989. 175 pp. ISBN 0-87727-704-4.

Number 3   *Thai Radical Discourse: The Real Face of Thai Feudalism Today*, Craig J. Reynolds. 1987. 2nd printing 1994. 186 pp. ISBN 0-87727-702-8.

Number 1   *The Symbolism of the Stupa*, Adrian Snodgrass. 1985. Revised with
            index, 1988. 3rd printing 1998. 469 pp. ISBN 0-87727-700-1.

SEAP Series

Number 23   *Possessed by the Spirits: Mediumship in Contemporary Vietnamese
            Communities.* 2006. 186 pp. ISBN 0-877271-41-0 (pb).

Number 22   *The Industry of Marrying Europeans*, Vũ Trọng Phụng, trans. Thúy
            Tranviet. 2006. 66 pp. ISBN 0-877271-40-2 (pb).

Number 21   *Securing a Place: Small-Scale Artisans in Modern Indonesia*, Elizabeth
            Morrell. 2005. 220 pp. ISBN 0-877271-39-9.

Number 20   *Southern Vietnam under the Reign of Minh Mạng (1820-1841): Central
            Policies and Local Response*, Choi Byung Wook. 2004. 226pp. ISBN 0-0-
            877271-40-2.

Number 19   *Gender, Household, State: Đổi Mới in Việt Nam*, ed. Jayne Werner and
            Danièle Bélanger. 2002. 151 pp. ISBN 0-87727-137-2.

Number 18   *Culture and Power in Traditional Siamese Government*, Neil A. Englehart.
            2001. 130 pp. ISBN 0-87727-135-6.

Number 17   *Gangsters, Democracy, and the State*, ed. Carl A. Trocki. 1998. Second
            printing, 2002. 94 pp. ISBN 0-87727-134-8.

Number 16   *Cutting across the Lands: An Annotated Bibliography on Natural Resource
            Management and Community Development in Indonesia, the Philippines,
            and Malaysia*, ed. Eveline Ferretti. 1997. 329 pp. ISBN 0-87727-133-X.

Number 15   *The Revolution Falters: The Left in Philippine Politics after 1986*, ed.
            Patricio N. Abinales. 1996. Second printing, 2002. 182 pp. ISBN 0-
            87727-132-1.

Number 14   *Being Kammu: My Village, My Life*, Damrong Tayanin. 1994. 138 pp., 22
            tables, illus., maps. ISBN 0-87727-130-5.

Number 13   *The American War in Vietnam*, ed. Jayne Werner, David Hunt. 1993.
            132 pp. ISBN 0-87727-131-3.

Number 12   *The Voice of Young Burma*, Aye Kyaw. 1993. 92 pp. ISBN 0-87727-129-1.

Number 11   *The Political Legacy of Aung San*, ed. Josef Silverstein. Revised edition
            1993. 169 pp. ISBN 0-87727-128-3.

Number 10   *Studies on Vietnamese Language and Literature: A Preliminary
            Bibliography*, Nguyen Dinh Tham. 1992. 227 pp. ISBN 0-87727-127-5.

Number 8   *From PKI to the Comintern, 1924–1941: The Apprenticeship of the Malayan
            Communist Party*, Cheah Boon Kheng. 1992. 147 pp. ISBN 0-87727-125-9.

Number 7   *Intellectual Property and US Relations with Indonesia, Malaysia, Singapore,
            and Thailand*, Elisabeth Uphoff. 1991. 67 pp. ISBN 0-87727-124-0.

Number 6   *The Rise and Fall of the Communist Party of Burma (CPB)*, Bertil Lintner.
            1990. 124 pp. 26 illus., 14 maps. ISBN 0-87727-123-2.

Number 5   *Japanese Relations with Vietnam: 1951–1987*, Masaya Shiraishi. 1990.
            174 pp. ISBN 0-87727-122-4.

Number 3   *Postwar Vietnam: Dilemmas in Socialist Development*, ed. Christine White,
            David Marr. 1988. 2nd printing 1993. 260 pp. ISBN 0-87727-120-8.

Number 2   *The Dobama Movement in Burma (1930–1938)*, Khin Yi. 1988. 160 pp.
            ISBN 0-87727-118-6.

Cornell Modern Indonesia Project Publications

Number 75   *A Tour of Duty: Changing Patterns of Military Politics in Indonesia in the
            1990s.* Douglas Kammen and Siddharth Chandra. 1999. 99 pp.
            ISBN 0-87763-049-6.

Number 74   *The Roots of Acehnese Rebellion 1989–1992*, Tim Kell. 1995. 103 pp.
            ISBN 0-87763-040-2.

Number 73   *"White Book" on the 1992 General Election in Indonesia*, trans. Dwight
            King. 1994. 72 pp. ISBN 0-87763-039-9.

Number 72   *Popular Indonesian Literature of the Qur'an*, Howard M. Federspiel. 1994.
            170 pp. ISBN 0-87763-038-0.

Number 71   *A Javanese Memoir of Sumatra, 1945–1946: Love and Hatred in the
            Liberation War*, Takao Fusayama. 1993. 150 pp. ISBN 0-87763-037-2.

Number 70   *East Kalimantan: The Decline of a Commercial Aristocracy*, Burhan
            Magenda. 1991. 120 pp. ISBN 0-87763-036-4.

Number 69   *The Road to Madiun: The Indonesian Communist Uprising of 1948*,
            Elizabeth Ann Swift. 1989. 120 pp. ISBN 0-87763-035-6.

Number 68   *Intellectuals and Nationalism in Indonesia: A Study of the Following
            Recruited by Sutan Sjahrir in Occupation Jakarta*, J. D. Legge. 1988.
            159 pp. ISBN 0-87763-034-8.

Number 67   *Indonesia Free: A Biography of Mohammad Hatta*, Mavis Rose. 1987.
            252 pp. ISBN 0-87763-033-X.

Number 66   *Prisoners at Kota Cane*, Leon Salim, trans. Audrey Kahin. 1986. 112 pp.
            ISBN 0-87763-032-1.

Number 65   *The Kenpeitai in Java and Sumatra*, trans. Barbara G. Shimer, Guy Hobbs,
            intro. Theodore Friend. 1986. 80 pp. ISBN 0-87763-031-3.

Number 64   *Suharto and His Generals: Indonesia's Military Politics, 1975–1983*, David
            Jenkins. 1984. 4th printing 1997. 300 pp. ISBN 0-87763-030-5.

Number 62   *Interpreting Indonesian Politics: Thirteen Contributions to the Debate, 1964–
            1981*, ed. Benedict Anderson, Audrey Kahin, intro. Daniel S. Lev. 1982.
            3rd printing 1991. 172 pp. ISBN 0-87763-028-3.

Number 60   *The Minangkabau Response to Dutch Colonial Rule in the Nineteenth
            Century*, Elizabeth E. Graves. 1981. 157 pp. ISBN 0-87763-000-3.

Number 59   *Breaking the Chains of Oppression of the Indonesian People: Defense
            Statement at His Trial on Charges of Insulting the Head of State, Bandung,
            June 7–10, 1979*, Heri Akhmadi. 1981. 201 pp. ISBN 0-87763-001-1.

Number 57   *Permesta: Half a Rebellion*, Barbara S. Harvey. 1977. 174 pp.
            ISBN 0-87763-003-8.

Number 55   *Report from Banaran: The Story of the Experiences of a Soldier during the
            War of Independence*, Maj. Gen. T. B. Simatupang. 1972. 186 pp.
            ISBN 0-87763-005-4.

Number 52   *A Preliminary Analysis of the October 1 1965, Coup in Indonesia (Prepared in January 1966)*, Benedict R. Anderson, Ruth T. McVey, assist. Frederick P. Bunnell. 1971. 3rd printing 1990. 174 pp. ISBN 0-87763-008-9.

Number 51   *The Putera Reports: Problems in Indonesian-Japanese War-Time Cooperation*, Mohammad Hatta, trans., intro. William H. Frederick. 1971. 114 pp. ISBN 0-87763-009-7.

Number 50   *Schools and Politics: The Kaum Muda Movement in West Sumatra (1927–1933)*, Taufik Abdullah. 1971. 257 pp. ISBN 0-87763-010-0.

Number 49   *The Foundation of the Partai Muslimin Indonesia*, K. E. Ward. 1970. 75 pp. ISBN 0-87763-011-9.

Number 48   *Nationalism, Islam and Marxism*, Soekarno, intro. Ruth T. McVey. 1970. 2nd printing 1984. 62 pp. ISBN 0-87763-012-7.

Number 43   *State and Statecraft in Old Java: A Study of the Later Mataram Period, 16th to 19th Century*, Soemarsaid Moertono. Revised edition 1981. 180 pp. ISBN 0-87763-017-8.

Number 39   Preliminary Checklist of Indonesian Imprints (1945-1949), John M. Echols. 186 pp. ISBN 0-87763-025-9.

Number 37   *Mythology and the Tolerance of the Javanese*, Benedict R. O'G. Anderson. 2nd edition, 1996. Reprinted 2004. 104 pp., 65 illus. ISBN 0-87763-041-0.

Number 25   *The Communist Uprisings of 1926–1927 in Indonesia: Key Documents*, ed., intro. Harry J. Benda, Ruth T. McVey. 1960. 2nd printing 1969. 177 pp. ISBN 0-87763-024-0.

Number 7   *The Soviet View of the Indonesian Revolution*, Ruth T. McVey. 1957. 3rd printing 1969. 90 pp. ISBN 0-87763-018-6.

Number 6   *The Indonesian Elections of 1955*, Herbert Feith. 1957. 2nd printing 1971. 91 pp. ISBN 0-87763-020-8.

Translation Series

Volume 4   *Approaching Suharto's Indonesia from the Margins*, ed. Takashi Shiraishi. 1994. 153 pp. ISBN 0-87727-403-7.

Volume 3   *The Japanese in Colonial Southeast Asia*, ed. Saya Shiraishi, Takashi Shiraishi. 1993. 172 pp. ISBN 0-87727-402-9.

Volume 2   *Indochina in the 1940s and 1950s*, ed. Takashi Shiraishi, Motoo Furuta. 1992. 196 pp. ISBN 0-87727-401-0.

Volume 1   *Reading Southeast Asia*, ed. Takashi Shiraishi. 1990. 188 pp. ISBN 0-87727-400-2.

Language Texts

INDONESIAN

Beginning Indonesian through Self-Instruction, John U. Wolff, Dédé Oetomo, Daniel
Fietkiewicz. 3rd revised edition 1992. Vol. 1. 115 pp. ISBN 0-87727-529-7. Vol.
2. 434 pp. ISBN 0-87727-530-0. Vol. 3. 473 pp. ISBN 0-87727-531-9.

Indonesian Readings, John U. Wolff. 1978. 4th printing 1992. 480 pp.
ISBN 0-87727-517-3

Indonesian Conversations, John U. Wolff. 1978. 3rd printing 1991. 297 pp.
ISBN 0-87727-516-5

Formal Indonesian, John U. Wolff. 2nd revised edition 1986. 446 pp.
ISBN 0-87727-515-7

TAGALOG

Pilipino through Self-Instruction, John U. Wolff, Maria Theresa C. Centeno, Der-Hwa
V. Rau. 1991. Vol. 1. 342 pp. ISBN 0-87727—525-4. Vol. 2., revised 2005, 378 pp.
ISBN 0-87727-526-2. Vol 3., revised 2005, 431 pp. ISBN 0-87727-527-0. Vol. 4.
306 pp. ISBN 0-87727-528-9.

THAI

A. U. A. Language Center Thai Course, J. Marvin Brown. Originally published by the
American University Alumni Association Language Center, 1974. Reissued by
Cornell Southeast Asia Program, 1991, 1992. Book 1. 267 pp. ISBN 0-87727-506-
8. Book 2. 288 pp. ISBN 0-87727-507-6. Book 3. 247 pp. ISBN 0-87727-508-4.

A. U. A. Language Center Thai Course, Reading and Writing Text (mostly reading), 1979.
Reissued 1997. 164 pp. ISBN 0-87727-511-4.

A. U. A. Language Center Thai Course, Reading and Writing Workbook (mostly writing),
1979. Reissued 1997. 99 pp. ISBN 0-87727-512-2.

KHMER

Cambodian System of Writing and Beginning Reader, Franklin E. Huffman. Originally
published by Yale University Press, 1970. Reissued by Cornell Southeast Asia
Program, 4th printing 2002. 365 pp. ISBN 0-300-01314-0.

Modern Spoken Cambodian, Franklin E. Huffman, assist. Charan Promchan, Chhom-
Rak Thong Lambert. Originally published by Yale University Press, 1970.
Reissued by Cornell Southeast Asia Program, 3rd printing 1991. 451 pp. ISBN
0-300-01316-7.

Intermediate Cambodian Reader, ed. Franklin E. Huffman, assist. Im Proum. Originally
published by Yale University Press, 1972. Reissued by Cornell Southeast Asia
Program, 1988. 499 pp. ISBN 0-300-01552-6.

Cambodian Literary Reader and Glossary, Franklin E. Huffman, Im Proum. Originally
published by Yale University Press, 1977. Reissued by Cornell Southeast Asia
Program, 1988. 494 pp. ISBN 0-300-02069-4.

HMONG

White Hmong-English Dictionary, Ernest E. Heimbach. 1969. 8th printing, 2002. 523 pp.
ISBN 0-87727-075-9.

VIETNAMESE

Intermediate Spoken Vietnamese, Franklin E. Huffman, Tran Trong Hai. 1980. 3rd
printing 1994. ISBN 0-87727-500-9.

* * *

Southeast Asian Studies: Reorientations. Craig J. Reynolds and Ruth McVey. Frank H. Golay Lectures 2 & 3. 70 pp. ISBN 0-87727-301-4.

Javanese Literature in Surakarta Manuscripts, Nancy K. Florida. Vol. 1, *Introduction and Manuscripts of the Karaton Surakarta.* 1993. 410 pp. Frontispiece, illustrations. Hard cover, ISBN 0-87727-602-1, Paperback, ISBN 0-87727-603-X. Vol. 2, *Manuscripts of the Mangkunagaran Palace.* 2000. 576 pp. Frontispiece, illustrations. Paperback, ISBN 0-87727-604-8.

Sbek Thom: Khmer Shadow Theater. Pech Tum Kravel, trans. Sos Kem, ed. Thavro Phim, Sos Kem, Martin Hatch. 1996. 363 pp., 153 photographs. ISBN 0-87727-620-X.

In the Mirror: Literature and Politics in Siam in the American Era, ed. Benedict R. O'G. Anderson, trans. Benedict R. O'G. Anderson, Ruchira Mendiones. 1985. 2nd printing 1991. 303 pp. Paperback. ISBN 974-210-380-1.

To order, please contact:

Cornell University
Southeast Asia Program Publications
95 Brown Road
Box 1004
Ithaca NY 14850

Online: http://www.einaudi.cornell.edu/southeastasia/publications/
Tel: 1-877-865-2432 (Toll free – U.S.)
Fax: (607) 255-7534

E-mail: SEAP-Pubs@cornell.edu
Orders must be prepaid by check or credit card (VISA, MasterCard, Discover).

Lightning Source UK Ltd.
Milton Keynes UK
UKHW051506170822
407425UK00007B/427

9 780877 271413